SUSTAINABLE DEVELOPMENT IN A DEVELOPING WORLD

Sustainable Development in a Developing World

Integrating Socio-economic Appraisal and Environmental Assessment

Edited by

Colin Kirkpatrick

Institute for Development Policy and Management, University of Manchester, UK

Norman Lee

Environmental Impact Assessment Centre and Institute for Development Policy and Management, University of Manchester, Manchester, UK

Edward Elgar
Cheltenham, UK • Northampton, MA, USA

333.714
S964

Published by
Edward Elgar Publishing Limited
8 Lansdown Place
Cheltenham
Glos GL50 2HU
UK

Edward Elgar Publishing, Inc.
6 Market Street
Northampton
Massachusetts 01060
USA

A catalogue record for this book
is available from the British Library

Library of Congress Cataloguing in Publication Data

Sustainable development in a developing world: integrating socio-economic and environmental appraisal/edited by Colin Kirkpatrick, Norman Lee.

  Includes bibliographical references.
  Papers presented at a conference in May 1996.
  1. Sustainable development — Congresses. 2. Environmental impact analysis — Congresses. 3. Economic development — Environmental aspects — Congresses. I. Kirkpatrick, C.H. (Colin H.), 1944–   . II. Lee, Norman, 1936–   .
  HD75.6.S866 1998
  333.7 14—dc21   97–22295
                                                                              CIP

ISBN 1 85898 581 1

Printed and bound in Great Britain by
Biddles Limited, Guildford and King's Lynn

Contents

List of figures   x
List of tables   xi
List of contributors   xii
Preface   xiv

PART I INTEGRATING APPRAISAL WITHIN THE
DEVELOPMENT PROCESS

1 Integrating environmental assessment with other forms of appraisal in
the development process
Norman Lee and Colin Kirkpatrick
1.1   Introduction   3
1.2   An overview of different forms of appraisal   4
1.3   Weak and strong forms of integration   11
1.4   Review of papers   13
1.5   Conclusions and recommendations   18

2 Integration of sustainability objectives in structural adjustment
programmes through the use of strategic environmental assessment
Hussein Abaza
2.1   Introduction   25
2.2   Strategic environmental assessment   26
2.3   Structural adjustment programmes (SAPs)   29
2.4   Structural adjustment programmes and the environment   33
2.5   Integration of environmental and social considerations in
      SAPs   38
2.6   Conclusion   43

3 Environmental assessment of trade liberalization: an OECD
perspective
Michel Potier
3.1   Introduction   46
3.2   The analytical framework for assessing the environmental
      implications of trade liberalization   46
3.3   Policy application   52
3.4   Conclusions   56

PART II APPRAISAL AND INTEGRATION: FRAMEWORKS AND
METHODS

4 Assessing the environmental impacts of national development
   Alan Grainger
   4.1 Introduction   61
   4.2 The new challenges to development   61
   4.3 The evolution of environmental impact assessment   62
   4.4 Sustainable development theories   63
   4.5 A comprehensive integrated assessment of the environmental
        impacts of national development   67
   4.6 Improving the equity of international regimes   73
   4.7 Conclusions   83

5 A methodology for investigating the impact of policy decisions on the
   natural resource environment of developing countries
   Jamie Morrison and Richard Pearce
   5.1 Introduction   88
   5.2 A descriptive framework   89
   5.3 The dynamic context   92
   5.4 A methodology for tracing the impacts of policy decisions   93
   5.5 Analysing the impacts of price policy   94
   5.6 The central role of farming practice   95
   5.7 The relationship between farming practice and environmental
        indicators   96
   5.8 The effect of policy changes   99
   5.9 Incorporating the existing state of technology   100
   5.10 Implications of non-price policies   104
   5.11 A framework for the analysis of potential impacts of
        alternative policies   105
   5.12 Conclusions   109

6 Economic valuation of environmental impacts: the temptations of
   EVE
   James Winpenny
   6.1 Introduction   112
   6.2 Applications   112
   6.3 Outstanding issues   115
   6.4 Suggestions for better integration   121

7 The relevance and consistency of EIA and CBA in project appraisal
   Norman Lee and Colin Kirkpatrick
   7.1 Introduction   125
   7.2 Relevance and consistency in specified theoretical contexts   125
   7.3 Relevance and consistency in practice   126
   7.4 Improving relevance and consistency in the use of EIA and
        CBA in project appraisal   132
   Annex: the treatment of socio-economic impacts within EIA   133

8 Community impact evaluation in the development process
   Nathaniel Lichfield and Dalia Lichfield
   8.1 Some reasons for the lack of integration   139
   8.2 Origins of CIE   141
   8.3 Integrating environmental assessment within CIE   143
   8.4 The CIE method in outline   144
   8.5 Nesting of stakeholders within the CIE   146
   8.6 Summary   150

PART III APPRAISAL AND INTEGRATION: CASE STUDIES

9 Environmental assessment and economic valuation of ground water
   remediation projects
   Larry W. Canter
   9.1 Introduction   155
   9.2 Traditional methodology for assessing ground water impacts   155
   9.3 Economic concepts basic to ground water valuation   157
   9.4 Ground water valuation studies   162
   9.5 Ground water remediation projects – an opportunity to
        integrate impact assessment and economic valuation   164
   9.6 Summary   171

10 Integrated management of the environmental assessment process for
   projects in the water environment
   David Hickie
   10.1 Introduction   175
   10.2 Information management   176
   10.3 Management of the EA process in the Midlands Region   177
   10.4 Communication plan   180
   10.5 Scoping stage   182
   10.6 Environmental action plan   185
   10.7 Summary   187

11 Integrated environmental assessment applied to river sand harvesting in Kenya
John Kitetu and John Rowan

11.1	Introduction	189
11.2	Methods	190
11.3	Baseline environmental data	191
11.4	Distribution, nature and economics of river sand harvesting	191
11.5	Scoping survey of local experiences in the main mining area	193
11.6	Magnitude and significance of environmental impacts	194
11.7	Mitigating measures	196
11.8	Strategic environmental assessment	196
11.9	Conclusions	198

12 Potential uses of contingent valuation in the evaluation of dryland resource development projects: a small-scale irrigation case study from south-east Zimbabwe
Chris Lovell, Dominic Moran and Dominic Waughray

12.1	Introduction	200
12.2	Key economic benefits of the schemes	201
12.3	Economic concerns surrounding the project	202
12.4	Key non-market-based benefits of the project	204
12.5	The use of CV methods	208
12.6	Conclusions	214

13 Public valuation of solid waste impacts: a case study in Bangkok
Ian Blore and Fiona Nunan

13.1	Solid waste management in Bangkok	217
13.2	Landfill externalities and their economic valuation	218
13.3	Estimation of disamenity effects	220
13.4	Questionnaire and survey design	220
13.5	Results of the open-ended survey	222
13.6	Results of the dichotomous-choice survey	223
13.7	Discussion of the results	224
13.8	What are valid CV results?	225
13.9	Dose–response and CV methods	226
13.10	CV methods and public policy	227
13.11	CV methods and risk	228

14 The environmental impact of irrigation: the social dimension. A case
   study of Sultanpur, India
   Behrooz Morvaridi
   14.1 Introduction   231
   14.2 The case study: Sultanpur District   232
   14.3 The Sarda Sahayak Irrigation Project   234
   14.4 Assessment of the environmental impact of poorly managed
        irrigation: increases in wasteland   235
   14.5 The socio-economics of degradation: access to resources   237
   14.6 Environmental degradation, gender and social relations   240
   14.7 What can be learnt from the case study?   241

   Index   245

Figures

4.1 The national land use transition 76
4.2 Unified model of national land use transition, forest transition and replenishment period 76
4.3 Distribution of forest cover in Thailand, 1992 78
4.4. Forest divided into six degradation classes, Thailand 80
5.1 A descriptive framework 91
5.2 Production possibility frontier 95
5.3 Hypothetical scatter plot of farm practices 96
5.4 Farming practices and environmental implications 98
5.5 Change under different technologies 101
5.6 Technology-specific zones 102
5.7 Effects of barriers to resource access 105
5.8a Propensity of a policy to impact on specific environmental indicators 107
5.8b Propensity of a policy to impact on specific environmental indicators 108
8.1 Impact chain: generalized diagram for all effects 147
9.1 Conceptual approach for a traditional study focused on ground water impacts 156
9.2 Framework for valuation of ground water 158
11.1 Distribution of sand harvesting sites south-east of Nairobi, Kenya 192
11.2 Environmental management issues in the Kenyan river sand industry, and relevant agencies 195
11.3 SEA framework applied to river sand mining in Kenya 197
12.1 Predicted logit function 211
13.1 The potential externalities of landfill sites and possible economic evaluation techniques 219
13.2 Iterative bidding for DC questionnaire 221

Tables

1.1 Weak and strong forms of integration of environmental, social and economic assessments in overall appraisal and decision making within the development process 12

8.1 Methods of project appraisal used by different decision takers and stakeholders 140

8.2 Manchester Airport Second Runway: extract from summary of sectoral preferences 148

8.3 The nesting principle in CIE 151

9.1 Examples of valuation techniques for several ground water services 160

9.2 Chronological listing of examples of economic or other valuation studies conducted on ground water related issues 162

9.3 Suggested steps for incorporating environmental cost–benefit analysis into site-specific decision making regarding Superfund sites 165

9.4 Relationships between the proposed integrative methodology, the traditional EIA process and the valuation framework 169

9.5 Information sources for the seven-step method for incorporating cost–benefit analysis into Superfund site decision making 170

10.1 Project management of issues 177

10.2 Stages in the EA process for projects in the Midlands Region of the Environment Agency, using SI No. 1217 Land Drainage Regulations 179

10.3 Communication plan – forms of communication 181

10.4 Typical communications plan for a flood defence project 183

10.5 Elements of an environmental action plan 186

11.1 Key stages in research 190

11.2 Results of scoping analysis and impact ranking by local resident groups 193

12.1 Multivariate logit single bid (well maintenance), double-bounded mean (scheme membership) 210

13.1 Main reason for not being 'willing to pay' in OE and DC surveys 222

13.2 Main reason for WTP responses 223

13.3 Mean values of WTP 224

14.1 Costs of land reclamation 239

14.2 Average yield per acre by size and crops 240

List of contributors

Hussein Abaza is Chief, Economics, Trade and Environment Unit, United Nations Environment Programme, Geneva, Switzerland.

Ian Blore is a member of the School of Public Policy, University of Birmingham.

Larry W. Canter is the Sun Company Chair of Ground Water Hydrology at the Environmental and Ground Water Institute at the University of Oklahoma, Norman, Oklahoma, USA.

Alan Grainger is Lecturer, School of Geography, University of Leeds.

David Hickie is Regional Environmental Assessment Co-ordinator for the Midlands Region of the UK Environment Agency and Research Associate in the Department of Geography, Loughborough University.

Colin Kirkpatrick is Professor of Development Economics, Institute for Development Policy and Management, University of Manchester.

John Kitetu is a researcher in the Environmental Science Division, Institute of Environmental and Biological Science, Lancaster University.

Norman Lee is Senior Research Fellow, EIA Centre and Institute for Development Policy and Management, University of Manchester.

Dalia Lichfield is Senior Partner in the firm of Dalia & Nathaniel Lichfield Associates, Urban, Environmental and Development Planners.

Nathaniel Lichfield is Partner in the firm of Dalia & Nathaniel Lichfield Associates, Urban, Environmental and Development Planners and Professor Emeritus of the Economics of Environmental Planning, University of London.

Chris Lovell is Irrigation Engineer, Institute of Hydrology, Natural Environmental Research Council, Wallingford, UK.

Dominic Moran is Environmental and Resource Economist currently working in the Economic Planning Unit of the Prime Minister's Department in Malaysia. He was previously a Research Associate at the Centre for Social and Economic Research on the Global Environment, University College London and University of East Anglia.

Jamie Morrison is Lecturer, Department of Agricultural Economics, Wye College, University of London.

Behrooz Morvaridi is Lecturer at the Development and Project Planning Centre, University of Bradford.

Fiona Nunan is Research Associate in Environmental Management, School of Public Policy, University of Birmingham.

Richard Pearce is Programme Director, Agricultural Development in the External Programme, and Senior Lecturer, Department of Agricultural Economics, Wye College, University of London.

Michel Potier is Head of the Economics Division in the Environment Directorate at the Organization for Economic Cooperation and Development, Paris.

John Rowan is Lecturer in Environmental Management, Environmental Science Division, Institute of Environmental and Biological Science, Lancaster University.

Dominic Waughray is Environmental Economist, Institute of Hydrology, Natural Environment Research Council, Wallingford, UK.

James Winpenny is Research Fellow, Overseas Development Institute, London.

Preface

Recent years have seen a profound change in our understanding of the links between economic development and the environment. Post-Rio, there is a general recognition of the need to incorporate environmental concerns into policy making, and to strive to achieve a sustainable development path, which gives equal consideration to the goals of economic development, improved quality of the environment, and a more equitable distribution of benefits.

The application of appraisal procedures to the planning of projects, programmes and policies has become an important means of anticipating economic, social and environmental impacts, and provides the basis for prioritizing policies which, if implemented, will contribute to a more sustainable development process.

Environmental assessment, initially in the form of environmental impact assessment (EIA) for projects and much more recently in the form of strategic environmental assessment (SEA) for policies, plans and programmes, has become an important method of appraisal within different types of economy (developed, developing and transitional) and different aid agencies and development banks. Equally, economic assessment, especially of projects, has been widely applied using the methodology of cost–benefit analysis (CBA). The status and practice of social impact assessment (SIA) has grown more slowly than in the case of EIA and CBA; nevertheless, it is now recognized as an essential part of the overall assessment process.

However, the bringing together of environmental, social and economic assessment procedures has focused attention on a number of issues relating to appraisal theory and practice, notably:

- What is, and should be, the relationship between environmental assessment and the other forms of assessment?
- How might these different forms of assessment be integrated, or used in combination, in influencing the sustainable development process?
- To what extent do the answers to these questions vary according to the type of economy involved and the stage in the planning process at which the proposed action is being appraised?

In May 1996, a conference was held to consider these issues. The conference was organized as part of the Collaborative Programme in Environmental Assessment and Economic and Social Appraisal in the Development Process, which brings together the resources of the Development and Project Planning Centre, University of Bradford, and the EIA Centre and Institute for Development Policy and Management, University of Manchester. Sixty papers were presented, from which 13 have been selected and revised for inclusion in this volume.

We are grateful to Clive George, Will Banham and Sylvia Dransfield for assistance in the organization of the conference, and to Jane Reeves in preparing the manuscript for publication.

Colin Kirkpatrick
Norman Lee

PART I

INTEGRATING APPRAISAL WITHIN THE DEVELOPMENT PROCESS

1 Integrating environmental assessment with other forms of appraisal in the development process

Norman Lee and Colin Kirkpatrick

1.1 Introduction

The last 25 years, since the enactment of the National Environmental Policy Act (1969) in the USA, have seen a worldwide extension in the use of different forms of environmental assessment within the development process. However, it is not the only form of appraisal that is applied; others include technical, economic and social appraisals. How, then, do these different forms of appraisal relate to each other, and how should they be jointly used to provide satisfactory overall appraisals of the proposed actions to which they relate? Furthermore, appraisals are not undertaken in a vacuum but are carried out to assist in reaching decisions relating to the planning, appraisal and implementation of actions. How, then, is the environmental assessment 'taken into account', in conjunction with other appraisals, in decision making?

This collection of studies is concerned with two aspects of the integration of environmental assessment in the development process:

- How environmental assessments should be integrated with other forms of appraisal, notably economic and social appraisals, in the overall appraisal of policies, plans, programmes and individual projects.
- How environmental assessments, together with other forms of appraisal, should be integrated into decision making at different stages in the development process.

Compared with other, more specialized, aspects of project appraisal, these linkages *within* appraisal and *with* decision making have been less extensively analysed and documented. Nevertheless, sufficient is known to suggest that they may be 'weak links' in the appraisal–decision making–development process. Hence, there is a need to review and evaluate the state of knowledge and practice in this area, to identify any major weaknesses and to put forward possible remedies. In so doing, it is also necessary to consider how far the analysis should be specific to the type of action being appraised and to the type of country in which the appraisal is taking place. For example, it may be necessary to differentiate between appraisal and decision-making relating to projects and to more strategic-level actions, such as policies, plans and programmes, and between appraisal and decision-making situations in developed economies, developing economies and transitional economies.

In May 1996, a conference was held, jointly organized by the Universities of Bradford and Manchester, to examine these two integration issues. Over 130 delegates attended from a variety of developing, transitional and developed economies. Sixty papers were presented,[1] from which 13 have been selected and revised for inclusion in this publication. They have been organized into three main sections. This section (Part I) contains two additional chapters which examine the role of strategic forms of environmental assessment in the appraisal of structural adjustment programmes and trade liberalization measures. Part II (Appraisal and Integration: Frameworks and Methods) contains five chapters which mainly examine methodological aspects of the two integration issues identified above. Part III (Appraisal and Integration: Case Studies) contains six chapters which present case studies relating to a variety of developing and developed country situations, which exemplify different policy, procedural and methodological approaches to these integration issues.

The contents of the individual chapters are summarized in Section 1.4 below and proposals for remedying deficiencies in integration practice are presented in Section 1.5. Before then, in Section 1.2, we briefly review the origins, development and current status of the main constituent forms of appraisal (environmental, social and economic). Then, in Section 1.3, we explore different forms, 'weak' and 'strong', of integration that may be used in overall appraisal and in its linkage with decision making.

1.2 An overview of different forms of appraisal

In a recent review of environmental and social assessment (Vanclay and Bronstein, 1995) separate papers were presented, in addition to those on environmental impact assessment (EIA) and social impact assessment (SIA), on technology assessment, policy assessment, economic and fiscal assessment, demographic impact assessment, health impact assessment, risk assessment, climate impact assessment, development impact assessment and environmental sustainability assessment. Inevitably, where there is a proliferation of different forms of appraisal, the scope for duplication and methodological inconsistency is considerable. In this chapter, we confine our review to three main forms of appraisal – environmental impact assessment, social impact assessment and economic appraisal – and assume that the others can be accommodated within one or more of these categories. Even so, as will be shown, a number of difficulties still remain.

Environmental impact assessment

EIA, as a formalized appraisal requirement, dates from the enactment of the National Environmental Policy Act (NEPA, 1969) in the USA. Subsequent to this, but especially after the adoption of Directive 85/337/EEC in the European Union, similar provisions for EIA have been made in virtually all developed economies and in a large and increasing number of newly industrializing economies, developing economies and transitional economies (Lee, 1995; Sadler, 1995). Additionally, most bilateral and multinational agencies and development banks have established their own formal EIA procedures (OECD, 1996).

To date, most formal environmental assessment requirements, as well as assessment practice, have related to project-level appraisal. However, particularly during the 1990s, the scope of environmental assessment regulation and practice has been extending to include the appraisal of certain policies, plans and programmes (PPPs), which require approval at earlier stages of the development process (Sadler and Verheem, 1996; Therivel and Partidario, 1996). To distinguish this type of appraisal from EIA at the project level, it is frequently called strategic environmental assessment (SEA). The types of PPPs to which SEA may be applied are extremely diverse: they include sectoral plans (for example, transport, water, forest, tourism plans), land use plans and national or international development strategies and agreements (for example, structural adjustment programmes and multinational trade agreements).[2] What they have in common is the likelihood that their subsequent implementation may give rise to significant environmental impacts which are considered relevant to their overall appraisal and approval.

Although EIA and SEA provisions and practice vary considerably in their detailed features, they possess a number of common characteristics, certain of which distinguish them from other forms of appraisal, as follows:

1. In comparison with many other forms of appraisal, EIA is more often a legal requirement for certain types of projects in the countries in which it is applied and this gives it a special status.
2. EIA and SEA are each considered to be both a *process* and a *method* of appraisal. Particularly in the case of projects, the constituent stages and procedures of the process are fairly well defined and may have legal standing. These may cover the scope of the appraisal, which typically defines its coverage of environmental impacts quite broadly but

may not require the coverage of certain economic and social impacts. Hence, environmental assessments will often include some of the impacts which may be included in a social impact assessment, a risk assessment, a health impact assessment or an economic appraisal – but not all these impacts. Similarly, the EIA regulations will typically require that the findings of the EIA, which are presented in the environmental impact statement (EIS), are made publicly available, and are subject to consultation and public comment, and that the combined findings are then 'taken into consideration' in decision making. Such provisions, which may influence both the content and importance attached to the EIA (and SEA) in decision making, are often absent in the case of other forms of appraisal.

3. The methodology of EIA and SEA involves predicting the expected magnitude of the environmental impacts and evaluating their significance for decision-making purposes (Canter, 1996). Although the significance of the environmental impact may be expressed in economic terms, this is not a requirement and, in the majority of cases at present, this is not considered to be practical, partly because of concerns over the technical reliability of the economic valuation methods available and the quality of data available for their use, and partly because of concern over their likely public acceptability for consultation and decision-making purposes. In the absence of a generally agreed methodology for combining environmental impacts with other types of impacts in the overall appraisal of proposed actions, a range of different kinds of approaches to overall appraisal and decision making are to be found. Some emphasize the procedural requirements of appraisal and decision making – for example, the importance of transparency in the process, of the opportunities for stakeholders and interest groups to be involved in the consultative process, of the public accountability of the decision makers for reaching a reasoned and informed decision and of the need for post-project monitoring to ensure compliance with the conditions of the decision during project implementation (Canter, 1996 ch.16; Lichfield and Lichfield, Chapter 8, this volume). Others may express a preference for a well-developed appraisal framework and methodology using some form of multi-objective or multi-criteria analysis in preference to a single-criterion technique, such as the net present value (NPV) criterion commonly used in economic appraisal (Canter, 1996, ch. 15; Nijkamp *et al.*, 1990; Phaneuf, 1990). These methodological characteristics of EIA may well differ from those observed in other forms of appraisal.

Social impact assessment

Burdge and Vanclay (1995) define social impact assessment (SIA) as a process for assessing the social consequences to human beings and their communities which are likely to result from specific policy actions or project developments. They date the formulation of SIA from shortly after the enactment of NEPA (1969); however, its subsequent relationship to EIA has been rather uncertain and imprecise.

There is ongoing uncertainty over the extent to which SIA is to be regarded as an integral component of the EIA process or as a separate process functioning in its own right. In many regulatory regimes, there is broad agreement that impacts on human beings and their communities, which result from environmental changes brought about by proposed new actions, do fall within the scope of an environmental impact assessment (Council on Environmental Quality, 1978). However, opinion is divided on whether or not the social impacts of new developments which are not associated with environmental changes are to be included in an EIA, although there may be broad agreement that they are relevant to the overall appraisal of such developments.

In practice, the status and influence of SIA have grown more slowly than in the case of EIA, even in countries such as the USA, Canada, Australia and New Zealand which use SIA both as a component of environmental assessment and as a stand-alone process. Burdge and Vanclay comment: 'the fact remains that in the two decades since SIA became a recognised subfield of research and policy application, there are few examples where its use has made a difference in the project/policy decision process. On the other hand, EIA has been shown to be one of the most far-ranging and significant methodologies to improve projects and policies' (Burdge and Vanclay, 1995, p.37).

There are many reasons for this situation, which continues to exist despite a substantial and expanding SIA literature.[3] These include: continuing uncertainties and ambiguities in a number of countries over its legal status; the existence of a wide diversity of different methodologies and approaches for undertaking SIAs; poor quality and inadequate data available for use in SIAs; and a lack of expertise in carrying out SlAs and using them effectively for decision-making purposes.

However, a number of more recent developments may strengthen SIAs' future role and influence. For example, some progress has been made in systematizing the stages in the SIA process and the assessment methods to be used which could lead to improvements in the quality and effectiveness of SIA, either within the framework of the EIA process or in parallel with it. This has been promoted in the Inter-organizational Committee's report *Guidelines and Principles for Social Impact Assessment* (Inter-organizational Committee, 1994) which identifies ten steps in undertaking an SIA which correspond to similar steps in the EIA process, as described in the Council on Environmental Quality's guidelines (CEQ, 1978). Additionally, in response to growing concerns over the social consequences of new developments, including impacts on human health and the well-being of women, and over the need to achieve greater local community involvement in the development process, new SIA guidelines are being developed or existing guidelines are being updated and strengthened by an increasing number of national and international aid-related organizations such as the Asian Development Bank (1992a,b), the World Bank (1994), the Overseas Development Administration (1995) and the United States Agency for International Development (1994). However, it remains to be seen how successfully, in practice, these strengthened forms of social impact assessment can be integrated into overall appraisal and decision making at the project and PPP levels.

Economic appraisal
Economic appraisal, as a formalized method of project appraisal, has the longest history of the three assessment methods under consideration in this chapter. Partly because of this it is, in a technical sense, the most developed and refined appraisal method and, in economic and financial circles, it undoubtedly has the highest status. Commercial investment appraisal methods (that is, those which consider only costs and revenues to project developers) have evolved over a number of decades from simple 'pay back' and 'book rate of return' methods to more sophisticated 'net present value' and 'internal rate of return' methods (Devine *et al.*, 1985, ch. 7). Broader social cost–benefit (CBA) methods (that is, those which cover costs and benefits to society as a whole) date back to the 1930s, when they were first systematically applied to water resource projects in the USA.[4] Since then, the CBA methodology has been further developed and refined, in particular, by adapting the methods used to reflect the special conditions and characteristics of developing countries. This developing country cost–benefit literature has focused attention on the pervasive market failures and other imperfections in developing countries, which have made prevailing market prices an inadequate guide to the full costs and benefits to society.[5]

The CBA methodology is now well developed and is described in a considerable number of economic investment manuals prepared in their own countries and by international aid agencies and development banks for use when appraising and approving their own funding activities.[6] Most of the differences in approach and detailed requirements that arose in the earlier literature have now been resolved. The alternative approaches adopted by Little and Mirrlees (1974) and UNIDO (1972) to the choice of the unit of valuation (the 'numeraire' debate), are now recognized as being almost identical. Similarly, the differences between the Anglo-Saxon CBA and French 'effects methods' of investment appraisal are now widely regarded as being relatively trivial (Franck, 1996).

In principle, because CBA aims to encompass all benefits and costs to society, it should include all the environmental and social benefits and costs (externalities) which would also be covered in environmental impact and social impact assessments. Similarly, in principle, CBA also considers the timing of benefits and costs (through the use of discounting procedures), takes account of the risk of accidents (by incorporating the findings of a risk assessment), makes allowance for different sources of uncertainty (for example, through the use of sensitivity analysis), and considers distributional effects (by, for example, weighting the benefits and costs to different socio-economic groups).

In practice, however, the extent to which each of the above elements in the economic appraisal is, or can be, performed to the satisfaction of those with interests in the overall appraisal and authorization of the proposed actions is quite variable. In particular, there is concern over the extent to which environmental and social impacts can be valued in economic terms for inclusion in CBAs. There already exists a substantial literature on the economic valuation of environmental impacts, in addition to the papers relating to the topic included in this volume.[7] What, collectively, they appear to indicate is that, despite the considerable methodological advances over the past two decades, not all environmental impacts can yet be satisfactorily valued in economic terms. Also, the extent to which they can be valued varies according to type of impact and type of country. Furthermore, securing public and political acceptance for the use of economic values of environmental impacts within economic appraisals can be difficult. This often leads to the use of hybrid forms of economic appraisal which incorporate information on some environmental and social impacts in a non-monetary form. Where this is the case, the overall appraisal begins to take on a more multi-objective or multi-criteria character (Department of the Environment, 1991, 1994).

Debate continues, also, on the choice of discount rates, particularly where the project may have significant environmental impacts. The case for applying a low discount rate to long-term environmental benefits (Cline, 1992, 1993) is countered by the argument that an adjustment to the discount rate is not an efficient way of protecting the interests of future generations. Alternatively, it has been suggested, a more effective approach may be to incorporate an environmental damage, or sustainability, constraint into the CBA which requires any environmental damage caused by a project to be offset by other compensating environmental improvements (Markandya and Pearce, 1991, 1994).

The appropriate treatment of the distributional consequences of a project is an additional unresolved issue. Some of the literature relating to CBA in the developing country context recommends the quantification and valuation of income flows to different groups, which are then assigned different distributional weights, before being incorporated in the overall estimate of net social benefit (Londero, 1996). In practice, however, the distributional weighting approach has never been applied on a systematic or consistent basis (Little and Mirrlees, 1990; Squire, 1990). Nor is there a general consensus on how the weights should be calculated. More recently, attention has switched to the process approach to project appraisal as an alternative way of taking account of the distributional, or 'people', impact of projects (Picciotto and Weaving, 1994), but, so far, it has proved difficult to integrate the process approach into the more traditional CBA appraisal methodology (Wilmshurst, 1996).

The CBA methodology, in principle, should be equally applicable at the level of policies, plans and programmes, with the net benefits, or rate of return, of a proposed policy change being calculated by comparing the projected 'with policy' and 'without policy' outcomes (Kanbur, 1990). In practice, the use of cost–benefit methods for policy analysis has been limited.[8] The benefits of policy changes are widely dispersed through the economy, and difficult to measure accurately. In the same way, the costs have an economy-wide impact, often with significant distributional effects. There is also the additional problem of allocating costs and benefits to particular policy changes, where a set of policy changes is introduced together as a policy reform programme. More fundamentally, the rational-choice model, which underlies the CBA approach, provides little insight into how societal interests and political economy considerations shape the decision-making process (Grindle and Thomas, 1991; Rodrik, 1996).

Additionally, economic appraisal is often distinguishable from EIA and SIA in being less open to public inspection. Furthermore, its provisions for consultation and public participation are much less developed and its procedural linkage with decision making and implementation may be of a different, and sometimes, weaker nature.

Hence important issues of scope, method and procedure are likely to arise when considering the integration of economic appraisal with other forms of environmental and social assessment in overall appraisal and decision making.

1.3 Weak and strong forms of integration

To a considerable extent, the concerns which need to be addressed, when analysing the integration of environmental assessment with other forms of social and economic assessment in appraisal and decision making, can be deduced from the reviews in the previous section. However, this can be further assisted by making use of a conceptual framework which incorporates both the integration of the different forms of assessment and the integration of appraisal with decision making. This is elaborated below.

The starting point in constructing such a framework is to identify the particular decision which is to be made. In reality, there are many decision points in the development process: they relate to different types of actions (policies, plans, programmes, projects), different sectoral activities (agriculture, energy, transport, and so on) and different stages in the planning and authorization process (project design, approval, implementation and so on). The legal and institutional context in which appraisal and decision making take place will also vary between and within countries according to the type of decision under consideration. Therefore, there is unlikely to be a single 'best' way, methodologically or procedurally, in which to address the two main integration issues with which this volume is concerned.

In Table 1.1, we illustrate two polar cases of integration, 'weak' and 'strong', within which the appraisal and the authorization decision for a particular development project are assumed to take place. In the 'weak' case, separate forms of assessment (environmental, social and economic) are undertaken and the decision-making authority possesses very considerable discretion in how it uses these when making its decision. In the 'strong' case, the environmental, social and economic assessments are fully integrated with each other for the duration of the appraisal process and the decision-making authority is explicitly required to use (and show it has used) the overall appraisal in reaching its decision.

Each of these approaches has its advantages and disadvantages, the relative importance of which varies from one appraisal and decision-making situation to another.

Table 1.1 Weak and strong forms of integration of environmental, social and economic assessments in overall appraisal and decision making within the development process

Weak	Strong
1. Environmental, social and economic objectives are separately defined for the proposed action (some simple consistency checks of the likely compatibility and attainability of the three sets of objectives are carried out). ↓	1. An integrated set of environmental, social and economic objectives is defined for the proposed action (its consistency is checked against overall sustainable development objectives for the economy). ↓
2. Environmental, social and economic data are gathered separately (there is some recognition of the need for consistency in data collection and in their subsequent analysis and interpretation). ↓	2. A combined programme of environmental, social and economic data gathering is undertaken (data are to be collected and subsequently analysed and interpreted according to a consistent set of criteria derived from the above integrated set of objectives). ↓
3. Predictions of the environmental, social and economic consequences of the proposed action are separately undertaken (major 'knock-on' effects between environmental, social and economic systems are also identified, where possible). ↓	3. Predictions of the environmental, social and economic consequences are undertaken within an integrated environmental–social–economic framework (the principal interactions and 'knock-on' effects between the environmental, social and economic systems are systematically analysed and taken into account when making the predictions). ↓
4. Separate environmental, social and economic appraisals of the proposed action are prepared, each based on its own set of appraisal criteria (each set of appraisal criteria should be derived from the corresponding, environmental, social and economic objectives identified above whose compatibility and attainability should have been checked previously). ↓	4. The overall appraisal of the proposed action is undertaken according to a set of criteria consistent with the above integrated set of objectives (this appraisal may be in the form of a CBA [if there is a sole NPV criterion] or, more likely, use multi-criteria analysis [if there are multiple criteria to apply]). ↓
5. Decision makers have considerable discretion in how they 'take into account' the findings of the separate appraisals in reaching their decision on the authorization of the proposed action. Typically, they use informal, non-explicit methods and do not provide justified reasons for their decision.	5. Decision makers are required to 'take into account' the results of the overall appraisal (which is published) in reaching their decision and are required to publish the justified reasons for the decision.

- The weak integration model is technically and organizationally less demanding. It provides a measure of independence to each form of appraisal which may be particularly important for the less well-established forms of appraisal, and it may be more acceptable to decision makers since it allows them more discretion when making their decision. On the other hand, separate appraisals increase the risks of overlap, omissions and inconsistencies occurring between them; they may reduce the influence of overall appraisal on project selection and design during the early stages of the appraisal process; and the lack of a strong link with decision making may seriously weaken the practical effectiveness of the appraisal process as a whole.
- The 'strong' integration model is better able to address the kinds of weaknesses that have been identified in the 'weak' model but it has its own drawbacks. It is more technically demanding (for example, because of the requirement to specify and quantify linkages and interactions between systems) and, potentially at least, it is also more demanding in its data requirements. The less well-developed and supported elements within the overall appraisal (for example those relating to certain environmental and social impacts) may be neglected in the construction and application of the integrated model. Also, decision makers may resent their more circumscribed decision making rôle if their decisions are to be largely determined by the findings of the overall appraisal.

Understandably, then, the choice between weak and strong brands of integration (and between intermediate brands) will vary according to the type of action and the appraisal and decision-making context in which it is being considered. Additionally, there will be important variations in the quality of application of whichever model is chosen. For example, as Table 1.1 shows, there is a variety of ways in which relevance and consistency can be strengthened within the weak integration model, and there are various ways, through further research and surveys, by which the more demanding technical and information requirements of the strong integration model may be better met. The means of achieving such improvements are considered further, following a review of the remaining chapters in this volume.

1.4 Review of papers
The papers which have been selected for inclusion in this volume have been chosen because of the contribution they make to understanding the need to integrate environmental assessment with other forms of appraisal

in the development process, to understanding the frameworks and methods of appraisal and integration that may be used, or which exemplify these through case studies relating to different types of actions and country situations.

The two other chapters in this opening section support the use of environmental assessment, in conjunction with other forms of appraisal, in more strategic forms of appraisal and decision making for certain types of policies, plans and programmes. Abaza, in Chapter 2, reviews the role of strategic environmental assessment (SEA), used in conjunction with other forms of appraisal, in the assessment and modification of structural adjustment programmes (SAPs). He suggests that SEA is a process which can assist in the integration of social, economic and environmental considerations at various stages in the preparation and approval of development policies, plans and programmes. More specifically, he argues for its application to SAPs which are being introduced in a considerable number of developing countries where they are having both positive and negative environmental consequences. He recommends that SAPs should be screened for their likely conformity with sustainability objectives, that both their socio-economic and environmental costs and benefits should be assessed and that alternative development scenarios and options should be evaluated from both environmental and economic perspectives.

Potier, in Chapter 3, focuses on the environmental assessment of trade liberalization policies. He draws attention to the conflicts which have arisen in the past between trade experts who have celebrated the virtues of trade liberalization and the environmental benefit to be gained in the process and the environmental specialists who have accused trade liberalization of leading to a systematic degradation of the environment. He then describes how the OECD has attempted to promote a more systematic and balanced approach to the trade liberalization–environment relationship. This has been undertaken through the development of an analytical framework for considering the possible environmental effects of trade liberalization and the preparation of case studies relating to trade in particular industries, to provide supporting empirical evidence. Additionally, the OECD has developed guidelines, based upon these studies, on how to assess the environmental effects of trade policies.

Part II contains chapters mainly concerned with analytical frameworks and assessment methods for use in integrated appraisal and decision making. Grainger, in Chapter 4, highlights the need to integrate environmental assessment and socio-economic appraisal at the national level, particularly in relation to developing countries, where he considers partiality in analysis has previously led to damaging policy interventions. In order to meet this need, he advocates the development of national environmental indices to be used when monitoring environmental performance. More specifically, he argues that such indices should be used in monitoring and evaluating the environmental impacts of macroeconomic policies adopted by such organizations as the International Monetary Fund and the World Bank and recommends a new National Index of Sustainable Development be used for this purpose.

Morrison and Pearce, in Chapter 5, develop a methodology for appraising the likely environmental impacts of policy decisions in the agricultural sectors of developing countries. This is to be used to examine how agricultural policy reforms are likely to affect farming practices, which, in turn, bring about changes in the environmental impacts of the agricultural sector. They demonstrate that a given policy change can have widely varying environmental consequences, depending on the broader policy context in which it is initiated and the type of agricultural technology which is currently applied. However, despite these complexities, they suggest that with relatively limited information it should be possible, using simple flow charts, to trace the likely environmental consequences of a new agricultural policy initiative. Then, it should also be possible to identify the modifications to the proposed new policy, and/or the additional complementary measures, which may be needed to offset any unacceptable environmental impacts.

Winpenny, in Chapter 6, examines the current state of knowledge and practice in the economic valuation of environmental impacts. He reviews the different uses of such economic valuations, which include the appraisal of both individual projects and broader based policies. He notes that, despite considerable progress, certain features of these valuations continue to be controversial both within the economics profession and in relations among economists, environmental professionals and the general public. A number of outstanding methodological issues are then examined relating to the use of contingent valuation techniques, the valuation of health and life, the use of discounting procedures and of benefit transfer methods. The chapter concludes with a number of suggestions to make the economic valuation of environmental impacts more credible and acceptable.

Lee and Kirkpatrick, in Chapter 7, examine a variety of relevance and consistency issues which arise in the selection and combined use of environmental assessment and economic appraisal methods. Their analysis mainly concentrates on the joint use of EIA and CBA at the project level. They demonstrate how the selection and joint application of different appraisal methods may be defective either because they are not entirely relevant in the decision-making context in which the appraisal is to be used or because of incompatibilities between the methods and/or procedures used in the two types of appraisal. The chapter concludes with a number of recommendations for improving the relevance and consistency of combined, project appraisals in the future.

Lichfield and Lichfield, in Chapter 8, present a different approach to integrated appraisal and decision making which has been developed for use within the UK land use planning and development control system. Originally known as the planning balance sheet approach, it has recently been modified and renamed community impact evaluation (CIE). Its main features, which are described and illustrated within the chapter, include: all types of benefits and costs (environmental and non-environmental) relevant to making planning decisions are included in the CIE; benefits and costs are not necessarily all expressed in monetary units; and benefits and costs are presented separately for each of the categories of stakeholders and other interested parties. The authors suggest that presenting the project or plan appraisal in this form assists the parties involved to identify its likely consequences for them, and facilitates identifying any modifications which may help in achieving a consensus for approval at the decision-making stage.

Part III contains a selection of case studies which illustrate different approaches, methodological and procedural, to meeting the integration needs which have been identified above. Canter, in Chapter 9, demonstrates how economic valuation methods and cost–benefit analysis may be used as integrating tools within the EIA process for ground water remediation projects at Superfund sites within the USA. He develops an integrative methodology, based on the principal stages in the EIA process, and then shows how the necessary information may be acquired and used at each stage in an overall appraisal of this type of project. He emphasizes that, for the integrative approach to work effectively, hydrogeological, engineering, environmental and economic professionals must each be willing to 'interact with and learn from related disciplines'.

Hickie, in Chapter 10, describes the provisions being made for strengthening the integration of the environmental assessment process into the overall planning, management and implementation of flood defence projects in the UK. He explains the environmental assessment process which is now applied in the Midlands Region of the recently established Environmental Agency which seeks to integrate technical, environmental and economic considerations into the assessment process from the early stages of project development. He then elaborates how this is to be achieved using, in particular, three supporting instruments. These are: a *communication plan* (to improve the management of communications with all appropriate parties, internal and external to the Agency, throughout project development and implementation); a *scoping report* (prepared at an early stage in project planning, before feasibility studies have begun); and an *environmental action plan* (to secure satisfactory implementation of the project in accordance with environmental and social requirements).

Kitetu and Rowan, in Chapter 11, present a study concerning the integrated environmental assessment of sand harvesting for construction purposes, from the beds of seasonally dry rivers in rural districts close to major urban centres in Kenya. Whilst these activities provide important employment and other economic opportunities in the rural areas concerned, excessive and inappropriate forms of sand harvesting do have serious, adverse, environmental, social and economic consequences associated with water losses, channel instability and damage to bridge piers. The authors support the use of strategic environmental assessments within the framework of a more comprehensive and strengthened planning strategy. This strategy, they suggest, should be applied at different levels of public administration and should take full account of the interdependences between different sectors such as the construction sector, sand harvesting, transport and water resources. Until this can be made operational, they recommend support for river sand harvesting cooperatives which will encourage the participation of the local community in the management of their communal sand resources.

Lovell, Moran and Waughray, in Chapter 12, show how contingent valuation methods can be used to quantify the total (market and non-market) economic benefits of a project. Using a case study located in the drylands area of south-east Zimbabwe, where rural households were provided with communal wells, the authors illustrate how survey and questionnaire responses can provide sufficient information to estimate the economic value attached to the non-market benefits resulting from the improved household food and income security associated with access to secure, high-quality water supply. The inclusion of these non-market values with the market value of the increased sales of agricultural products substantially increased the project's net present value.

Blore and Nunan, in Chapter 13, use contingent valuation (CV) techniques to estimate the economic value of the environmental (disamenity) costs associated with a landfill urban refuse site in Bangkok, Thailand. Using a comparatively small sample of respondents, the authors were able to derive estimates which were used to inform the public policy decision-making process. The study highlights the problems that can arise in interpreting CV responses, where the affected parties are not fully aware of the environmental impacts. In the case of landfill sites, there are potential health risks linked to leachate, landfill gases and particulate air pollution, about which individuals may not be informed. Where this is the case, the respondents' valuations may be restricted to the disamenity effects and therefore understate the total economic value of the environmental costs.

Morvaridi, in Chapter 15, is concerned with the integration of social assessment and environmental impact assessment. Using a case study of an irrigation project in Sultanpur, Uttar Pradesh, India, he shows how the progressive environmental deterioration in the quality of land, caused by irrigation-induced salinization, has led to a major impact on household nutrition and poverty levels, the utilization of household labour, gender relations, the migration of labour to alternative sources of employment, and the consolidation of land holdings. He concludes that, for the purpose of assessment, social impact and environmental impact should be integrated within a common interdisciplinary framework.

1.5 Conclusions and recommendations

On the basis of the chapters contained in this volume, supplemented by the additional documentation cited in this chapter, the case for more effective, integrated appraisal and decision making has, in our judgement, been conclusively established. This holds both for different stages in the development process (the preparation and approval of policies, plans, programmes and projects) and for different types of economy (developed, developing, transitional). However, the diversity of situations in which more effective integration is needed means that there is no single integration model which will be universally applicable – in some cases a 'strong' version may be chosen; in other cases a 'weak' version will be more appropriate. Yet, in most circumstances, the underlying principles and purposes of integration will be essentially the same.

The studies which have been reviewed in this introductory chapter have revealed an interesting and potentially important discrepancy in knowledge and practice:

- Over the past quarter century, important advances in knowledge and its application have been made in each of the three main forms of appraisal – environmental impact assessment, social impact assessment and economic appraisal.
- Yet, over the same period of time, there have not been commensurate advances in integrated appraisal and decision making.

The consequence is that the advances in EIA, SIA and CBA have been much less influential in their effects on the development process than they could otherwise have been. While this is more apparent at the project level of appraisal and decision making, it is also believed to apply at the policy, plan and programme level.

Given this situation, there is a need to consider what further measures might be taken to remedy the deficiencies which have been identified. Although there are many specific suggestions in the following chapters and the accompanying literature, there is not yet a consensus on the over-all strategy which should be followed. Below, we indicate some of the components that we believe should be included in such a strategy.

1. *Awareness raising* The extent of the deficiencies, and their conse-quences for the quality of overall appraisals and decision making, are not yet sufficiently widely appreciated among those involved in deci-sion making, consultation activities relating to appraisals and decision making, and technical studies for appraisals. In all these cases, the benefits from a more interdisciplinary approach need to be empha-sized through awareness-raising initiatives. This applies equally to policies, plans and programmes as it does to project appraisal and decision making.

2. *Guidance, case studies and training* Simple, practical guidelines (proce-dural and methodological) should be prepared on how to undertake the two recommended forms of integration. These will need to be sensitive to the different contexts (type of action, authorization procedures, country and so on) in which they are likely to be used. Their application should be illustrated by a number of realistic 'inte-gration' case studies. Their use should be reinforced through training programmes, which include the guidelines and appropriate case stud-ies as training materials.

3. *Research and other studies* Both the above proposals should be sup-ported by a programme of research and other related studies. These should serve the following purposes:

   - Improving knowledge of the relevant subsystems (environmental, social and economic) and of the linkages (causal and procedural) between them, which is necessary to the more effective development of integrated appraisal and decision-making models. These study and modelling activities need to be carried out at different levels of generality and with different information requirements to take account of the different types of actions and country situations to which they may be applied.
   - Evaluating the procedures and methods of appraisal and decision making currently in use for particular types of action. The evalua-tion should be undertaken from the standpoint of their intended

integrated use, having regard to such criteria as consistency, relevance, effectiveness, practicality and so on. Such studies should result in recommendations for improvements to current practice.

- Improving data availability for integrated appraisal and decision making. This would first require a comparison, on a type of action and/or type of country basis, between current information needs and availability in order to identify the major information deficiencies needing the most urgent attention.
- Preparing case studies, illustrating both good and bad integration practice in appraisal and decision making. These may then be used for training and awareness raising purposes as well as improving guidance on best practice.

It is hoped that the publication of the chapters in this volume, and the proposals they contain, will stimulate further activity leading to practical improvements in this area. The present intention is to hold a follow-up conference in two to three years' time which will review and evaluate the progress which has been made over the intervening period.

Notes

1. These are contained in Development and Project Planning Centre (University of Bradford) and Environmental Impact Assessment Centre (University of Manchester) (1996), *Integrating Environmental Assessment and Socio-Economic Appraisal in the Development Process: Conference Papers*, 3 vols, DPPC, University of Bradford, Bradford.
2. The literature relating to SEA is now quite extensive. Recent relevant studies include Sadler and Verheem (1996), de Boer and Sadler (1996), Therivel and Partidario (1996), Lee and Hughes (1995), Kirkpatrick and Lee (1997), Reed (1996), Munasinghe and Cruz (1995), OECD (1994).
3. The SIA literature includes the following relevant studies: Vanclay (1989 continuing), Inter-organizational Committee on Guidelines and Principles for Social Impact Assessment (1994), Burdge *et al.* (1994), Overseas Development Administration (1995), Asian Development Bank (1992a,b), USAID (1994), World Bank (1994).
4. The early contributions to the development of the CBA methodology were reviewed in Prest and Turvey (1965). The more recent theoretical CBA literature is surveyed by Dreze and Stern (1987), Squire (1989).
5. The best-known early contributions to the developing country CBA literature are Little and Mirrlees (1968, 1974), UNIDO (1972), Squire and van der Tak (1975). Curry and Weiss (1993) gives a detailed, up-to-date account of the methodology and specific appraisal methods; Chowdhury and Kirkpatrick (1994, ch. 4) provides an introductory treatment of the same issues. The various contributions in Kirkpatrick (1994) and Kirkpatrick and Weiss (1996) examine a range of issues being currently debated concerning cost–benefit analysis and project appraisal in developing countries.
6. CBA manuals prepared by development agencies include: ODA (1988), Ward and Deren (1991), World Bank (1995), Asian Development Bank (1996b). Devarajan *et al.* (1996) give a useful summary of current World Bank thinking on economic project appraisal methodology and practice.

7. The economic valuation of environmental effects is dealt with in: Asian Development Bank (1996a), Abelson (1996), Winpenny (1991), Pearce (1993), Hanley and Spash (1993), Weiss (1994), OECD (1995).
8. For an early empirical attempt to apply shadow pricing to policy analysis, see Squire. Little and Durdag (1979).

References

Abelson, P. (1996), *Project Appraisal and Valuation of the Environment*, London: Macmillan.

Asian Development Bank (1992a), *Guidelines for Social Analysis of Development Projects*, Manila: ADB.

Asian Development Bank (1992b) *Guidelines for the Health Impact Assessment of Development Projects*, Manila: ADB.

Asian Development Bank (1996a), *Economic Evaluation of Environmental Impacts*, Manila: ADB.

Asian Development Bank (1996b), *Guidelines for the Economic Analysis of Projects*, mimeo, Manila: ADB.

Burdge, R.J. and F. Vanclay (1995), 'Social Impact Assessment' in F. Vanclay, and D.A. Bronstein (eds), *Environmental and Social Impact Assessment*, Chichester, UK: Wiley.

Burdge, R.J. *et al.* (1994), *A Conceptual Approach to Social Impact Assessment: Collection of Readings*, Middleton, WI: Social Ecology Press.

Canter, L.W. (1996), *Environmental Impact Assessment*, second edition, New York: McGraw-Hill.

Chowdhury, A. and C. Kirkpatrick (1994), *Development Policy and Planning: An Introduction to Models and Techniques*, London: Routledge.

Cline, W. (1992), *The Economics of Global Warming*, Washington, DC: Institute for International Economics.

Cline, W. (1993) 'Give Greenhouse Abatement a Fair Chance', *Finance and Development*, **30** (1), March, 3–6.

Council on Environmental Quality (1978), 'National Environmental Policy Act – Regulations', *Federal Register*, **43** (230), 55978–6007.

Curry, S. and J. Weiss (1993), *Project Analysis in Developing Countries*, London: Macmillan.

de Boer, J. and B. Sadler (eds) (1996), *Strategic Environmental Assessment: Environmental Assessment of Policies*, No. 54, VROM Series, Ministry of Housing, Spatial Planning and the Environment, The Hague.

Department of the Environment (1991), *Policy Appraisal and the Environment*, London: HMSO.

Department of the Environment (1994), *Environmental Appraisal in Government Departments*, London: HMSO.

Devarajan, S., L. Squire and S. Suthiwart-Narueput (1996), 'Project Appraisal at the World Bank', in C. Kirkpatrick, and J. Weiss (eds), *Cost–Benefit Analysis and Project Appraisal in Developing Countries*, Cheltenham, UK and Brookfield, US: Edward Elgar.

Devine, P.J., N. Lee, R.M. Jones and W.J. Tyson (1985), *An Introduction to Industrial Economics*, fourth edition, London: Unwin Hyman.

Dreze, J. and N. Stern (1987), 'The Theory of Cost–Benefit Analysis', in A. Auerbach and M. Feldstein (eds), *Handbook of Public Economics*, Amsterdam: North-Holland.

Franck, B. (1996), 'The Effects Method and Economic Cost–Benefit Analysis: Substitutes or Complements?' in C. Kirkpatrick and J. Weiss (eds), *Cost–Benefit Analysis and Project Appraisal in Developing C ountries*, Cheltenham, UK and Brookfield, US: Edward Elgar.

Grindle, M.S. and J.W. Thomas (1991), *Public Choices and Policy Change*, Baltimore, MD and London: The Johns Hopkins University Press.

Hanley, N. and C. Spash (1993), *Cost–Benefit Analysis and the Environment*, UK: Edward Elgar.

Inter-Organizational Committee on Guidelines and Principles for Social Impact Assessment (1994) 'Guidelines and Principles for Social Impact Assessment', *Environmental Impact Assessment Review*, **15** (l), 11–43.

Kanbur, R. (1990) 'Projects Versus Policy Reform', *Proceedings of the World Bank Annual Conference on Development Economics, 1990*, Washington, DC: World Bank.

Kirkpatrick, C. (ed.) (1994), 'Special Issue on Project Appraisal in Developing Countries', *Journal of International Development*, **6** (1).

Kirkpatrick, C. and N. Lee (1997), 'Market Liberalization and Environmental Assessment in Developing and Transitional Economies', *Journal of Environmental Management*, **50** (3), July.

Kirkpatrick, C. and J. Weiss (eds) (1996), *Cost–Benefit Analysis and Project Appraisal in Developing Countries*, Cheltenham, UK and Brookfield, US: Edward Elgar.

Lee, N. (1995), 'Environmental Assessment in the European Union: A Tenth Anniversary', *Proiect Appraisal*, **10** (2), 77–90.

Lee, N. and J. Hughes (1995), *Strategic Environmental Assessment Legislation and Procedures in the Community*, 2 vols, mimeo, Brussels: European Commission (DGXI).

Little, I.M.D. and J. Mirlees (1968), *Manual of Industrial Project Analysis in Developing Countries*, Vol. 2, Paris: OECD.

Little, I.M.D. and J. Mirlees (1974), *Project Appraisal and Planning for Developing Countries*, London: Heinemann.

Little, I.M.D. and J. Mirlees (1990), 'Project Appraisal and Planning Twenty Years on' *Proceedings of World Bank Annual Conference on Development Economics*, Washington, DC: World Bank.

Londero, E. (1996) 'Reflections on Estimating Distributional Weights', in C. Kirkpatrick and J. Weiss (eds), *Cost–Benefit Analysis and Project Appraisal in Developing Countries*. Cheltenham, UK and Brookfield, US: Edward Elgar.

Markandya, A. and D. Pearce, (1991), 'Development, the Environment and the Social Rate of Discount', *World Bank Research Observer*, **6** (2), 137–53.

Markandya, A. and D. Pearce (1994), 'Natural Environments and the Social Rate of Discount', in J. Weiss (ed.) *The Economics of Project Appraisal and the Environment*, Aldershot, UK: Edward Elgar.

Munasinghe, M. and W. Cruz (1995), *Economy-wide Policies and the Environment: Lessons from Experience*, World Bank Environmental Paper No.10, Washington, DC.

Nijkamp, P., P. Riebveld and H. Voogd (1990), *Multicriteria Evaluation in Physical Planning*, Amsterdam: North-Holland.

OECD (1994), *Methodologies for Environmental and Trade Reviews*, Paris: OECD.

OECD (1995), *The Economic Appraisal of Environmental Projects and Policies: A Practical Guide* (author J. Winpenny), Paris: OECD.

OECD (1996), *Coherence in Environmental Assessment: Practical Guidance on Development Co-operation Projects*, Paris: OECD.

Overseas Development Administration (1988), *Appraisal of Projects in Developinq Countries*, London: HMSO.

Overseas Development Administration (1995), *A Guide to Social Analysis for Projects in Developing Countries*, London: HMSO.

Pearce, D. (1993), *Economic Values and the Natural World*, London: Earthscan.

Phaneuf, Y. (1990), *EIS Process and Decision Making*, Canadian Environmental Assessment Research Council, Hull, Quebec.

Picciotto, R. and R. Weaving (1994), 'A New Project Cycle for the World Bank', *Finance and Development*, **31** (4), December, 42–5.

Prest, A. and R. Turvey (1965), 'Cost–Benefit Analysis: A Survey', *Economic Journal*, **75**, 685–705.

Reed, D. (ed.) (1996), *Structural Adjustment, the Environment and Sustainable Development*, London: Earthscan.

Rodrik, D. (1996), 'Understanding Economic Policy Reform', *Journal of Economic Literature*, **XXXIV** (1), March.

Sadler, B. (1995), *Environmental Assessment in a Changing World: Evaluating Practice to Improve Performance*, final report, International Study of the Effectiveness of Environmental Assessment, Canadian Environmental Assessment Agency, Hull, Quebec.

Sadler, B. and Verheem, R. (1996), *Strategic Environmental Assessment: Status, Challenges and Future Directions*, No. 53, VROM series, Ministry of Housing, Spatial Planning and the Environment, The Hague.

Squire, L. (1990), 'Comment on "Project Appraisal and Planning Twenty Years on"', *Proceedings of World Bank Annual Conference on Development Economics*, Washington, DC: World Bank.

Squire, L., I. Little and M. Durdag (1979), 'Application of Shadow Pricing to Country Economic Analysis with an Illustration from Pakistan', *World Bank Staff Working Paper No. 330*, Washington, DC: World Bank.

Squire, L. and H. van der Tak (1975), *Economic Analysis of Projects*, Baltimore, MD: Johns Hopkins University Press.

Squire, N. (1989) 'Project Evaluation in Theory and Practice', in H. Chenery and T.N. Srinivasan (eds), *Handbook of Development Economics*, Vol. 11, Amsterdam, North-Holland.

Therivel, R. and M. Partidario (eds) (1996), *The Practice of Strategic Environmental Assessment*, London: Earthscan.

United Nations Industrial Development Organisation (UNIDO) (1972), *Guidelines for Project Evaluation*, New York: UN.

United States Agency for International Development (1994), *Social Soundness Analysis*, Washington, DC: USAID.

Vanclay, F. (1989 continuing), *Social Impact Assessment Bibliography*, A Database and Interrogation Program for DOS-Based Personal Computers, Wagga Wagga: Centre for Rural Social Research, Charles Stuart University.

Vanclay, F. and D.A. Bronstein (eds) (1995), *Environmental and Social Impact Assessment*, Chichester, UK: Wiley.

Ward, W.A. and B. Deren (1991), *The Economics of Project Analysis: A Practitioner's Guide*, EDI Technical Materials, EDI of the World Bank, Washington, DC.

Weiss, J. (ed.) (1994), *The Economics of Project Appraisal and the Environment*, Aldershot, UK: Edward Elgar.

Wilmshurst, J. (1996) 'An ODA Perspective on the Past and Future of Project Appraisal' in C. Kirkpatrick and J. Weiss (eds), *Cost–Benefit Analysis and Project Appraisal in Developing Countries*, Cheltenham, UK and Brookfield, US: Edward Elgar.

Winpenny, J.T. (1991), *Values for the Environment*, London: HMSO.

World Bank (1994), *The World Bank Participation Sourcebook*, Washington, DC: World Bank.

World Bank (1995), *Economic Analysis of Investment Operations*, mimeo, Washington, DC: World Bank.

2 Integration of sustainability objectives in structural adjustment programmes through the use of strategic environmental assessment

Hussein Abaza

2.1 Introduction

The Earth Summit in Rio demonstrated worldwide support for the principle of sustainable development. Under the banner of sustainable development, governments, environmental activists and development bankers now scrutinize the possible environmental impacts of investment decisions. Although the results of such assessments are often controversial and sometimes unsatisfactory, it is now considered important to assess the possible environmental impacts of such projects, programmes and policies. However, until quite recently, the environmental consequences of macroeconomic policies have not been rigorously analysed.

This chapter focuses on the uses of strategic environmental assessment (SEA) and, more specifically, on the assessment of the environmental impacts of structural adjustment programmes (SAPs). It analyses the linkages between macroeconomic policies, the use of natural resources and environmental degradation. It is clear that the design of SAPs has failed to take account of environmental and social considerations in any meaningful way. Nevertheless, structural adjustment remains the principal vehicle for restructuring struggling economies, and failure to appreciate its environmental impacts will only help to perpetuate the social and economic trends that have already generated environmental problems of crisis proportions.

The chapter argues the need for a thorough reform of structural adjustment policies which would incorporate environmental concerns, institutional changes, reforms in lending policies and the identification of priorities for future work to enhance their effectiveness. This can be facilitated by applying SEA to all countries undergoing macroeconomic reforms. The broad objectives of SEA should be to review the existing development strategy of each country, identify the foundations of its future economic and social development, identify the role that the environment and natural resources play in its development strategy, and to design adjustment programmes tailored to those specific conditions.

2.2 Strategic environmental assessment

The main emphasis of environmental assessment (EA) since its emergence more than a decade ago has been on improving the design of projects and mitigating their negative environmental impacts. EA extended the range of environmental planning tools to cover a wider range of decisions and decision makers, but still only affected a minute proportion of types of decisions that influence the environment. Project-level EA has proved to be inadequate, and the need to promote the use of EA beyond the project level has been receiving wide acceptability and recognition. EA beyond the project level has generally been referred to as strategic environmental assessment (SEA). It includes EAs of policies, sectors, regional EAs, and programmes relating to privatization and SAPs. SEA can also be applied to operations of transnational corporations, national budgets and to global conventions and treaties (Goodland and Tillman, 1995). It has been defined as:

> The formalized, systematic and comprehensive process of evaluating the environmental impacts of a policy, plan or programme and its alternatives, the preparation of a written report on the findings, and use of the findings in publicly-accountable decision-making. (Therivel *el al.*, 1992)

> EA of strategic actions – all government actions at higher level of organization than the construction project, including policies, plans and programmes and non-binding guidelines. (European Commission, 1994)

> Consideration of environmental impacts on policies, plans and programmes applied to higher levels of decision-making with the object of attaining ecologically sustainable development. (Commonwealth of Australia EPA, 1994)

SEA has emerged as a significant and necessary form of EA. The aims it serves have been acknowledged for some time, but practice is relatively recent. Nevertheless, a number of countries have already developed SEA approaches to assess systematically the environmental impacts of policies, plans and programmes (Bregha *et al.*, 1990; Holtz, 1991; Therivel *et.al.*, 1992; Wood and Djeddour, 1992; Partidario, 1995). However, the application of EA principles to the policy and planning levels has been raising some concerns amongst policy makers as well as practitioners. It has been argued, in countries such as Sweden, Australia and Denmark, that physical planning already covers EA requirements. In other words, its analysis covers natural and socio-economic considerations, alternative solutions, and conflict resolution approaches. However, in the view of others, significant differences between EA and planning justify the distinctive role of the former (Lerman, 1994). Further, the use of SEA, particularly in developing countries, is hampered by the misconception that it is a constraint on development, rather than a positive tool to ensure the attainment of sustainability objectives.

In this chapter it is acknowledged that the environment is inseparable from the socio-economic fabric of any system, and it is therefore essential to take both into account for sound decision making. Unfortunately, environmental management and planning, as initially understood and interpreted, were taken to imply a completely different process from natural resource management and socio-economic planning. Furthermore, the development and application of different tools and appraisal methodologies for environmental assessments, distinct from social and economic analysis, have contributed to the segregation of those disciplines and this has further led to an artificial dichotomy between environment and development. This is now beginning to change, and has to change, if sustainable development is to be achieved.

Therefore, it is now more appropriate to refer to SEA as a process which promotes the integration of social, economic and environmental considerations in development plans, policies and programmes. SEA not only provides recommendations for mitigating measures; it also identifies and assesses the environmental, social and economic implications of alternative policies and actions, and helps in the selection of those policies and programmes which promote the attainment of sustainability objectives.

Two basic mechanisms have been identified through which SEA may be introduced into national decision-making procedures. In some countries SEA is introduced by applying existing project EA procedures to higher-level decisions. A variation, occurring in those countries with no EA systems, is to introduce an EA system which covers all types of proposed development actions. Another approach is to adopt a policy and planning rationale whereby EA principles are applied in the formulation of policies and plans through the identification of needs and development options which are assessed according to the objective of achieving sustainable development (Partidario, 1995).

There is a number of different approaches to determining the planning initiatives where SEA should be used. According to Bisset (UNEP, 1996), these may include applying SEA to:

- those initiatives which are expected to cause significant adverse environmental impacts (this uses a similar criterion to that used in many project-level EA systems);
- those initiatives which are likely to affect the number, location, type and characteristics of projects which would subsequently be subject to project-level EA (for example, thermal power stations or highways); and
- those initiatives affecting particular sectors (such as the transport sector) which have been defined as priorities in environmental terms.

SEA may be applied to major new policy proposals and to existing policies, programmes or plans, which contain long-term commitments where these have potentially significant impacts (UNEP, 1996).

SEA needs to be institutionalized to ensure cooperation and coordination of the process across and within institutions. This will be very much influenced by the political will of the government concerned, the existing institutional set-up, and the decision-making system in place. It is important that the definition of the types of actions to which EA may be applied is sufficiently broad to include such actions as structural adjustment programmes, trade policies, and multilateral and bilateral agreements.

At the policy-making level, the key challenge is to gain high-level government commitment to establish a policy-making structure that both enables and encourages the application of SEA at all necessary stages, taking into account that the policy-making process may not correspond to a rational step-by-step process moving from broad strategies, via plans and programmes, to concrete projects (UNEP, 1996).

SEA has a significant role in shaping the development process and in decision making. Policy, programme and plan preparation and implementation is a continuous process which follows a spiral or cyclical track through time. Theoretically, there is no end point. Policies and similar initiatives are continually being revised, renewed and 'reinvented' as experience is gained and new circumstances and social goals and objectives become determining priorities. SEA should, therefore, be viewed as a continuous process (Goodland and Sadler, 1993).

SEA is a powerful tool which can be applied both at the level of broad policy initiatives and to more concrete programmes and plans that refer to specific developments and locations. These could be rolling national or regional development plans, which are prepared regularly in many countries. Similarly, town plans or sectoral investment strategies are a common component of the development process. There are also other non-project-level actions which are not part of a formal policy or plan-making process, but which can have significant environmental consequences. Some actions can occur relatively unexpectedly and/or intermittently and this can sometimes make anticipatory assessments more difficult to implement. Included among such types of actions are: certain SAPs, emergency budgets, certain trade agreements, and fundamental political changes and accompanying policy initiatives (for example, the early initiatives when first moving from centrally planned toward market-oriented economies) (UNEP, 1996).

There is, then, a range of challenges and barriers to the adoption of SEA. Perhaps, however, difficulties are associated with the perceived newness of the environmental assessment tool. That is why it may be more appropriate to refer to SEA as a modified process aimed at achieving sustainability objectives, rather than as a new process which requires a completely different apparatus.

There are strong reasons why SEA should be applied in all countries undergoing macroeconomic reforms. The main objectives of SEA in such situations should be to review the development strategy of each country, identify the foundations of future economic and social development, identify the role that the environment and natural resources play in the development strategy, and to design adjustment programmes tailored to those specific conditions. Issues to be considered in this assessment should include the significance of poverty reduction, intra-generational equity considerations, performance indicators such as health, education, and the likely effect on general welfare of the population and the ecological support system (Partidario, 1995).

This chapter focuses on SAPs for a number of reasons. It is estimated that about US$30 billion had been disbursed by the International Monetary Fund (IMF) and the World Bank on SAPs by 1995. There has also been a shift in the lending operations of other regional development banks and bilateral aid agencies to support these programmes. So far SAPs have largely failed to incorporate environmental considerations into the design of policy-based lending. This was because the environment was not considered a priority at the time. It was also viewed as an extra financial burden and it was believed that there was no relation between macroeconomic crises and environmental degradation, and that economic policies could easily reverse any negative environmental impacts resulting from development projects (Reed, 1992). However, in practice, a great deal of debate and controversy has been generated by the results and implications of such programmes, not only concerning the environment but also for the welfare of the economies and populations of the countries involved.

2.3 Structural adjustment programmes (SAPs)
For many developing countries, the 1980s represented a period of hardship. Internal mismanagement of economies, combined with prevalent adverse international relations, resulted in what was referred to as the 'debt crisis'. This was aggravated by increases in oil prices during the period between 1974 and 1979 and by restrictive monetary policies which were adopted by Western countries during the late 1970s and early 1980s to curtail their own inflation rates. The latter caused real interest rates to rise, which made it very difficult for developing countries to service their debts. As a result, developing countries experienced balance of payment

difficulties, which forced them to rely even more heavily on external funding to maintain their economies. Economic growth rates declined and some countries even experienced negative growth.

The IMF and the World Bank agreed to provide financial assistance with the primary objective of enabling countries to service their debts. Assistance, however, was conditional on the adoption of stringent economic and fiscal reform measures designed to reorient faltering economic policies towards growth. Within a broad framework, referred to as structural adjustment, both short-term 'stabilization' and more medium-term 'adjustment' measures were proposed. Structural adjustment began in 1979, and within a decade represented 25 per cent of total World Bank lending. This was reflected in 187 operations in 67 countries costing about US$30 billion (Goodland and Tillman, 1995).

There has been a great deal of debate regarding the environmental impacts of SAPs. According to the World Bank, although adjustment programmes have not focused on environmental issues, most of them included measures which, on balance, appeared more likely to help than hurt the environment. It has also been argued that with adequate complementary measures, policies can be introduced to achieve environmental as well as economic objectives (Hansen, 1990a, 1990b). On the other hand, in an article reviewing the environmental impacts of SAPs, Ridell (1992) concluded that adjustment programmes, which have altered the organization of the state, food supply, the meaning of development, the environment, and urban–rural interaction, in most cases led to the failure of the state, environmental degradation, and an increase in poverty.

A major emphasis of stabilization policies was to reduce the pressure on foreign reserves by reducing domestic demand. Balance of payment problems were addressed through a monetary approach. The idea was to control inflation and reduce imports by maintaining fiscal contractionary policies and restraining the supply of money. Simultaneously, currency devaluation policies were adopted to improve the terms of trade and make exports more competitive in international markets. Although these were expected to cause short-term recessionary effects, it was argued that economic growth would resume as soon as export-led growth increased.

Stabilization programmes generally had short-term macroeconomic objectives such as reduction in: balance of payment deficits, inflation, and government budget deficits. The objectives of SAPs are: the diversification of the production base, improved efficiency, increased competition, a shift towards the market system, and rapid economic growth.

The principal instruments of stabilization and adjustment have been:

1. Currency devaluation
2. Monetary discipline
3. Reduction of public spending
4. Price reforms
5. Trade liberalization
6. Reduction and/or removal of subsidies
7. Privatization of public enterprises
8. Wage restraints
9. Institutional reforms (Panayotou and Susangkarn, 1991).

Although circumstances in individual countries have varied, adjustment programmes – generically defined to include IMF-supported stabilization and World Bank-supported adjustment programmes – have generally had three principal objectives:

1. To attain macroeconomic balance by bringing expenditures in line with national income.
2. To allocate resources more efficiently, which involves switching resources across economic sectors.
3. To mobilize more resources over the longer term to raise rates of economic growth and living standards, particularly for the poor.

The policy instruments used in adjustment programmes have depended on the weight and immediacy given at the time to each of these objectives. It is axiomatic that a government's success in reducing an unsustainable gap between aggregate supply and demand will depend on the policies chosen and the ability to coexist with, or to modify, the country's institutional and policy setting. The particular policy path chosen has generally involved placing constraints on national expenditures through monetary and fiscal instruments, as well as expanding supply by changing the market and institutional environment to eliminate bottlenecks. Under these circumstances, policy makers face the challenge of selecting the best combination of policies, not simply choosing between alternatives to restrain demand or enhance supply (World Bank, 1994a,b).

As in Latin America, the initial round of adjustment programmes in Africa, which occurred from 1981 to 1984, concentrated mainly on restoring macroeconomic balances. The imbalances were precipitated by over-expansionary monetary and public finance policies in the past, underwritten by levels of foreign borrowing well beyond the debt-servicing capacity of the countries. This situation was compounded by a history of distortionary trade and price policies that discriminated against the production of tradables in general and the rural sector in particular.

The second phase of adjustment programmes retained most of the same policy instruments but recognized that it would take longer to achieve the intended objectives. More emphasis was therefore placed on improving resource allocation and growth. Governments increasingly sought to change the structure of economic incentives through a comprehensive revision of trade and exchange rate policies as well as through institutional reforms, especially in marketing. In addition, they paid more attention to improving the efficiency of the public sector and the planning and implementation of public investments. This growth orientation was facilitated by increased flows of external financing in support of adjustment programmes.

It was during the second generation of programmes that more attention was focused on the social dimensions of adjustment. Once it was seen that the transition could well take longer than initially anticipated, public policy began to explore ways to assist poor and vulnerable groups affected by the adjustment process. Governments and donors recognized that vulnerable groups could not wait for the benefits of adjustment to accrue to them and that they would need various kinds of assistance during, the process. However, social dimensions programmes were seen as *parallel* activities to be undertaken alongside ongoing adjustment programmes. Moreover, these early projects and programmes with social dimensions emphasized protecting poor and vulnerable groups during adjustment, through welfare and consumption interventions. This is mere mitigation, rather than promoting integration into the newly emerging economic environment.

The current third phase of adjustment programmes carried the second phase one critical step further. The programmes explicitly incorporate poverty reduction as a *fundamental objective* of adjustment policy, along with improved efficiency and economic growth. This represents a major challenge for policy design, since it explicitly touches the core of the adjustment programme and requires an understanding of the effects of alternative adjustment packages on poverty. This in turn demands a much more comprehensive data base than is generally now available (World Bank, 1994a,b).

Based on this record of adjustment programmes, the current phase will probably evolve towards an even stronger focus on poverty-oriented adjustment, in which increasing the participation of the poor in the growth process would be one of the key components. To achieve this, it will be necessary to broaden the design of the adjustment programme itself. Four main aspects of the adjustment programme are particularly open to review:

1. Phasing price and institutional reforms to identify the optimal sequencing of macro policy necessary to incorporate poverty considerations.
2. Reforming public finance – both its expenditure and revenue dimensions. A critical component of this is protecting core funding for public expenditures that benefit mainly the poor.
3. Strengthening the institutional capacity-building component of adjustment, including participatory programmes for community organizations and local non-governmental organizations (NGOs).
4. Exploring new forms of external financing to support both the widened objectives of a poverty-sensitive adjustment process and the direct costs of project and programme interventions.

In short, it appears that future adjustment programmes will require refinement of policy instruments in the light of accumulated experience, particularly with respect to making macroeconomic policy formulation itself more conscious of its effect on social welfare and the environment. Experience has shown that when first-generation adjustment programmes simply emphasized restraining demand, there was less emphasis on social and environmental considerations and public involvement (World Bank, 1994a,b).

2.4 Structural adjustment programmes and the environment
The links between structural adjustment and the environment are complex and multifaceted. Furthermore, to establish the linkage clearly, it is necessary to quantify and value environmental changes and to establish causal relationships with economic policy changes that are introduced by SAPs.

A further issue concerning the linkage between structural adjustment and the environment has to do with the implementation gap. Since structural adjustment policy prescriptions and conditionalities are rarely observed as agreed upon or intended, it is often not clear whether the identified environmental impacts are due to the prescribed policies or to their incomplete implementation. This is particularly important since structural adjustment policies are designed as a package of complementary, compensatory and mutually reinforcing policies; a partial, selective or incomplete implementation may result in greater or smaller environmental impacts than the full package of policies, depending upon which parts were dropped or were not fully implemented. Similarly, failing to follow the prescribed sequence of policy reforms may result in radically different results from those intended or anticipated. For example, if improved security of property rights was intended to take place before trade liberalization, but was postponed due to institutional delays, the effects of trade liberalization on deforestation and natural resource management will be different from those anticipated (Panayotou and Susangkarn, 1991).

SAPs typically call for changes in:

1. Trade policy – to encourage exports, the exchange rate is devalued, export restrictions are lifted and import tariffs are reduced to increase the competitiveness of domestic production.
2. Fiscal policy – public expenditure is reduced to eliminate the fiscal deficit, the tax system is reformed and higher prices are charged for public services to increase government revenues.
3. Public enterprises – privatization or closure of inefficient parastatals; reform of public enterprises to improve profitability.
4. Financial sector – restructuring institutions to facilitate resource mobilization; improving the regulatory framework to restore public confidence.
5. Industrial policy – reducing protection to boost industrial competitiveness internationally; liberalizing price control; devaluing the currency to promote exports.
6. Agricultural policy – liberalizing agricultural prices; promotion of export cash crops; deregulation of agricultural trade to smooth the circulation of agricultural inputs and products.
7. Land reforms – have not been commonly emphasized in the SAPs. When undertaken, the aim has been to secure property rights to land among the rural poor in order to reduce rural poverty and income inequalities.
8. Energy policy – improve energy conservation and decrease imports of energy by removing energy subsidies and supporting the development of domestic energy sources.
9. Infrastructure reforms – these include expanding infrastructure in order to reduce transport costs and facilitate a more efficient allocation of resources (Reed, 1992).

It is argued that there is ample evidence that adjustment programmes are having the desired effects on adjusting countries. These include, according to the set of indicators established by IMF and the World Bank: increased aggregate production and per capita GDP in most countries; increased agricultural exports which have become somewhat more diversified; increased revenues from extractive industries such as timber, fossil fuels, minerals and semi-precious stones, with fledgling industrial sectors given new market opportunities and incentives in some countries; and declining budget deficits with inflation brought under control in many countries. These are believed to indicate that anticipated supply-side benefits will bring greater economic benefits in the future.

On the other hand there are consistent and disturbing trends in the increase of poverty in rural and urban areas in virtually all countries. Unemployment, decrease in social services and other support systems, environmental degradation, and the incidence of poverty have grown with increasing distributional inequalities.

Moreover, while price reforms have led, in some instances, to positive environmental impacts, others have generated negative outcomes, exemplified by widespread extensification of subsistence farming, accelerated deforestation and overtaxing soil productivity. SAPs have also resulted in increased reliance and pressure on natural resources and environmental services.

Market, policy and institutional failures within host countries are not the only issues that models and theory need to address. Provisions for the exogenous factors that threaten the sustainability of development strategies also need to be made. Adherence to loan conditionality under SAPs has generally taken precedence over mitigation measures to deal with unforeseen natural disasters such as floods and droughts and their impact on the environment, and on the productive capacity of the country concerned and its population.

At the 1995 UN Social Summit, it was claimed by some that SAPs resulted in increased poverty and inequality; others claimed the contrary. Some claimed that growth is a prerequisite for alleviating poverty and, to achieve growth, economic reforms are required (Goodland and Tillman, 1995). Mahbub Ul Haq (1994) states:

> To address poverty, economic growth is not an option: it is an imperative. The needs of people must take precedence over the needs of the environment. It is rather difficult, however, to see a marked difference between both, since people derive their basic needs from the environment and its life support system. In that sense one does not see sustained development in conflict with poverty alleviation. On the contrary it is a necessary prerequisite to reduce poverty and enhance the welfare of people.

The disregard for social and environmental considerations in the design and implementation of SAPs – especially in the early days – is a key to understanding the long-term impacts that adjustment policies are having on the natural resource base of reforming countries, and the consequence this has on sustained growth and the welfare of the population. Negative environmental impacts resulting from SAPs which have generally been identified include:

- *Stabilization measures* Price changes have occurred primarily in the stabilization phase of the economic restructuring process and, consequently, the promised benefits of the supply-side response of the adjustment process have not developed fully. This has resulted in exacerbating the economic conditions for the poorest segments of society, forcing them to over-exploit natural resources that were available to them and to move on to marginal lands.

- *Production choices* By promoting exports through better prices for cash crops, farmers switched from low-input subsistence agriculture to high-input cash crop farming; the promotion of beef exports has had a major impact on land use through the spread of cattle ranching. Devaluation of currencies, resulting in increased prices of imports, may also lead the poor to expand small-scale agriculture into marginal lands.

- *Trade liberalization* Exchange rate policy resulted in both production and substitution effects. The environmental impacts of trade liberalization were, therefore, reflected in the environmental consequences of the resulting increased direct foreign investment in the extractive, industrial, agricultural, forestry, tourist and transport sectors. An increased orientation towards the primary commodity export sector has resulted in accelerated rates of deforestation, soil erosion, desertification and water pollution. It is argued, however, that export-oriented agricultural policies have a positive effect on the environment because, with some exceptions, such as groundnut and cotton, export crops tend to be less dangerous to soils than basic food crops (Repetto and Cruz, 1992).

- *Removal of subsidies* Environmental economists encourage the removal of subsidies because it is a move in the direction of internalizing all resource costs which, in turn, should increase efficiency and innovation, reduce waste, resource depletion and environmental damage. However, the impact of the removal of subsidies on basic commodities such as food, fuel and agricultural inputs, if not compensated by other measures, represents an increased burden on the poor. Also the removal of fuel subsidies may lead to increased fuelwood use, with the resulting deforestation, loss of biodiversity, soil erosion and possible intensification of desertification. Removal of agricultural subsidies, if not accompanied by other substitute measures, may result in the more intensive use of land, which may also have negative environmental impacts, and extension into marginal lands.

- *Institutional capacities* Sharp reductions in public expenditure, apart from involving cutbacks in the provision of social services, have often entailed a shrinking of the environmental management and protection apparatus and institutions – including enforcement capacity. Together, these trends imply greater environmental deterioration within and outside formal markets and a public sector that is handicapped to address the problem. Illegal logging in forest reserves and increased poaching of wildlife have commonly escalated.

- *Debt and degradation* Debt that cannot be amortized forces raw materials-dependent countries to accelerate the rate of extraction and conversion of natural resources to meet their external financial obligations. The need to repay debt is literally forcing most governments to mortgage their environment to finance the interest on loans (Dei, 1993).
- *Investment decisions* SAPs favour export-oriented growth. International competitiveness requires heavy investment in the productive sector. Investments in domestic environmental assets such as national parks, primary forests, reserves or wildlife usually lose out, since their supposed rate of return does not match that of export products.
- *Poverty and unemployment* Structural adjustment through its deflationary policies generally increases unemployment, at least during the shorter term, and impoverishes large sections of the population through the removal of subsidies. In order to cope, many people resort to farming on marginal lands, opening up new land in forest reserves, using timber illegally, and poaching wildlife. This results in unsustainable land use patterns (Panayotou, 1995).

It should be noted, however, that SAPs may include policy directives and packages which, if properly designed and complemented with necessary policy measures and incentives, could result in positive environmental impacts. These measures include: the removal of perverse subsidies that encourage waste or over-intensive resource exploitation; the introduction of greater economic and price stability, which promotes sound resource management and lower marginal time preference; and higher standards of living, which may entail increased demand for better environmental quality, general efficiency, and technology gains.

Though the structural adjustment era (1979 to the present) initially failed to address environmental issues adequately, it is evolving to integrate the environment more broadly and with more depth, as environment–economy interactions manifest themselves over time and as both North and South develop greater awareness of the productive capacity and inherent value of the environment.

Goodland and Tillman (1995) recommend that 'EAs be systematically applied to all adjustment and policy lending, first by strengthening the policy requiring EA of adjustment lending, then by reviewing proposed loans to ensure that policy has been met'.

Munasinghe and Cruz (1995) state:

The following are immediate steps that can be taken by decision makers:

- More systematic efforts are needed to monitor environmental trends and anticipated emerging problems when policy reforms are being prepared.
- Serious potential environmental impacts of proposed economywide reforms identified earlier should be carefully assessed ...
- Where potential adverse impacts of economywide reforms can be identified and analyzed successfully, targeted environmental policies of investments need to be implemented to mitigate predicted environmental damage and enhance beneficial effects.
- A follow-up system for monitoring the impacts of economic reform programmes on environmentally sensitive areas should be designed and resources made available to address environmental problems that may arise during implementation.

2.5 Integration of environmental and social considerations in SAPs

It must be emphasized that structural reforms are central to improving the long-term productivity and stability of many developing countries. Thus, it is not the intention to diminish the importance of implementing policy reforms, but to secure a change in how the costs and benefits of adjustment, and of the emerging development process, are distributed. Specifically, it is essential to ensure a more equitable distribution of costs and benefits and that social and environmental costs are integrated into the calculus of development strategies.

With the experience so far gained from the implementation of SAPs, it is now becoming more feasible to anticipate the impacts of price changes on rates and composition of resource use under adjustment programmes. Social and institutional changes can be anticipated and their subsequent impacts on natural resource use can also be foreseen in general terms. EA of SAPs should be able to identify these changes clearly and ensure that the design of structural programmes avoids significant negative impacts, and enhances the attainment of environmental and socioeconomic objectives. Special attention must be given to the impact of macroeconomic reforms on poverty. Further, specific measures and programmes must be implemented to ensure that poverty-induced environmental damage is minimized.

EA needs to be integrated with other existing policy and planning instruments, and directed towards full-cost accounting of natural capital. This necessitates the careful analysis of the effects on the environment as part and parcel of the wider economy at the macro as well as micro policy level. As stated by Richardson (1989), 'full-cost accounting of development programmes must be "ecologically grounded" by regional planning that spatially adjusts land uses to resource potentials' and provides an integrated context for project assessment (Sadler and Jacobs, 1990).

Cost internalization of environmental and social externalities should be central to the assessment process in order to reflect the true costs of environmental goods and services and to arrive at the actual full costs and benefits of development programmes. This will involve the adoption of a package of policy, command and control, and market-based instruments. It will also involve decisions on such matters as timing, how much of the externalities to internalize, and the use of market-based instruments such as taxes, subsidies and charges.

Poverty

Efforts to reduce poverty can have large payoffs for the environment, since poverty and environmental degradation are interlinked. As pointed out by the 1992 *World Development Report*, the poor are both the victims and the agents of damage to the environment. Because the poor – especially poor women – tend to have access only to more environmentally fragile resources, they often suffer high productivity declines due to soil degradation or loss of tree cover. And because they are poor, they may have little recourse but to extract what they can from the resources available to them. The high fertility rates of poor households further strain the natural resource base.

One of the underlying justifications of adjustment programmes is to remove biases against the poor, particularly the rural poor, and to encourage expansion of agricultural and tradable goods sectors. Many small farmers are not able to respond to new price incentives in a timely manner and, when faced with the disruptions in market systems, respond by overtaxing their productive assets in order to survive.

To reverse this trend, a sustainability assessment of SAPs might seek to ensure that government mechanisms are put in place to provide credit, extension support services and advice during this transition period to help small farmers respond effectively to the new price structures and market mechanisms (WWF, 1996). The promotion of sustainable development also has to be coupled with the improved provision of basic education and health services to the population. This is because such basic social services should eventually lead to an increase in incomes of the poor, hasten the transition to lower fertility rates, and enable the poor to protect the environment by making investments that are in their long-term social and economic interests. Although broad-based growth is essential, it will need to be complemented by government action in specific areas to spur poverty reduction and protect the environment. Educating girls may have the highest payoff for poverty reduction because it raises the economic productivity of women and leads to healthier, better-nourished, and better-educated children. Higher levels of education also lead to lower fertility levels, reducing population growth and pressure on the environment. Policies to protect the environment will often be specific to the diverse ecological conditions prevailing. Appropriate incentives to preserve rather than mine the soil, economic energy pricing and sensible tax policy for forestry are examples of policies that may benefit the environment and be consistent with poverty-reducing growth.

A sustainability assessment of policies, programmes and plans should, therefore, consider the need for provision of basic social services such as education and health care, particularly to the poorer segments of the population; introduce programmes and mechanisms for promoting distributional equity and ensure that social mitigation and safety nets actually reach the poor and are not captured by the middle class; create jobs and provide income-generating opportunities, particularly for women; and create transitional employment and training programmes, and targeted food-assistance programmes.

Role of the state
Structural adjustment programmes have sought to reduce the state's dominant role of initiating and implementing economic activities and providing basic services to the public. This entails the need to identify a different role for the state in each country, particularly in countries in which the state has hitherto played a major economic role. Such a role should be intended to support and complement the privatization of public-owned institutions, the dismantling of public service systems, and the replacement of controlled market systems by a free market one.

A strategic assessment of adjustment programmes needs to ensure that programmes are not designed solely from an economic point of view, but also consider the political realities of the situation. This entails taking into account the needs of the largest segments of the population and major groups likely to be affected by the reforms.

Macroeconomic stability, by building confidence in the future, tends to lower the discounting of the future. However, SAPs can produce extremely unstable political conditions which can create more uncertain conditions for the future.

Furthermore, the state is responsible for ensuring that trade policies are consistent with sustainable development, recognizing that the international market is structured according to short-term profit, not long-term sustainability. Other important functions of the state include: its role as an economic agent until such time as the private sector takes over; strengthening the government's managerial and administrative capacity in the environmental sector; enforcing environmental regulations and establishing a market system of environmental incentives.

Closely tied to strengthening the contribution of the state to sustainable development is its role in addressing institutional constraints, particularly in low-income countries. The dislocations and problems associated with the adjustment process draw attention not only to policy and market failures, but to institutional problems as well. Among these are issues of uncertain property rights, inadequate population planning policies and programmes; deficiencies in environmental data collection and monitoring systems; difficulties in integrating national environmental action plans and social development programmes into macroeconomic development strategies; and weakened capacity to enforce existing environmental laws and regulations. Adjustment programmes should identify the areas where institution development must occur so that a country's integration into the global economy is undertaken on a sustainable basis. Furthermore, designers of adjustment programmes should identify where economic reforms must be preceded by institutional reforms and strengthened to ensure that the economic benefits of adjustment are not offset by institutional and policy failures.

Role of local communities and the private sector
The importance of local interest groups has grown and will continue to grow in response to the inability of governments and the private sector to deliver many services to the different segments of the population. Strategic planning and assessment of adjustment programmes should ensure:

1. The involvement of local communities in order to secure their input and support for the proposed programmes, their involvement in identifying priorities and development options and in the implementation of projects and activities emanating from the proposed programmes.
2. The involvement of community groups and NGOs in the delivery of social services, which increases responsibility for managing local resources to formulate local development plans, administer mitigation programmes, strengthen local participation, and build the capacity of local groups.
3. The expansion of the scope of activities of community groups to address growing environmental challenges, to identify costs and benefits of development activities, and to mobilize support for long-term environmental protection activities (WWF, 1996).

International considerations
Incorporating environmental considerations in policy and decision making not only has implications at the national level, but also at the international level. Measures need to be introduced at the international

level to support policy reforms aimed at promoting sustainable development at the national level.

Over the last few decades, the need to account for the contributions of activities made by all sectors of the economy and their impact on resource depletion and degradation has become increasingly apparent. The current national accounts system provides misleading information on national economic growth. The system does not differentiate between economic growth due to increases in income, and economic growth due to the use and degradation of the natural stock or natural capital of a country. The commonly used depreciation adjustment for man-made assets is not applied to natural assets in the national income accounts; in fact, their depreciation is estimated as income as it is the result of economic activity (Tietenberg, 1994). Since sustainable development includes social, economic and environmental dimensions, it is essential that national income accounting also reflects any degradation and depletion of natural resources. As the current system of national accounts (SNA) does not take these considerations into account, steps need to be taken to adjust the SNA in order to provide a true indicator for development (WWF, 1996).

Though internalization of environmental costs, which should be one of the main assessment tools for policies, programmes and projects, is believed to be beneficial to developed and developing countries alike, it also involves costs, especially in the short term. This is in addition to the strictly political and economic considerations involved. Therefore, unless governments more generally are committed to cost internalization, it is very unlikely that unilateral action would be taken by individual governments. International cooperation through a multilateral internalization process is, therefore, likely to be essential to induce governments to introduce and adopt cost internalization measures. It provides the necessary political support and leverage against domestic interests (Panayotou, 1995).

The globalization of the world economy has implications for sustainable development which need to be addressed at the international level. *Inter alia,* this requires consideration of the environmental impacts of trade policies and agreements, ensuring, that environmental considerations are taken into account in the negotiation of bilateral and multilateral trade agreements, and the assessment of the actual costs and benefits of trade agreements and policies. It also entails the introduction of measures to secure the internalization of environmental costs, monitoring and assessment of impacts at the national and international level, the introduction of mechanisms for the transfer of financial resources and environmentally sound technologies between countries adopting sustainable trading systems.

It needs to be emphasized that the adoption of sound environmental planning and management practices, leading to sustainable development patterns, cannot be expected unless other adverse international policies are reversed. This will require measures to address issues relating to unfavourable terms of trade, conditionality of aid, the impacts of transnational investment, the debt crises facing developing countries, and the evolving consumption and production patterns and lifestyles in different parts of the world. The present reality is that prevailing international economic relations make it very difficult for most developing countries to allocate adequate investment resources, or introduce the necessary policy adjustment measures to promote sustainable development.

2.6 Conclusion

In most countries, SAPs have had two major effects. First, there has been a strong substitution effect in favour of exports. Second, there has been a strong distributional effect through change in both public expenditures and relative prices. The second effect has exacerbated poverty at least in the short and medium term. Both effects may result in increased environmental damage. This is the case, for example, in low-income countries dependent on natural resource exports which lack (a) appropriate property rights in environmental resources and (b) adequate environmental protection measures.

Emphasis is rightly given to the need for adjustment policies and reforms. However, the different kinds of costs and benefits of these adjustments must be taken into account in their evaluation. Specifically, there is a need to ensure that social and environmental costs are integrated into the calculus of alternative development strategies. SEA has a central role to play in this.

When SEA is applied to structural adjustment programmes, it needs to screen them for their conformity with sustainability objectives, assess both their socio-economic and environmental costs and benefits (Goodland and Sadler, 1993), evaluate alternative scenarios and development options, explore different options for environmentally and economically sound technology use, assess cost internalization measures (including the removal of subsidies and distorting price signals) and provide proper quantification to the extent possible of social and welfare gains and long-term benefits to the economy and to its constituent socioeconomic groups. This needs to be integrated into the hierarchy of plans and planning activities among different levels of government and across the diversity of plans undertaken within each level of government (McDonald, 1995).

Taking its direction from the Rio Declaration, Agenda 21, as well as from its own mandate, UNEP has reoriented and focused its activities on advancing the use of EA as a practical and effective tool to achieve sustainable development. Emphasis is now placed on addressing the challenges facing the integration of EA in the design, implementation and evaluation of policies, programmes, plans as well as projects; on promoting the development and implementation of SEA; on monitoring, audit and *ex-post* evaluation; on providing practical, clear and concrete metholies; on developing techniques for the integration of physical, social, economic and environmental analysis and assessment; on encouraging the use of SEA for regional and international activities and programmes likely to have trans-boundary effects; and on strengthening national capacities in this area.

References

Bregha, François, Jamie Bendickson, Don Gamble, Ton Shillington and Ed Weick (1990), 'The Integration of Environmental Considerations into Government Policy', report prepared for the Canadian Environmental Research Council.

Dei, George (1993) 'Sustainable Development in the African Context: Revisiting some Theoretical and Methodological Issues', *Africa Development*, **XVIII** (2), 97–110.

European Commission (1994), *Strategic Environmental Assessment: Existing Methodology*, Brussels: European Commission (DGXI).

Goodland, Robert and Barry Sadler, (1993), '*The Use of Environmental Assessment in Economic Development Policy Making*', Washington, DC: World Bank; Victoria: The Canadian Environmental Research Council.

Goodland, Robert and Gus Tillman (1995), '*Strategic Environmental Assessment – Strengthening the Environmental Assessment Process*', Washington, DC: World Bank.

Hansen, S. (1990a), 'Macroeconomic Policies: Incidence on the Environment', in James T. Winpenny (ed.), *Development Research: The Environmental Challenge*, London: ODI, Victoria: Assessment Research Council.

Hansen S. (1990b), 'Macroeconomic Policies and Sustainable Development in the Third World', *Journal of International Development*, **2** (4), special issue, 533–57.

Holtz, Susan (1991), 'Issues in the Environmental Assessment of Policy: A Research Prospectus', draft paper prepared for the Canadian Environmental Assessment Research Council.

Lerman, Peggy (1994), 'Physical Planning Linked to EIA: A Method for Processing Knowledge that Promotes Sustainability and Efficient Procedures', paper presented at the Third EU Workshop on Environmental Impact Assessment, Delphi, 1994, subsequently published in C. Cassios (ed.) (1995), *Environmental Impact Assessment Methodology and Research*, Brussels: European Commission (DGXI).

McDonald, G.T. (1995), 'Integrating EIA into the Planning Process', Brisbane, Australia: University of Queensland.

Munasinghe, Mohan and Wilfrido Cruz (1994), *Economywide Policies and the Environment: Emerging Lessons from Experience*, Vols I and II, Washington, DC: World Bank.

Panayotou, Theodore (1995), '*Internalization and Competitiveness*', Cambridge, MA: Harvard Institute for International Development.

Panayotou, Theodore and Chalongphob Susangkarn (1991), 'The Debt Crisis, Structural Adjustment and the Environment: The Case of Thailand'. Cambridge, MA: Harvard Institute for International Development.

Partidario, Maria Rosario (1995), 'Strategic Environmental Assessment – Highlighting Key Practical Issues Emerging from Recent Practice'. Portugal: New University of Lisbon.

Reed, David (ed.) (1992), *Structural Adjustment and the Environment*, World Wildlife Fund. London: Earthscan.

Repetto, Robert and Wilfrido Cruz (eds) (1992), *The Environmental Effects of Stabilization and Structural Adjustment Programs: The Philippines Case*, Washington, DC: World Resources Institute.

Richardson, N. (1989), *Land Use Planning and Sustainable Development in Canada*, Ottawa: Canadian Environment Advisory Council.

Ridell, J.B. (1992), 'Things Fall Apart Again: Structural Adjustment Programmes in Sub-Saharan Africa', *Journal of Modern African Studies*, **30** (1), 53–68.

Sadler, B. and P. Jacobs (1990), 'A Key to Tomorrow: On the Relationship of Environmental Assessment and Sustainable Development' in P. Jacobs and B. Sadler (eds), *Sustainable Development and Environmental Assessment: Perspectives on Planning for a Common Future*, Hull, Quebec: Canadian Environmental Assessment Research Council.

Therivel, R. *et al.* (1992), *Strategic Environmental Assessment*. London: Earthscan.

Tietenberg, T.H. (1994), *Economics and Environmental Policy*, Aldershot, UK: Edward Elgar.

Ul Haq, M. (1994), Barbara Ward Lecture, (1994).

United Nations Environment Programme (UNEP), Environment and Economics Unit (EEU) (1996), *Environmental Impact Assessment: Issues, Trends and Practice*, prepared by Ron Bisset, Nairobi: UNEP.

Wood, Christopher and Mohammed Djeddour (1992), 'Strategic Environmental Assessment: EIA of Policies, Plans and Programmes', *Impact Assessment Bulletin*, **10** (1), 3–21.

World Bank (1992), *World Development Report*, New York and London: Oxford University Press for the World Bank.

World Bank (1994a), *Adjustment in Africa: Lessons from Country Case Studies*, Washington, DC: World Bank.

World Bank (1994b), *Adjustment in Africa: Reforms, Results, and the Road Ahead*, Washington, DC: World Bank.

World Wildlife Fund (WWF) (1996), *Structural Adjustment, the Environment and Sustainable Development*, London: Earthscan.

3 Environmental assessment of trade liberalization: an OECD perspective

Michel Potier

3.1 Introduction

The environmental effects of trade liberalization have proved to be a particularly controversial topic where *a priori* views often prevail over rigorous analysis. The trade experts community has celebrated the virtues of trade liberalization and underlined the environmental benefits to be gained from such a process, while the environmentalists have accused trade liberalization of leading to a systematic degradation of the environment.

Trade and environment issues have been analysed and discussed in the OECD since 1991 in a forum of government representatives from environment and trade ministries, as part of the OECD's work to integrate environmental concerns into economic and sectoral policies such as trade, energy, agriculture, transport, development aid and taxation.

The OECD's role in this field has been two-fold. The first aim was to provide an analytical framework for considering the possible environmental effects of trade and trade liberalization and to undertake case studies in particular industries to illustrate the issues further. This was a particularly daunting task, to the extent that methods for assessing the environmental implications of a programme or of a policy are much less developed than for a project. Ideally, in this context, we should introduce a clear distinction between the impact on the environment of trade flows and of trade liberalization. It appears that in practice, however, it is very difficult to disentangle the effect on the environment of trade flows and trade liberalization at the sectoral level, and for this reason we shall consider simultaneously the effects on the environment of both trade flows and trade liberalization.

The OECD's second role has been to develop a set of guidelines on how to assess the environmental effects of trade policy, based on the results of the analytical work. This chapter will illustrate these two main aspects of the work.

3.2 The analytical framework for assessing the environmental implications of trade liberalization

The environmental effects of trade and trade liberalization have been analysed as product, scale, structural and regulatory effects. The case studies that have been undertaken cover agriculture, transport, wildlife and endangered species, fisheries and forestry.

Product effects
The most direct and obvious way that the environmental impacts of trade and trade liberalization can be transmitted across borders is through the actual products and services that find their way into the international market place. In terms of *positive effects*, trade provides the mechanism for faster diffusion of goods and services which contribute to environmental protection. For instance, an OECD study on the environment industry has estimated that the market for environmental equipment and services is about US$200 billion worldwide and growing at a rate of 5.5 per cent per year. Trade also expands markets for goods produced by more environmentally sound production methods and fosters commerce in environmentally sound inputs, thereby raising environmental protection levels in producing as well as consuming countries. Trade liberalization in the form of a relaxation of coal import restrictions, for example, would facilitate a greater use of low-sulphur as opposed to higher-sulphur coal. The OECD case study on transport indicates that liberalizing trade could reduce the relative cost and increase the availability of environmentally friendly technologies such as catalytic converters, thereby accelerating the transition to a less polluting and more efficient car fleet. Trade liberalization also occurs through regional agreements. The North Atlantic Free Trade Association (NAFTA), for example, will result in relaxed constraints on imports of heavy trucks and buses into Mexico from Canada and the USA; such vehicles are less polluting than many Mexican ones.

Trade and trade liberalization may have *negative* product effects through the international movement and exchange of goods which can cause damage to the environment or harm ecosystems, such as hazardous wastes, dangerous chemicals or introduction of endangered species. Trade in hazardous wastes can obviously be at the source of environmental damage in the form of emissions to water, air and land if there are inadequate means of disposal, recycling or reusing such waste, as in the developing countries. These concerns were central to the 1989 Basel Convention provisions for a prior informed consent mechanism, coupled with fairly detailed prior informed notification procedures. They were also reflected in the subsequent 1995 decision of the Conference of the Parties to the Basel Convention to introduce a trade ban on all waste trade intended for final disposal between developed and developing countries and a ban on waste intended for waste recovery and recycling, by 1997. Certain chemicals harmful to man and the environment, through their explosive, flammable, toxic, corrosive or carcinogenic characteristics, are currently transported and traded internationally. Freer cross-border trade will require enhanced cooperative efforts to avoid or mitigate environmental accidents.

Trade in living organisms used in agriculture has led to environmental problems, either by spreading of diseases or as a result of competition between an introduced species and the existing fauna. While it is generally acknowledged that the over-exploitation of wildlife is due mainly to habitat destruction and domestic wildlife consumption, there are cases where international trade significantly affects certain endangered species. There is substantial demand for wildlife species and their products emerging in rapidly developing Asian countries, for example, for elephant ivory and rhino horn in China, Singapore and Macau. The loss of birds through illegal trade is likely to be as much as 50 per cent greater than in legal trade.

Scale effects

Some of the environmental effects of trade can be attributed to the expansion of the overall scale of economic activity and market growth. Again those effects can turn out to be positive or negative. The conventional view of many economists is that trade induced by an expansion of economic activity and trade liberalization increases the efficiency of international markets through a freer flow of goods and services which permits a better allocation of resources and thereby provides countries with the financial resources to tackle environmental problems. According to this view, trade can have *positive scale effects* on the environment by contributing to a rise in environmental awareness through increases in per capita income and by making available more funds to be spent on environmental protection.

However, the expansion of economic activity concomitant with an increase in trade and trade liberalization implies more use of natural resources and more pollution. In the absence of a full internalization of environmental costs, or a proper valuation of ecosystems and of well-defined and assigned property rights, the increased resource use and pollution will impose social costs not factored in to the private decision-making processes of the market. In this context, a trade-driven growth will unavoidably exacerbate existing market and policy failures in such sectors as fisheries, agriculture, forestry or transport, and lead to negative scale effects.

- In the fisheries sector, international trade and trade liberalization policies have contributed to the overfishing of high-value species such as cod or haddock and slow-growing marine animals such as certain species of whales and turtles. The problems are rooted in the 'tragedy of the commons' and lack of clear property rights, but international trade makes the over-use problems larger in scale.

- In the agriculture sector, it is interesting to note that both positive and negative scale effects have been reported. Trade liberalization has increased environmental pressures on land, water and soils in developing countries while in some other countries it has led to increased agricultural incomes. This has reduced the incentive for poor farmers to cultivate marginal lands or to deforest them for firewood.

- In the forestry sector, it is extremely difficult to distinguish the impact on the environment of timber harvested for international trade from total domestic timber harvests. The direct impact of timber extraction on the state of the forests of many tropical and temperate countries appears to be relatively insignificant. However, the indirect impact of timber extraction – through road building and opening up forests – has more significant implications for forest conservation and environmental degradation, in particular in developing countries. A study carried out on the removal of export restrictions across the major economic sectors in the Philippines indicated that trade liberalization could increase deforestation and that the effects through industrial logging would be particularly significant.

- In the transport sector, trade liberalization will imply higher transport levels to take care of an increased flow of goods. In general, such scale effects will require the adoption of appropriate environmental measures to mitigate the negative environmental effects associated with an increase in the transportation of goods (particularly in terms of air emissions and impact on the infrastructure).

Structural effects
The structural effects of trade and trade liberalization are more indirect than the scale and product effects. They are related to the patterns of production and resource use. Although it is very difficult to single out the specific role of trade relative to other factors, it is believed that trade has an impact on the environment in altering the international location and intensity of production and consumption activities via national and international market prices. If environmental assets were properly valued and measured and if environmental costs were properly internalized, trade would probably play its role and have positive structural effects in allocating economic activities among nations according to the environmental endowments and conditions of different countries. But in the absence of this ideal case, trade may have negative structural effects in encouraging production and consumption in regions which are unsuited to the nature or intensity of the activity.

In the same vein, trade liberalization, through the removal of trade-distorting policies (subsidies and tariff and non-tariff barriers), has the potential to cause positive structural effects as demonstrated in the case studies.

- In the forestry sector, it has been shown that in many countries conditions have been created for short-term harvesting by private concessionaires, and also subsidies have been given, thus allowing industry to extract more timber than socially optimal. For example, in Malaysia and Indonesia government policies to encourage the switching from the export of raw logs to processed timber products have led to substantial economic losses, the establishment of inefficient processing operations and accelerated deforestation. In Indonesia the use of export taxes and restrictions to encourage processing activities has led to counterproductive effects on forest management and depletion because of the poor management techniques of the domestic processors.
- In the transport sector, liberalization of trade will induce not only scale effects related to an increased growth of production and consumption but also changes in the composition of goods and services demanded. More items of lower lot size with higher value-to-weight ratios will displace larger lot size and low-value/weight goods in international trade. Such change in the structure of the demand will result in more trucks and air transport relative to rail, ship and barge transport. Liberalization of the transport sector itself is likely to induce intermodal shifts in transport demand and supply.
- In the agricultural sector, trade measures are normally used as a means to ensure the effectiveness of domestic support arrangements. Pressures from trade liberalization can therefore lead to domestic policy reforms which would bring about structural change in the economy and reduce incentives to overproduction. It has also been suggested that if trade liberalization were pursued by both developed and developing countries, the net effect would be a shift of production from developed to developing countries. With such a shift, not only would fertilizer and chemicals use decline in the North, but labour would be substituted for them in the South, which would reduce substantially the use of chemicals in world food production. Shifts to less bought-in feeds in livestock production would also reduce environmental problems of waste disposal in developed countries, and would move livestock production to the extensive margin in both developed and developing countries with

more pasturing, often a substitute for cereals. While environmental benefits could be derived from such reforms, it is worth noting that higher commodity prices arising from market forces could also lead to environmental stress on land and water resources. Evidence from unilateral policy reform in New Zealand suggests mixed outcomes. Phosphate fertilizer, pesticide use and land conversion on pastoral lands fell significantly. Total pesticide use in all agricultural sectors rose, land management quality declined in certain farms due to income pressures, and weeds and other pests increased due to a decline in pest control assistance.

The evidence collected to date does not suggest that production changes under trade liberalization will lead to broad short-term environmental benefits or damages. Some improvements can be expected from agricultural policy reform but localized problems from concentrated production or land abandonment are also likely to occur. The introduction of harmful non-indigenous plant, animal and insect species through new trade routes is likely to damage environmental resources. The situation may be worse for many developing countries which do not have in place extensive environmental protection measures to protect against damages from their growth in agricultural protection. Larger risks lie in the future when trade liberalization will be further advanced and when a rapidly growing world population will push up food demand and prices. Even greater specialization in food production is likely to cause environmental problems arising from monoculture environments and loss of biodiversity.

Regulatory effects

Regulatory effects relate to the impact of changes in trade policies on existing environmental policies and standards. They can also be positive or negative.

Although trade liberalization should help to raise overall levels of environmental protection as more attention and resources are devoted to the protection of the environment, there is a widespread concern that the regulatory effects of trade may not be entirely positive.

Trade liberalization agreements may affect environmental policies in promoting harmonization of national policies in particular environmental standards to facilitate trade. Concerns have been raised among the environmental community that such harmonization will lead to the lowest common denominator. However, experience tends to show, in particular in the EU, that harmonization of standards has been working upward rather than downward. National law, and procedures dealing with environmental subsidies, environment-related fiscal measures or environment-related import and export measures, may be affected by trade liberalization. For instance, the process of harmonization of the various fiscal regimes of the countries of the EU turned out to limit the scope of the adoption by members of the EU of new environmental taxes. On a more positive note, the NAFTA included provisions aiming at strengthening the level and the enforcement of environmental standards. International agreements in areas such as foreign investment may circumscribe the scope for national governments to impose environmental controls.

3.3 Policy application

The analytical work initiated in the OECD on the environmental effects of trade and trade liberalization found an immediate policy application in 1991 and 1992 when the OECD Council instructed the Organization to develop procedural guidelines to help governments improve the mutual compatibility of trade and environmental policies and policy making. The procedural guidelines on integrating trade and environment policies agreed by OECD governments stress the following issues: transparency and consultation; trade and environmental examinations; reviews and follow-up; international environmental cooperation; dispute settlement.

We shall briefly review the content of this guideline, describe the general methodology suggested for conducting environmental reviews of trade policies and agreements, and report on progress made by OECD countries to implement them.

The 'trade and environmental examinations, reviews and follow-up' guideline
According to this guideline, governments should examine or review trade and environmental policies and agreements with potentially significant effects on the other policy area early in their development in order to assess the implications for the other policy area and to identify policy options for addressing concerns. Governments may cooperate in undertaking such examinations and reviews. Governments should follow up as appropriate to implement policy options, to re-examine the policies, agreements and any measures in place, and to address any concerns identified in the conclusions of such re-examinations.

This guideline concerns, therefore, both the trade implications of environmental policies and agreements and the environmental implications of trade policies and agreements. It calls for the development of methodologies for the conduct of examinations or reviews in both areas.

General methodology for conducting environmental reviews of trade policies and agreements

Using the work described in the first part of this chapter as a starting point, the Secretariat developed an analytical framework for conducting environmental reviews of trade policies and agreements.

It must be emphasized first that it is not evident which trade policies and agreements should be subject to environmental reviews, which means it is necessary to establish *screening criteria* reflecting particular country trade and environmental policy concerns. A selection will have to be made from among the main types of national trade measures or instruments (tariffs and related measures, non-tariff measures, trade-related subsidies, trade-related intellectual property rights (TRIPS) and trade-related investment measures (TRIMS)); and main types of trade agreements (trade liberalization agreements, commodity agreements, preferential trade agreements, sectoral trade agreements) as potential candidates for environmental reviews. At the same time, there will be a need to consider the nature and magnitude of potential environmental impacts. Screening criteria may be developed with respect to products, processes, sectors and regions within a country affected by the trade policy or agreement.

Second, the *scope* of the review (its extent and complexity) will vary according to the type of trade measure or agreement and the legal and administrative structure of the country concerned. It will also vary with the type, extent and significance of the potential environmental impacts associated with the trade policy or agreement.

Third, with respect to the *timing*, it must be said that as a general rule environment reviews should be conducted as early as possible in the policy-making process so that the results of such reviews can be taken into account in the final form of the trade measure or agreement.

Fourth, *participants* to the environmental review process will also vary with the type of trade measure or agreement and the country or countries concerned. They will include national and sub-national government participants (trade and environment governmental experts) private-sector participants (for example, environmentalists, industry representatives, trade unions, consumer groups and academics) and international participants (trading partners) as appropriate.

Fifth, many different types of *methodologies* can be used in conducting such reviews (methodologies borrowed or adapted from traditional environment impact assessments, models and other forecasting techniques, scenario analysis, evaluation techniques, and so on). However, environmental reviews will depend upon, to a large extent, the information available from the economic assessment of the trade measures or agreement, which are themselves difficult to conduct.

Finally, it will be of paramount importance to include in environmental reviews provisions for *monitoring* how the results of the reviews are taken into account and implemented, and for *follow-up* to ensure that identified concerns are addressed.

Turning to the *environmental effects* to be looked for, there are three main types of physical environmental effects which can be reviewed: pollution, health and safety, and resource effects. These environmental effects may vary in their geographical scope and can be national, transboundary or global, although there is not always a clear distinction between these different types of effects. Finally, the main categories of trade-related environmental effects which have been identified for facilitating environmental reviews are those elaborated in the first section of this chapter: the product and technology effects, the scale effects, and the structural and regulatory effects.

Implementation of the guideline relating to the environmental reviews of trade policies and agreements
OECD member countries' responses to a questionnaire sent out at the end of 1994 by the Secretariat point to a number of interesting lessons in relation to the implementation of the guidelines on trade and environment.

The first is that in many countries there was already in place a forum for consultation on trade and environmental matters, with existing procedures for subjecting major policy proposals to environmental assessment, although not many details were given on how this assessment was carried out.

The second is that the adoption of the OECD (1993) procedural guidelines by the OECD Council in 1993 has fostered the process of consultation among the parties involved and has resulted in new studies being commissioned, or workshops organized, by governments, aiming particularly at understanding better the impact of trade and trade agreements on the environment.

Third, for some European countries no review was undertaken, where it is thought that it will be for the EU to undertake such reviews, to the extent that trade policy is an exclusive competence of the Union.

Fourth, most of the assessment work seems to have been carried out in North America. Canada undertook an environmental assessment of NAFTA in 1992 before the development of the OECD procedural guidelines. The USA released in February 1992 the final review of NAFTA, which set forth a series of recommendations to the US negotiators that 'would help NAFTA have an environmentally positive impact'.

Since June 1993, the USA has prepared two additional reports on environmental issues in connection with major international trade agreements. In November 1993, the Office of the US Trade Representative led an inter-agency team which produced a second report on the likely significance of the NAFTA for environmental issues (Office of the President, 1993). The report was sent to Congress in conjunction with the NAFTA implementing legislation. It concluded that, while implementation of the NAFTA might have some minor short-term adverse environmental impacts (for example, by leading to additional trade-related traffic in the border region), the NAFTA would have important beneficial effects on the environment which should outweigh these adverse impacts.

Follow-up examinations of the environmental effects of NAFTA will be undertaken jointly by the USA, Mexico and Canada through the North American Commission on Environmental Cooperation (the CEC). The NAFTA environmental side agreement provides that one function of the Commission is to 'consider on an ongoing basis the environmental effects of the NAFTA' (Article 10 (6) (d)). This function is to be implemented, in part, through a project in the Secretariat's 1995 work programme designed to collect information and acquire methodologies for identifying and measuring environmental effects of the NAFTA.

In August 1994, the Office of the US Trade Representative released a report similar to that prepared for the NAFTA on environmental issues associated with the General Agreement on Tariffs and Trade (GATT) Uruguay Round Agreement. That report, which was also sent to Congress, noted that the Uruguay Round Agreement, by strengthening world economic growth, was likely to have both positive and negative effects on the environment. The report found that by reducing government intervention in markets, the Uruguay Round will provide companies with an incentive to produce as efficiently as possible to stay competitive, thereby promoting the efficient use of global resources. It also suggested that by opening significant new market opportunities for developing countries, the Uruguay Round should reduce the dependence of such countries on resource-intensive activities which are often detrimental to the environment.

The report also observed that increased economic growth rates are likely to have negative effects on the environment, for instance, by increasing pressure on wildlife habitats around the world.

In Canada, because the Uruguay Round Agreement was substantially completed before the NAFTA review and the development of the OECD procedural guidelines, the full type of review envisaged in these procedural guidelines was not carried out. However, an *ex-post* review of the

Uruguay Round Agreement was published in April 1994. It was designed to identify the extent to which the results of the Agreement are consistent with the federal government's commitment to protect the environment and promote sustainable development (DFAIT, 1994).

3.4 Conclusions

The case studies which have been carried out as part of the OECD's work show how it is difficult to appraise the relative contribution of trade, trade policies and trade liberalization to environmental degradation. The direct environmental effects of trade and trade liberalization (product and scale effects) appear to be both positive and negative, although limited to some specified cases. The indirect environmental effects related to trade structural effects are probably more significant but more difficult to identify and to isolate from other contributing factors.

The environmental effects of trade liberalization, both positive and negative, will vary depending on the country, sector and particular circumstances. In order to reap the benefits of trade liberalization with a view to achieving sustainable development, the challenge for governments will be to improve the integration of environmental and trade policies and ensure better consistency among the various government policy interventions. Such a course of action will imply adjustments to both environmental and trade policies. Distorting trade practices will have to be corrected while environmental safeguard clauses will have to be introduced.

At the risk of gross generalization, the scale effects of trade liberalization may well be negative in environmental terms, and the net effect will depend on positive technology and product effects outweighing the scale effects in the short term, with structural changes being positive in the longer run. Environmental reviews at an early stage of trade policy development would alert policy makers to potential welfare losses on the environment side, and stimulate the search for mitigating environmental policies.

A fuller integration of environmental and trade policies would contribute to the enhancement of the positive environmental effects of trade and trade liberalization and the minimization of any negative effects.[1] This process could be facilitated by a better implementation of the OECD procedural guidelines on trade and environment adopted by ministers in 1993.

Note

1. The Development Centre at the OECD has undertaken some model simulations to demonstrate this point, using economy-wide models with environmental data incorporated for Mexico.

References

Department of Foreign Affairs and International Trade (1994), *Canadian Environmental Review of the Uruguay Round of Multilateral Trade Negotiations*, Ottawa, April.

OECD (1993), *Trade and Environment*, Paris: OECD GD(93)99, June.

OECD (1994), *The Environmental Effects of Trade*, Paris: OECD.

OECD (1994), *Methodologies for Environmental and Trade Reviews*, Paris: OECD GD(94)103.

OECD (1995), *Report on Trade and Environment to the OECD Council at Ministerial Level*, Paris: OECD GD(95)63.

Office of the President (1993), *The NAFTA – Expanding US Exports, Jobs and Growth – Report on Environmental Issues*, President of the United States, Washington, DC, November.

PART II

APPRAISAL AND INTEGRATION: FRAMEWORKS AND METHODS

4 Assessing the environmental impacts of national development

Alan Grainger

4.1 Introduction

Environmental impact assessment is now widely used in project formulation and regional planning but hardly at all in national development planning. However, this must change if developing countries are to respond positively to the rise in external environmentally related interventions into their development process, such as structural adjustment programmes that lead to environmental degradation, and calls for all tropical timber to come from sustainably managed forests. Environmental conditions may soon be included in world trade agreements and international environmental regimes made stronger than in the past, to mitigate global climate change or reduce the rate of biodiversity degradation.

The basic problem with all these interventions is their partiality: structural adjustment programmes neglect the environment, while environmental conditions in international environmental and trade regimes take no account of development realities. New planning techniques are therefore needed by national and international policy makers to integrate environmental assessment and socio-economic appraisal at the national scale if developing countries are to resist the most extreme impositions and choose the development path which balances wealth creation and environmental conservation in the way they want.

This chapter suggests how to extend the environmental economics theory of sustainable development to form the basis for these new techniques, shows how they may be applied to make the major external interventions more equitable to developing countries, and in each case discusses the problems of integrating environmental and socio-economic data.

4.2 The new challenges to development

It was previously implicitly assumed that developing countries were free to replicate the development trends of the developed countries – if only they could. This freedom included depleting natural resources and, in the short term, degrading the environment to generate economic growth without paying the associated external costs.

But over the last 20 years there have been growing calls to restrict this freedom in order to protect the global environment. Developing countries have been urged to practise 'more sustainable development' (IUCN, 1980; WCED, 1987); halt deforestation (Goldsmith, 1980); and manage their environments to ensure more sustainable forest management in the humid tropics and reduce the spread of desertification in arid areas (UN, 1978; Poore, 1989). Conserving tropical forests and expanding tropical forest plantations have also been proposed to mitigate future global climate change by conserving, and extending, present terrestrial carbon stocks (Sedjo and Solomon, 1989).

Common environmental policies, not the convergent policies characteristic of weak environmental regimes (Porter and Welsh Brown, 1991), are a necessary precondition for a truly global environmental management in which nations work together according to a single, binding plan. In progressing along the path of global environmental management, the governments of the developed countries are acting under pressure from their own environmentalist lobbies, and out of fear of the costs imposed on their economies by global climate change and the reduction in global biodiversity. Present per capita emissions of greenhouse gases in developing countries are small relative to those in developed countries. But the more that developing economies grow in the conventional sense, the more their overall emissions will rise. The environmental impacts of human activities are already at the stage where they are worrying the developed countries, but imposing global restrictions now will constrain the future development of the developing countries.

So while better global environmental management will undoubtedly benefit the world as a whole, the costs of this change will fall unequally on the developing countries because it will constrain their development. It is not surprising that such actions have been described as a new 'eco-imperialism' (Lal, 1989), following the formal imperialism of the colonial era and the informal imperialism (or neo-imperialism) that succeeded it (Taylor, 1989). The growing strength of international environmental regimes, and the prospect that environmental conditions will be included in international trade regimes, mean that developing countries are being asked to conform with the environmental ethics of the developed countries and internalize the external environmental costs of their development to benefit the whole world, rather than their own development.

4.3 The evolution of environmental impact assessment
The use of environmental impact assessment (EIA) has spread widely over the last 25 years and is now common in both developed and developing countries as a valuable complement to cost–benefit analysis (Wathern,

1988; Canter, 1996). Developing countries are increasingly making the use of EIA mandatory in the planning process, and overseas development agencies funding projects in developing countries are often required by the laws of their own countries to conduct an EIA at the appraisal stage.

But EIA is fundamentally an environmental assessment, and so its ability to cover socio-economic impacts in an integrated way is rather limited. It also suffers, in comparison with cost–benefit analysis, from an inability to take account of the timing and duration of different impacts, and so lacks a developmental context. So far it has been mainly applied to project planning, rather than on a larger scale.

In recent years there has been a growing demand for environmental assessment techniques at national level, which are the subject of this chapter. They generally come under the heading of strategic environmental assessment, defined by Therivel *et al.* (1992) as 'the formalized, systematic and comprehensive process of evaluating the environmental impacts of a policy, plan or programme and its alternatives, the preparation of a written report on the findings, and the use of the findings in publicly-accountable decision-making.'

4.4 Sustainable development theories

The environmental economics theory of sustainable development provides one framework within which to develop new national planning techniques. But it is often overshadowed by a more general understanding of what sustainable development entails. In this section the two approaches are referred to as the 'hard' and 'soft' approaches, respectively.

Soft approach
Soft approaches to sustainable development are popular among policy makers, but are usually based on vaguely defined aims traceable to the origins of the concept in the 1980s.

Sustainable development first emerged as a serious concept in the IUCN World Conservation Strategy in 1980. Many environmentalists previously opposed development because it harmed the environment. But they eventually accepted the inevitable, and took the view that if developing countries were to develop, they should try to do so in a more sustainable way that caused less harm to the environment. Sustainable development was therefore an explicit attempt by environmentalists to bridge the gap between environment and development, though they also had an implicit agenda to constrain the future development of developing countries in the interests of the global environment.

Sustainable development only became popular after the publication in 1987 of the report of the Brundtland Commission (WCED, 1987). It soon became the latest 'buzz word', even though no one could really explain what was meant in practice by WCED's definition of sustainable development as development that 'meets the needs of the present without compromising the ability of future generations to meet their own needs'. Nevertheless, it was the conceptual foundation for the UN Conference on Environment and Development (UNCED) held in Rio in 1992, and for the mammoth global action plan, Agenda 21, the Commission for Sustainable Development set up to monitor progress in achieving the goals agreed at Rio, country reports by national governments, and various endeavours by local councils and non-governmental organizations.

In developed countries sustainable development has become synonymous simply with better environmental management, but international programmes appear to want to place far more constraints on resource depletion and environmental degradation in developing countries, and the inequity of this been widely criticized by political ecologists and development economists (Redclift, 1987; Adams, 1990). Despite the injunctions of WCED (1987) to take account of the needs of the world's poor, sustainable development has so far focused more on intra-generational equity than core–periphery equity.

Hard approach
Natural capital and human capital Hard approaches to sustainable development are distinguished by a stronger theoretical basis. Environmental economists, such as David Pearce and other members of the CSERGE groups at University College London and the University of East Anglia, saw in sustainable development the germ of an important theoretical concept which, if developed, could have major practical applications. They initially defined it as development that 'leads to non-declining human welfare over time' but made a key theoretical advance in specifying it in terms of a relationship between human capital and natural capital (Pearce *et al.*, 1989; Pearce, 1991).

Human capital (also referred to as man-made capital) represents the total stock of material and intellectual capital accumulated by the growth of civilization. It can be conveniently divided into three main categories: productive capital (PC), for example, industrial capital, farmland; cultural capital (CC), for example, health care and education provision; and infrastructure capital (IC), for example, provision of roads and sewers. So total human capital is given by:

$$HC = PC + CC + IC \qquad (1)$$

Natural capital consists of two main parts:

1. Resources capital (*RC*), comprising the stocks of natural resources.
2. Environmental quality (*EQ*), determined by the quality of environmental sinks (land, atmosphere and water), the functioning of the world's major cycles and ecosystems, and human aesthetic perceptions.

So total natural capital is given by:

$$NC = RC + EQ = (RRC + NRC) + EQ \tag{2}$$

where *RRC* and *NRC* are renewable and non-renewable resources capital, respectively.

Economic growth versus economic development Not all environmental economists support the theories of Pearce and his colleagues. But most would acknowledge that: (a) transforming natural capital into human capital is an inevitable consequence of development; (b) society in general, and economists as well, have traditionally given priority – within the constraints of monetary policy – to promoting the growth in the output of goods and services (measured by gross domestic product or GDP) rather than paying the costs of environmental impacts like pollution. Indeed, national income is artificially inflated by the failure to correct for the depreciation of natural capital in the same manner used for human capital (Tietenberg, 1994).

Economic development is often monitored using the GDP index, for want of anything better. But it is not the same as economic growth, and is best thought of as an advance in the well-being of society as a whole, achieved by sharing the income generated by growth more equally among a country's population (Simpson, 1987). The new United Nations human development index (HDI) attempts to measure development in terms of indicators showing improvements in education, health care and so on (UNDP, 1991).

Development versus sustainable development Many policy makers, professionals and academics still focus on the conventional approach to the development of developing countries, rather than development that takes account of environmental impacts. For example, according to Ul Haq (1994): 'To address poverty, growth is not an option: it is an imperative. The needs of people must take precedence over the needs of the environment.'

Given the historical background this is understandable. The underdevelopment school (for example, Frank, 1967) and modernist school (for example, Rostow, 1960; Bauer, 1976) fundamentally disagree in their interpretation of the present and future role of the developing countries in the world economy, but both would view greater equity in the distribution of national GDP and the distribution of the fruits of economic activity in developing countries as progress, of which the HDI could provide an important measure.

However, the principal schools of development theory have been left behind by the recent growth of concern about the environmental dimension of development. This has led to a polarity between 'developmentalists' and 'environmentalists', apparent in divisions within development agencies and even between different types of non-governmental organizations in developing countries.

There is no reason why present development theories could not be modified to take account of the environment (Adams, 1990) and sustainable development is probably best understood against the background of established theory, as Redclift (1987) showed. But development can no longer be understood apart from the environment, and since HDI emphasizes human benefits, not the balance between these and environmental costs, it is not a good indicator of sustainable development. Another index is therefore needed to integrate the environmental and socio-economic components of the development process.

Linear and circular models The traditional growth and development approaches both stress the need to raise national output and resource consumption and pay little regard to how this affects resource capital, or how environmental quality is degraded when waste products generated by this utilization are deposited into the major environmental sinks. Macroeconomic models of national economies based on these traditional approaches show circular income flows, but assume a linear model of the role of natural resources in the national economy: resources appear to come from nowhere and go to nowhere after being used to generate income.

In contrast, the new world-view of environmental economics (and ecological economics) is best represented by a circular model, in which it does matter how rapidly natural capital is depleted and where waste products are deposited. Resources are extracted from resource stocks, and then after use and temporary storage in human capital they return either to resource stocks or environmental sinks. Sustainable development involves maintaining this circle by constraining the transformation of natural capital into human capital so that leakage is minimized as much as possible (Pearce and Turner, 1990).

Conditions for sustainable development Three alternative conditions have been proposed for sustainable development in the framework of environmental economics theory:

1. In the hyper-strong condition there is no decline at all in natural capital, that is,

$$\partial NC \geq 0$$

2. In the strong condition there is no decline in critical natural capital, that is, that which, like biodiversity, is essential for the health of the planet.
3. In the weak condition there is no decline in total capital, so the rise in human capital (∂HC) at least balances the decline in natural capital (∂NC), that is,

$$\partial NC \geq \partial HC$$

The third condition allows complete substitutability between natural and human capital; the second allows some; the first allows none at all. But could they ever be applied in practice in a developing country? Condition 1 seems totally impractical and Condition 2 seems difficult to achieve, though it depends on how critical natural capital is defined. Condition 3 seems the most feasible of the three, but questions remain about how changes in natural capital and human capital can be compared directly.

Sustainable development versus sustainable resource management The hard approach to sustainable development helps to overcome the common confusion between sustainable development and sustainable resource management. The sustainable management of a renewable resource is just one part of the all-embracing concept of sustainable development, and will ensure that the stocks of managed ecosystems remain constant over the long term. But this is only essential for all ecosystems if the hyper-strong condition is adopted, or just to those parts of ecosystems containing critical natural capital if the strong condition is adopted. It is not essential if countries develop under the weak condition, in which there is greater flexibility.

4.5 A comprehensive integrated assessment of the environmental impacts of national development
The first major problem to tackle using an integrated socio-economic–environmental assessment is to monitor the environmental impacts

of national development in an equitable way. This will have two key applications: monitoring compliance with international environmental regimes, and modelling the environmental impacts of external financial interventions.

The first of these applications needs a national index which can monitor environmental performance yet also take account of the needs and realities of development. Governments who committed themselves to practising sustainable development following UNCED require an index that will enable them to monitor the extent to which they are meeting their commitments so they can make progress reports to the Commission for Sustainable Development. If it is to have general support, the index must take account of generic features of development in developing and developed countries, use a common scale of measurement, and must not perpetuate core–periphery inequity.

In contrast, the second application needs a national index which can monitor the national environmental impacts of macroeconomic policies introduced to stabilize development. International agencies such as the International Monetary Fund and World Bank would insert such an index into national economic models so as to test the possible impacts of interventions into national economies before they are made. Between 1979 and 1995 their structural adjustment programmes provided financial assistance of US$30 billion to 167 countries (Goodland and Tillman, 1995) but took no account of the likely environmental impacts of the conditions imposed on governments. These typically required an increase in exports and a reduction in government spending, and the expansion of agriculture and mining, and the increase in poverty that resulted from these conditions, had significant impacts on resource stocks and environmental quality (Cruz and Repetto, 1992).

Both needs could be satisfied by an index that integrates the socio-economic and environmental components of development. This section suggests how one might be formulated, after reviewing previous attempts to devise sustainable development indices, which can be divided for convenience into the two categories of soft and hard indices.

Soft indices
The soft approach is one-sided in addressing only the environmental impacts of development without taking account of its social, economic and political dimensions. It follows the multiple-criteria approach typical of EIA, using a variety of environmental indicators with little integration and theoretical basis.

The World Resources Institute has used a small group of key environmental indicators, such as national carbon emissions per capita, the sustainability of forest management and so on. This has the advantage of being succinct, and uses data already available, but by focusing on physical environmental indicators alone it takes no account of socio-economic considerations, such as a country's level of development.

Trying to measure sustainability with environmental indicators alone will discriminate against developing countries, whose current rates of resource depletion and environmental degradation generally exceed those of developed countries. On the other hand, there would be greater similarity with rates achieved by developed countries at a comparable stage of their development. For example, in the 1970s Brazil had the highest deforestation rate of any tropical country, and the USA had a negative deforestation rate as a result of continuing reforestation. But in the 1850s, at a comparable stage in its own development, the USA had a deforestation rate similar to that of Brazil in the 1970s (Williams, 1989).

The governments of developed countries may believe that they can achieve sustainable development simply by reducing environmental degradation and restoring their environment, that is, by focusing only on the environmental quality component of natural capital. By not considering any radical change in current human–environment relationships they are conforming to the concept of sustainable growth identified by Turner (1988) as a more limited form of sustainable development – though the term is no longer generally used. It should therefore be no surprise if their approach to monitoring the sustainability of their own development is also rather partial.

The UK government recently published a compendium of 140 'Indicators of Sustainable Development' (DOE, 1996). But the indicators, which ranged from GDP, to the number of passengers passing through UK airports, out-of-town retail floorspace, emissions of greenhouse gases, and the area of ancient woodland, lacked integration. The need 'to go beyond environmental indicators to include indicators which specifically link environmental impacts with socio-economic activity' was acknowledged, but this simply meant equating a 'healthy economy', as measured by GDP growth, with a sustainable economy, which is not convincing.

The UK government fortunately saw its list of indicators as just the first stage in its indicator selection process, but the World Bank (1995) has also been engaged in a detailed exploration of a range of possible indicators, and the difference between the two exercises is that the World Bank appears more committed to eventually integrating socio-economic and environmental indicators that represent human and natural capital respectively.

Hard indices

In contrast, hard indices do integrate the environmental and socio-economic components of development. They are characterized by a stronger theoretical foundation and the use of single synthetic indices, of the kind typical of cost–benefit analysis.

Green GDP and ISEW Several researchers, including Robert Repetto at World Resources Institute (Repetto *et al.*, 1989), have estimated a country's Green GDP by correcting gross output for the costs of resource depletion and the environmental degradation associated with this. After subtracting the value of natural capital lost by the depletion of oil, soil and forest resources, Repetto estimated that Indonesia's mean GDP growth rate between 1971 and 1984 was only 4 per cent per annum, not 7 per cent, as in the conventional measure. It has been argued that, as long as the Green GDP is greater than zero, development is sustainable. But this approach is partial in its coverage and takes no account of core–periphery inequity. In contrast, the Index of Sustainable Economic Welfare (ISEW) is more comprehensive in adjusting per capita GNP for social as well as environmental welfare, but its value depends on the choice of indicators and data availability (Moffatt and Wilson, 1994).

Pearce and Atkinson's Z index In another approach, Pearce and Atkinson (1992) argued that for development to be sustainable, a country's annual savings should not be less than the total depreciation of natural and human capital. So they estimated an index Z for 21 countries, where:

$$Z = S/N - (\partial Km)/Y - (\partial Kn)/Y \qquad (3)$$

and S is savings, Y income, Km human capital and Kn natural capital. Development was sustainable if Z was greater than or equal to zero.

But this gave strange results. Countries developing sustainably included Japan ($Z = 17$), Costa Rica ($Z = 15$), the Netherlands ($Z = 14$), Brazil ($Z = 3$), the USA ($Z = 2$) and even the Philippines ($Z = 0$). Non-sustainable countries included Indonesia ($Z = -2$), Nigeria ($Z = -5$) and Mali ($Z = -14$). This approach is concerned with income and flows rather than capital and stocks, and as Pearce has admitted, it is essentially static, so Z could change from year to year and even shift from positive to negative. It may be a more equitable indicator than Green GDP but it is not very reliable.

Grainger's S index Grainger (1992) proposed estimating a national index of sustainable development, S, in terms of the weak condition for sustainable development, that is,

$$S = f(\partial NC + \partial HC) = f(\partial RC + EQ) + \partial HC) \qquad (4)$$

For development to be sustainable in a given year, S must be greater than or equal to zero, since the fall in natural capital must at least be balanced by the rise in human capital. However, sustainable development is a path, not an annual rate. So the sustainability of development must be judged by the trend in S, not its value in a single year.

This index potentially represents a major advance in integrating socio-economic and environmental assessments because it: (a) combines the socio-economic and environmental components of development and (b) measures the latter in terms of the depletion of major resource types and the degradation of major environmental sinks. It is also a dynamic index, and this overcomes one limitation of Pearce and Atkinson's static index.

But S is still not entirely suitable as it stands because it is a pure number with no relation to any point on a scale of development. A net increase of x units in S in a developed country will therefore mean the same as a similar rise in a developing country, which is clearly unsuitable. Sustainability would be expected to increase over time as a country becomes more developed, improves its efficiency of resource utilization, and spends more on reducing environmental degradation and reclaiming previously degraded environments. So merely comparing the S values of different countries will put developing countries at a disadvantage, as their S values will normally be inferior to those of developed countries.

The need for an improved index
None of these indices is therefore satisfactory. Ideally, what is needed is a new sustainable development index (SDI) which is 'hard', and measures the degree of sustainability, not whether development is either sustainable or not, and so takes account of the anticipated evolution of sustainability over time. It should be possible to construct a normative trend for each country to show how its raw index S should increase over time, and estimate the degree of sustainability by comparing how well the actual trend in S matches this ideal trend. Progress in improving sustainability would be evident from the convergence of the two curves. Because of the variation in socio-economic and environmental conditions between countries, individual national curves may be necessary, though it might also be possible to construct a normative curve showing S as a function of GDP per capita.

Improving data availability by natural resource accounting
Regular estimation of each country's SDI will demand good monitoring of a country's natural resource stocks and environmental quality. At the

moment, for most developing countries, the quality of data on natural resources and the environment is very poor. For example, estimates of tropical forest areas and deforestation rates are very inaccurate for most countries because of the low frequency at which national surveys are conducted – once every ten years at the most (Grainger, 1996a). A few countries, such as Brazil, the Philippines and Thailand, have had an excellent record of national forest monitoring over the last 25 years but reliable estimates are not available even for them before the mid-1960s. For other resources the situation is probably far worse, and the reliability of estimates of non-renewable resource stocks is particularly poor, with the historical spatial bias in prospecting playing a major role in this (Rees, 1990).

Once the SDI has been accepted internationally, governments would be motivated to collect data on a regular basis, as happened with collection of data for the national economic accounts needed to estimate GDP (O'Loughlin, 1971). Initial studies in this field spurred the Philippines and Costa Rica to pay greater attention to natural resource accounting (Repetto *et al*, 1989; Solórzano *et al.*, 1991). This is bound to spread over the coming decades, but it will take time before all countries have comparable data sets.

The initial SDI will probably be based on a restricted number of indicators for which data are readily available for most countries, for example, the stocks of forests, fisheries, fuel minerals and non-fuel minerals, and the quality of land, air and water sinks. The list will then gradually expand as data availability improves with time, enabling the value of the SDI to become a better approximation to the sustainability of development (Grainger, 1992).

Data integration challenges
Estimating the SDI raises a number of interesting challenges for integrating socio-economic and environmental data.

First, the difficulty of valuing natural capital and human capital in equivalent terms has been recognized for some time as the major obstacle to putting into practice the environmental economics theory of sustainable development (Maddox, 1994) and this problem is still unresolved.

Second, the low price of primary commodities (raw natural resources, like roundwood) relative to finished products inevitably means that non-market values of natural resources, such as those associated with the river flow stabilization function of forests on catchments, assume great importance in determining whether the rise in human capital exceeds the fall in natural capital. The total economic value methodology for obtaining a full evaluation of the market and non-market values of forests and other resources, in terms of direct and indirect use values, option values, and existence values, is now well understood (Pearce and Turner, 1990; Dixon and Sherman, 1990), and increasing attention is now being paid to appraising natural capital (Jansson *et al.*, 1994). But a major question is the extent to which non-market values are estimated by the contingent valuation method, with its known inaccuracies (Diamond and Hausman, 1994; Willis, 1995), and whether this can be gradually replaced by more objective approaches to valuation.

Applications
Once a practical SDI has been devised it should have major applications. For example:

1. All countries in the world could be ranked according to the level of their SDI, as well as their GDP, GDP per capita, and HDI, and annual reports published.
2. Governments could set target values of SDI to achieve, either in the course of their national five-year development plans, or to meet targets set by the Commission for Sustainable Development.
3. The environmental impacts of proposed interventions into the economies of developing countries, by the structural adjustment programmes of the World Bank or International Monetary Fund, could now be tested beforehand by including the SDI into a national econometric model of the country concerned. If the impact on the SDI was undesirable, as was all too common with such programmes in the 1980s, the financial conditions imposed on government policies would have to be relaxed. Banks providing development finance to countries could also measure the performance of their investment not only in pure financial terms, but also by its impact on the SDI.

4.6 Improving the equity of international regimes
An integrated approach to socio-economic and environmental appraisal is also needed to ensure that developing countries are treated equitably in future international environmental and trade regimes. Two main interventions are addressed here: the attempt to impose sustainable management of tropical forests and other resources, and a potential move to require large areas of tropical forests to be conserved to help mitigate global climate change. As they are viewed at present, both interventions are inequitable since they focus purely on the environmental impacts of resource exploitation and take no account of development aspects. Moreover, the forest set-aside proposal is mainly concerned with avoiding global, rather than local, environmental impacts.

Modelling national land use morphology

If models of national economies are to become circular with respect to natural resources and the environment, then these must be modelled on the same spatial scale as output and income – the national scale. This might be objectionable to those who believe that a 'bottom-up', rather than 'top-down', approach to development is essential. But national land use morphology – the broad pattern of national land use – evolves as an entity over time and studies of this can reveal generic patterns of spatio-temporal behaviour (Grainger, 1995a). The following discussion makes this assumption, but regards development as a continuum and does not assume the existence of specific stages, as in Rostow (1960).

International environmental regimes

Mitigating global climate change Six years of scientific discussions under the auspices of the Intergovernmental Panel for Climate Change (IPCC) have examined in detail the practicality of proposals for developing countries to contribute to international efforts to mitigate global climate change by setting aside large areas of high biomass density tropical forests to maintain terrestrial carbon stocks, or expanding these stocks by increasing their rate of timber plantation establishment (Andrasko *et al.*, 1991). If forest-based strategies of these kinds were indeed implemented on a large scale as part of an expanded climate change convention, it would represent a significant external intervention into the economies of developing countries.

Compensation schemes Developing countries would therefore be justified in requesting suitable compensation for agreeing to participate in such regimes. They would involve significant financial transfers to developing countries from the developed countries, which are responsible for the bulk of greenhouse gas emissions through fossil fuel combustion. Such transfers would be justified if greater terrestrial carbon sequestration were used to reduce the need to cut fossil fuel use, and might be funded by carbon taxes in developed countries (Hoel, 1993).

But how could the most appropriate level of compensation be estimated? It is possible that all countries in the world might simply be offered the same amount of money per tonne of carbon conserved. But this would place developing countries in an unfair position since they would not be able either to use income gained from exploiting these forests for timber or to use the land beneath them to contribute to their development, whereas forests conserved in temperate countries might already have been exploited many times for timber and consist of regrowth on previous agricultural land (Grainger, 1997).

To take account of this, normative trends for forest conversion to agriculture, and forest exploitation for timber, should be constructed for each country, based upon what should happen if it were to develop sustainably. (Such trends, incidentally, would need to be constructed for all resources to produce the overall normative trend in the sustainable development index.) The impact of set-asides on this normative trend could be assessed, and used to calculate the level of compensation for constraining the development process. For example, a normative deforestation trend might leave the country with a national forest cover of 30 per cent, but participation in the international environmental regime would require the government to ensure that 40 per cent remains instead; then the level of compensation could be based on the difference between these two figures.

Modelling generic trends in national land use morphology
Such normative trends can be understood using the theory of the national land use transition – a period of time in which a significant proportion of forest cover in a country is cleared. The transition ends when deforestation is brought under control and the agriculture and forest sectors of national land use come into a dynamic equilibrium (Grainger, 1995a). The range of possible transition scenarios can best be understood by reference to (a) a normative scenario, in which deforestation is controlled by a combination of improved agricultural productivity and proactive government forest protection, and ends with a substantial forest cover remaining; (b) a critical scenario, in which deforestation is controlled by market forces in the forest sector and reactive government forest protection, but ends with little forest cover remaining (Figure 4.1). The end of the transition may be followed – after some delay – by a forest replenishment period (Figure 4.2).

Until recently, the deforestation path taken by a particular country was not of major importance to it or to other countries. But this situation changed after concern grew about widespread tropical deforestation and its contribution to global climate change and the loss of global biodiversity. If a country undergoes a normative transition, corresponding to the normative forest depletion trend that is part of a sustainable development path, then when the transition ends it retains more forest – and larger stocks of carbon and biodiversity – than would otherwise be the case.

Ideally, in a country that was largely forested before the spread of human settlement, the normative transition would end with a national land use morphology corresponding to the optimum land suitability classification, so that all areas suitable for agriculture would be farmed, and all the unsuitable areas would be left under forest. Some tropical countries, such as Thailand, undertook a national land suitability

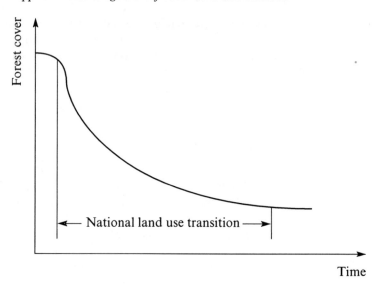

Figure 4.1 The national land use transition

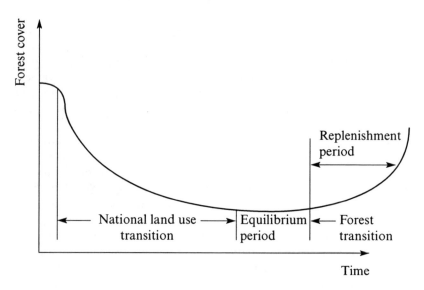

Figure 4.2 Unified model of national land use transition, forest transition and replenishment period

classification many years ago but others still lack one. The results of Thailand's survey showed that about 42 per cent of the country was unsuitable for agriculture (Government of Thailand/FAO, 1972), so in the Fifth National Development Plan (1982–86), the government adopted 40 per cent as the optimum national forest cover. In 1973, forest cover was actually 43 per cent, but by 1988 it had fallen to 28 per cent.

A geographical information systems (GIS) comparison of the distribution of forest cover in Thailand in 1992 with a map of its optimum national land suitability classification shows that forest was mainly confined to marginal upland areas which should remain under forest (called 'designated areas' in Figure 4.3). However, a large proportion of the designated area has been cleared of forest and so is not under its optimal land use. For countries still lacking a national land suitability classification, this technique could be used to determine the optimum minimum forest cover, provided basic map data on environmental factors are available (Grainger *et al.*, 1996).

Mapping degraded forest areas available for replenishment
Sustainable development theory places constraints on two parts of natural capital: resource capital and environmental quality. The normative national land use transition shows the ideal depletion path for forest resource stocks but does not say anything about lesser human impacts on the forest which degrade it but do not clear it.

Forest degradation is widespread throughout the world, and the component of environmental quality associated with degraded forest is lower than it would be under natural conditions. Little is known about the extent of degraded forests, but interest in them rose when it was realized that they are sub-optimal as far as their carbon stocks are concerned. Subsequently, IPCC (International Panel on Climate Change) deliberations have provoked considerable research into how much degraded forest there is in the world, where it is located, how much extra carbon could be taken out of the atmosphere if it were replenished, and whether it is available for inclusion in a global climate change mitigation programme.

This research has important lessons for integrated socio-economic and environmental assessment. The basic philosophy underlying the IPCC deliberations was that of physical science, which viewed degraded forests merely as unfilled carbon stores. But from this limited perspective, the physical suitability of forests for replenishment can be assessed by comparing the potential biomass density and actual biomass density of an area of forest.

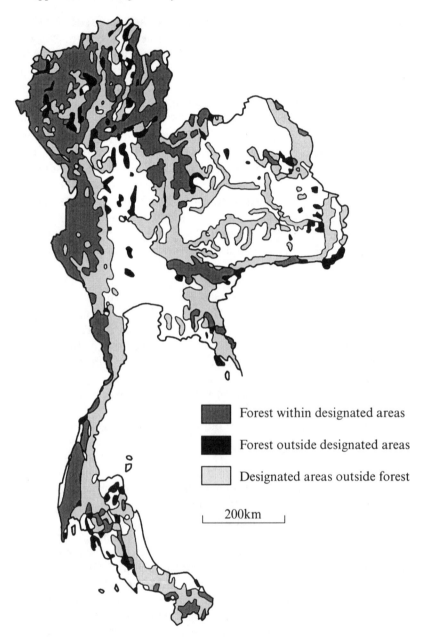

Forest within designated areas

Forest outside designated areas

Designated areas outside forest

200km

Figure 4.3 Distribution of forest cover in Thailand, 1992

This was the basis of GIS study undertaken for the whole of continental South and South-East Asia by Iverson *et al.* (1993). Potential biomass density was estimated as a function of climate and other environmental variables and represented by a potential carbon sequestration index (PCSI) on a scale of 1 to 100. Actual biomass density was represented on a similar scale by an actual carbon sequestration index (ACSI) estimated by: (a) a model based on climate and settlement data; (b) a global vegetation index derived from Advanced High Resolution Radiometer (AVHRR) satellite data (the two estimates showed good correlation). Maps of PCSI and ACSI were produced for remaining forests in the region and the latter subtracted from the former to give a map of forest divided into six degradation classes (Figure 4.4). The average degradation was 88 mg C per ha, compared with a mean regional biomass density of 185 mg C per ha. Two-thirds of all forest could sequester an extra 50–150 mg C per ha to help to mitigate global climate change. The quality of the estimate was limited by inaccurate forest maps and errors made in estimating ACSI and PCSI. But it was the first study to use direct measurements and models to estimate the large-area distribution of degraded forest.

Just because an area of degraded forest is physically suitable for replenishment does not mean that it is actually available. A variety of social, economic and political constraints would determine if such forest could be included in an international mitigation programme. Despite the difficulties and errors involved in studying these constraints, international policy makers do require estimates of how much degraded forest might be actually available. To achieve this requires a fully integrated socio-economic and environmental regional assessment that takes account of such constraints but does so using limited data.

Availability can be assessed in two stages. The first assesses technical availability based on the degree of degradation, the current land use, and the most appropriate form of replenishment treatment. Degraded forest is divided into two main classes according to the most appropriate form of replenishment: most forest in the low to medium degradation classes just needs protection as it is regenerating naturally; forest in higher degradation classes needs afforestation or intensive management. Degraded forest is then divided into its different land use types. Land is technically available if it is highly degraded (for example, rangeland and weedy grassland), so cultural factors will not impede its availability, or if it is covered by managed forest, when current management practices should be capable of modification. It is technically unavailable if it is only slightly degraded, or is being farmed (for example, tree crop plantations and forest fallow) and so is not culturally degraded.

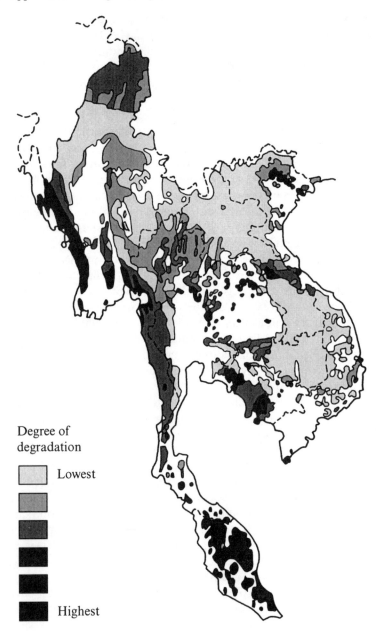

Degree of
degradation

Lowest

Highest

Figure 4.4 Forest divided into six degradation classes, Thailand

Only a proportion of the area of technically available land will be actually available, so the second stage of the assessment must estimate directly the influence of social, economic and political constraints. It can be assumed that all forest technically available for protection will be actually available, but much forest land that is technically available for afforestation is likely to be unavailable, either because it is too degraded to make afforestation economic, or for social reasons: much heavily degraded forest fallow is still used by shifting cultivators, and weedy grasslands and rangelands are often used for grazing. Political constraints will further reduce the actually available area. Procedures are now being developed to include relevant social, economic and political attributes of vegetation in such large-area mapping exercises (Grainger, 1996b).

The sustainability of resource management
Over the last ten years there has been growing interest in promoting more sustainable management of tropical forests for timber production. The First International Tropical Timber Agreement (1983) promoted collaboration between tropical timber-producing and importing countries to improve forest management in a non-coercive, partnership approach that essentially took an evolutionary view of forest management. But latterly environmentalist non-governmental organizations (NGOs) have campaigned to give developing countries firm deadlines to achieve fully sustainable development. Afterwards, only timber from sustainably managed forest could be traded worldwide.

NGO actions were based on a mistaken belief that imposing sustainable management would control deforestation. It would, by definition, require perfect protection of forests from encroachment, but selective logging itself does not lead to forest clearance, and various studies have argued that banning logging in tropical forests would probably raise deforestation rates, as governments would no longer protect forests for timber production and farmers would be more free to expand into forests (Grainger, 1993). However, owing to these pressures the Second International Tropical Timber Agreement (1994) included a deadline of the year 2000, although trade sanctions were omitted.

Regardless of whether or not the imposition of sustainable forest management will control deforestation, it is questionable in its own right on the basis of historical experience. If it took hundreds of years even for the USA to attain sustainable forest management, why should developing countries be expected to achieve it any faster (Williams, 1989)? Sustainable management requires sustainable institutions and not just perfect management techniques, and in developing countries sustainable state institutions can take many decades to evolve (Grainger, 1995b).

Some developing countries, such as the Philippines, are now abandoning as failures their attempts to improve centralized forest management and are decentralizing it (Poffenberger, 1990), though traditional communal institutions are largely gone and need to be replaced by new analogues that retain the best features of the old but are relevant to modern conditions. Unfortunately, environmentalists take no account of these realities. Management is either sustainable or not. How can developing countries respond?

Attempts to impose sustainable management are incompatible with the integrated approach in this chapter, as they focus purely on curbing (supposed) environmental impacts and take no account of development needs. Indeed, their limitations are even deeper, since their environmental impact assessment is very simplistic – bipolar rather than graduated.

An alternative, and more integrated, approach could be based on an extended form of sustainable development theory. In current theory sustainable resource management is only essential in the hyper-strong condition (see above) though it would help to meet the other conditions. But these restrictions only treat trends in natural capital and say nothing about how they may be achieved. As it distinguishes clearly between natural capital and human capital, it is difficult for current theory to accommodate issues like sustainable management which depend on both resource management and human institutions. The problem can be overcome by extending the scope of human capital to include a new sub-category of resource sustainability capital (RSC). Equation (1) now becomes:

$$HC = PC + CC + IC + RSC \qquad (5)$$

In this new approach the sustainability of renewable resource management would be regarded as an investment parameter. This seems reasonable, since introducing sustainable management systems generally requires investing in physical and institutional infrastructure as well as technical inputs. Sustainable management is therefore not just a requirement for improved social welfare, but also, because of the need for strong supporting human institutions, it is a component of investment in human capital itself. Sustainable land use in this guise becomes something 'attained' rather than 'given'. It takes time to evolve, depending on the pace at which human capital generally expands.

This implies that if the world community does decide to introduce environmental conditions into international trade regimes, these should take account of the level of development of each country, and not be imposed uniformly throughout the world. The focus of concern about the need for more sustainable management of forests and other resources would then switch back from strict distinctions between sustainable and non-sustainable management and the imposition of fixed limits on when sustainable management must be achieved, and look instead at the degree of sustainability of management and supporting efforts within each country to increase this by investing in the expansion of resource sustainability capital.

One of the difficulties involved in assessing the sustainability of forest management in a tropical country is the sheer time required – at least three rotations (or up to 120 years) for each area of forest (Poore, 1989). The degree of sustainable management in an entire country could be monitored more rapidly by: (a) estimating the proportion of national forest area conforming to International Tropical Timber Organization criteria for sustainable management; (b) using a single surrogate indicator.

A possible surrogate indicator is the ratio between the actual number of forest guards per ha of forest and some ideal number. Information on the institutional strength of forestry departments is often difficult to obtain, especially the number of foresters actually stationed in forested areas rather than at headquarters. In 1957 the Royal Forest Department in Thailand had only 1000 forest officers in the field to protect over 30 million ha of forest, but by 1991 this had at least quadrupled while the forest area had halved to only 14 million ha. So the density of forest guards was one for every 3500 ha (Poffenberger, 1990; Wongpakdee, 1991). In 1992 the Philippines had the same number of forest guards to protect 6 million ha of forest – a density of one guard for every 1700 ha of forest. This seems to lead to the conclusion that the sustainability of forest management in Thailand is only half that in the Philippines, but does not reflect informal assessments of the two situations and so reveals the inadequacy of surrogate indicators of this kind.

4.7 Conclusions

A paradigm shift in international environmental affairs has led to mounting intervention into the development process of developing countries and this could intensify in the future. Initially, it led to the greater use of environmental impact assessment in project and regional planning, but subsequent developments mean that new development planning techniques are required at national level to integrate environmental assessment and socio-economic appraisal. These techniques are needed as much for the benefit of the developing countries as for any other reason, in order to protect them from external impositions which unfairly discriminate against them and prejudice their sustainable development.

This chapter has suggested some principles upon which suitable techniques could be based. A national index of sustainable development could be used to monitor the increase in the degree of sustainable development over time in both developed and developing countries, and be included in national economic models to test the effect of proposed external intervention into national economies by the World Bank and International Monetary Fund to reduce the possibility of environmental degradation. New international trade regimes should not include environmental conditions that penalize developing countries for not having fully sustainable natural resource management, or impose deadlines to achieve this, but should instead focus on the degree of sustainable management and how this evolves over time. Finally, developing countries participating in international environmental regimes should be compensated for the lost development resulting from the need to set aside forests, land or other resources for global benefit.

Much additional research is needed before such an approach can be implemented. For example, the difficulties of valuing natural capital and human capital in equivalent terms must be overcome, and long-term national case studies are needed to learn how countries behave at different stages of their development process. However, studying national development from a more integrated human–environmental perspective will not only lead to improved development planning techniques but also shed new light on the development process, and so this research should be worthwhile from many perspectives.

References

Adams, W.M. (1990), *Green Development*, London: Routledge.

Andrasko, K., K. Heaton and S. Winnett (1991), 'Evaluating the costs and efficiency of options to manage global forests', in C. Sargent (ed.), *Proceedings of Technical Workshop to Explore Options for Global Forest Management*, Bangkok, 24–30 April 1990; 216–33, Office of the National Environment Board, Government of Thailand/US Environmental Protection Agency, Bangkok.

Bauer, P. (1976) *Dissent on Development*, London: Weidenfeld and Nicolson.

Canter, L.W (1996), *Environmental Impact Assessment*, second edition, New York: McGraw-Hill.

Cruz, W. and R. Repetto (1992), *The Environmental Effects of Stabilization and Structural Adjustment Programs: The Philippines Case*, Washington, DC: World Resources Institute.

Diamond, P.A. and J.A. Hausman (1994), 'Contingent valuation: is some number better than no number?' *Journal of Economic Perspectives* **8** (4).

Dixon, J.A. and P.B. Sherman (1990), *Economics of Protected Areas*, London: Earthscan.

DOE (1996), 'Indicators of sustainable development for the United Kingdom', consultation document, UK Department of the Environment, London: HMSO.

Frank, A.G. (1967), *Capitalism and Underdevelopment in Latin America*, New York: Monthly Review Press.

Goldsmith, E. (1980), 'World Ecological Areas Programme. A proposal to save the world's tropical rain forests', *The Ecologist*, **10**, 2–4.

Goodland, R. and G. Tillman (1995), 'Strategic environmental assessment – strengthening the environmental assessment process', Washington, DC: World Bank.

Government of Thailand/FAO (1972), *General Land Capability Map of Thailand*, Bangkok.

Grainger, A. (1992), 'The role of biophysical indicators in evaluating national progress in sustainable development', paper presented to a workshop on Global Environmental Indicators, World Resources Institute, Washington, DC, 7–8 December 1992.

Grainger, A. (1993), *Controlling Tropical Deforestation*, London: Earthscan.

Grainger, A. (1995a), 'National land use morphology: patterns and possibilities', *Geography*, **20**, 235–45.

Grainger, A. (1995b), 'Changes in land use and forest management in Southeast Asia – an evolutionary perspective', in S. Sandbukt (ed.), *Proceedings of the International Symposium on Management of Rain Forest in Asia*, University of Oslo, 23–26 March 1994, pp. 3–17, Centre for Development and the Environment, University of Oslo.

Grainger, A. (1996a), 'An evaluation of FAO's Tropical Forest Resource Assessment', *Geographical Journal*, **162**, 73–9.

Grainger, A. (1996b), 'Integrating the socio-economic and physical dimensions of global climate change mitigation', in M. Apps (ed.), *Proceedings of the NATO Advanced Research Workshop on The Role of Forest Ecosystems and Forest Resource Management in the Global Climate Cycle*, Banff, Alberta, 11–16 September 1994, pp. 335–48, Berlin: Springer Verlag.

Grainger, A. (1997), Compensating for opportunity costs in forest-based strategies to mitigate global climate change', *Critical Reviews in Environmental Science and Technology*, **27** (Supplement).

Grainger, A., H. Francisco, B. Malayang, C. Mehl and P. Tirasawat (1996), 'Population–environment dynamics at high population density in the humid tropics', final report, School of Geography, University of Leeds.

Hoel, M. (1993), 'Harmonization of carbon taxes in international climate agreements', *Environmental and Resource Economics*, **3**, 221–31.

IUCN (1980), *World Conservation Strategy*, International Union for the Conservation of Nature, Morges, Switzerland.

Iverson, L.R., S. Brown, A. Grainger, A. Prasad and D. Liu (1993), 'Carbon sequestration in South/Southeast Asia: an assessment of technically suitable forest lands using geographic information systems analysis', *Climate Research*, **3**, 23–38.

Jansson, A., M. Hammer, C. Folke and R. Constanza (1994), *Investing in Natural Capital*, Washington, DC: Island Press.

Lal, D. (1989), *The Limits of International Cooperation*, The Wincoft Lecture, Institute for Economic Affairs, London.

Maddox, B. (1994), 'Fading blueprint of a greener world', *Financial Times*, 26 February, p. 18.

Moffatt, I. and M.D. Wilson (1994), 'An index of sustainable welfare for Scotland, 1980–91', *International Journal of Sustainable Development and World Ecology*, **1**, 264–91.

O'Loughlin C. (1971), *National Economic Accounting*, Oxford: Pergamon Press.

Pearce, D.W. (ed.) (1991), *Blueprint 2. Greening the World Economy*, London: Earthscan.

Pearce, D.W. and G. Atkinson (1992), 'Are national economies sustainable? Measuring sustainable development', Centre for Social and Economic Research on the Global Environment, University College, London.

Pearce, D.W. and R.K. Turner (1990), *Economics of Natural Resources and the Environment*, London: Harvester Wheatsheaf.

Pearce, D.W., A. Markandya and E.B. Barbier (1989), *Blueprint for a Green Economy*, London: Earthscan.

Poffenberger, M. (1990), 'The evolution of forest management systems in Southeast Asia', in M. Poffenberger (ed.), *Keepers of the Forest*, West Hartford, CT: Kumarian Press.

Poore, M.E.D. (ed.) (1989), *No Timber Without Trees*, London: Earthscan.

Porter, G. and J. Welsh Brown (1991), *Global Environmental Politics*, Boulder, Co: Westview Press.

Redclift, M. (1987), *Sustainable Development: Exploring the Contradictions*, London: Methuen.

Rees, J. (1990), *Natural Resources: Allocation, Economics and Policy*, second edition, London: Routledge.

Repetto, R., W. Magrath, M. Wells, C. Beer and F. Rossini (1989), *Wasting Assets: Natural Resources in the National Accounts,* Washington, DC: World Resources Institute.

Rostow W.W. (1960), *The Stages of Economic Growth*, Cambridge: Cambridge University Press.

Sedjo R.A. and R.A. Solomon (1989), 'Climate and forests', in N.J. Rosenberg *et al.*, (eds), *Greenhouse Warming: Abatement and Adaptation*, Washington DC: Resources for the Future, pp. 105–19.

Simpson, E.S. (1987), *The Developing World: An Introduction*, London: Longman.

Solórzano, R., R. Camino, R. Woodward, J. Tosi, V. Watson, A. Vasquéz, C. Villalobos, J. Jimenez, R. Repetto and W. Cruz. (1991), *Accounts Overdue: Natural Resource Depreciation in Costa Rica*, Washington DC: World Resources Institute.

Taylor P.J. (1989), *Political Geography*, Harlow: Longman.

Therivel, R. *et al.* (1992), *Strategic Environmental Assessment*, London: Earthscan.

Tietenberg, T.H. (1994), *Economics and Environmental Policy*, Aldershot, UK: Edward Elgar.

Turner, R.K. (1988), 'Sustainability, resource conservation and pollution control: an overview', in R.K. Turner (ed.), *Sustainable Environmental Management*, London: Belhaven Press.

Ul Haq, M. (1994), Barbara Ward Lecture, (1994).

UN (1978), United Nations Conference on Desertification 1977, *Round-Up, Plan of Action and Resolutions*, New York: United Nations.

UNDP (1991), *Human Development Report 1991*, United Nations Development Programme. Oxford: Oxford University Press.

Wathern, P. (ed.) (1988), *Environmental Impact Assessment: Theory and Practice*, London: Unwin Hyman.

WCED (1987) *Our Common Future.* World Commission on Environment and Development, United Nations, New York.

Williams, M. (1989), *Americans and their Forests. A Historical Geography*, Cambridge: Cambridge University Press.

Willis, K.G. (1995), 'Contingent valuation in a policy context: the National Oceanic and Atmospheric Administration report and its implications for the use of contingent valuation methods in policy analysis in Britain', in K.G. Willis and J.T. Corkindale (eds), *Environmental Valuation: New Perspectives*, Wallingford: CAB International.

Wongpakdee, Somboon (1991), 'Thailand national parks and sanctuaries 1990', Tiger Paper, March, pp. 29–32, Bangkok: UN Food and Agriculture Organization.

World Bank (1995), *Monitoring Environmental Progress. A Report on Work in Progress*, Environmentally Sustainable Development Series, Washington DC: World Bank.

5 A methodology for investigating the impact of policy decisions on the natural resource environment of developing countries

Jamie Morrison and Richard Pearce

5.1 Introduction

One of the major issues concerning commentators and researchers involved with the problems of developing countries is the potential of poor countries to increase food output at a rate fast enough to meet the demands manifested by rising populations and incomes, and increasing urbanization.[1] Two central themes of the debates surrounding this issue are the influence of the technologies currently deployed and likely to be developed in the future, and the sustainability of the natural resource environment as it comes under increasing pressure from attempts to raise the productivity of the resources deployed in agricultural production. The relationship between the technological choices and the policy environment are well documented, but the link between policy change and the natural resource environment has received much less attention.

While the impacts of specific localized changes in the socio-economic context have received substantial focus, for example those stemming from the implementation of projects where the association between action and impact are both visible and measurable, the links between sectoral and macroeconomic policy and the sustainability of the natural resource environment are much harder to discern.

In analysing the impact of any policy change, policy makers would ideally take into account these environmental costs and benefits as well as the economic outcomes in terms of increased efficiency. Often, however, it appears difficult even to determine whether the impacts associated with such policy decisions will be positive or negative, let alone the magnitude of any effects.

One problem facing researchers is that their attempts to incorporate sustainability issues into policy analysis are likely to be static in nature because both technology and population growth rates are considered to be exogenous influences. Models which treat these variables endogenously are likely to be of little use to policy makers because they are both highly complex and intractable, while more simplified models are likely to prove unreliable. The assessment of the impacts of policy decisions on the natural resource environment has been hindered by the absence of a methodology for tracing these impacts (Munasinghe and Cruz, 1994). This absence of a satisfactory methodological approach has undoubtedly contributed to the difficulty of getting policy makers to recognize the existence of the potential policy–environment relationships at all (Lutz and Young, 1992).

Even where such relationships are recognized, they are rarely incorporated at the policy design stage as it is difficult to determine the magnitude of environmental effects until they become apparent. In the context of substantive economic policy reform, this implies that these effects are not taken into consideration until after the reform process has been implemented and the response is reactive rather than proactive. The latter point highlights the importance of both the environmental impact assessment and the analysis of the economic costs and benefits of policy decisions being completed at the same point in the policy formulation process, a theme central to the action impact matrix methodology (Munasinghe and Cruz, 1994).

In this chapter we restrict our discussion to the effects on the natural resource environment which occur as a result of policy decisions that affect the agricultural sector. While there has been substantive work carried out on the environmental impact of different farming practices, and the development of technical indicators to describe the direction and magnitude of these impacts (OECD, 1995), we focus on the other side of the link, that is, on the ability of policy makers to determine the likely implications of policy reforms on farming practice.

5.2 A descriptive framework

This section provides some idea of the complexity of the policy context affecting agricultural activity, and the multifarious influences of this context on farming practice and of the latter on the natural resource environment. Fox (1993) identifies three phases in the 'environmental assessment of agricultural policies':

- an analysis of the economic factors influencing farm production practices and of the outcome of farm production practices;
- an investigation of what he describes as 'resource depletion and transport and fate modelling'; and
- the valuation of these environmental effects.

A similar, although more general, approach views farming practices and rural resource management as being determined by a range of policy and non-policy factors, which in turn determine the environmental impact (Ministry of Agriculture and Food, New Zealand, 1993). The framework outlined below is an adaptation of these approaches intended to reflect more closely the concerns of this chapter.

While it is apparent that there is a range of policy variables which are likely to influence natural resource use, it should be remembered that the effect of policy will not only depend on its characteristics but also on the context in which it is introduced. In other words, there will be a range of parameters describing the scenario in which various policies interact, and these parameters will influence the outcome of these interactions.

These parameters, both environmental and non-environmental, economic and non-economic, may have a considerable bearing on the final outcome of changes in relevant policy variables. The latter will include policies likely to have an impact far wider than the agricultural sector and its natural resource environment, but which nevertheless can have a profound influence on agriculture, in some cases a greater influence than those policy interventions which are sector-specific. These macroeconomic influences, as well as having direct effects on agriculture, also provide the broad economic context in which sector-specific interventions, or agricultural policies *per se*, impact on agricultural activity.

This conjuncture of socio-economic and natural resource environments together with the policy context largely determines the way in which agricultural activity is conducted, which is loosely termed 'farming practice'. These form a crucial link in the framework and in any consequent analysis, since they provide a bridge between policy change and changes in the status of the natural resource environment.

This chain of events is summarized in the flow diagram depicted in Figure 5.1. Those elements which describe the context in which agricultural activity occurs, namely the socio-economic and natural resource variables which are unlikely to change in the short to medium term, or are not under the control of national governments, are described as socio-economic and natural resource parameters.

Since economic policy interventions (macroeconomic policies and agricultural policy variables) will have a feedback effect on these parameters, just as environmental impacts will have a feedback effect on the natural resource environment, these influences are also shown in the diagram. Two sets of interaction: socio-economic and natural resource, are illustrated by broken-line arrows. The natural resource parameters will additionally have a more direct effect on farming practices and this is also depicted in the diagram.

The bold arrows demonstrate the relationships with which we are most concerned in this chapter, that is, those between policy interventions and

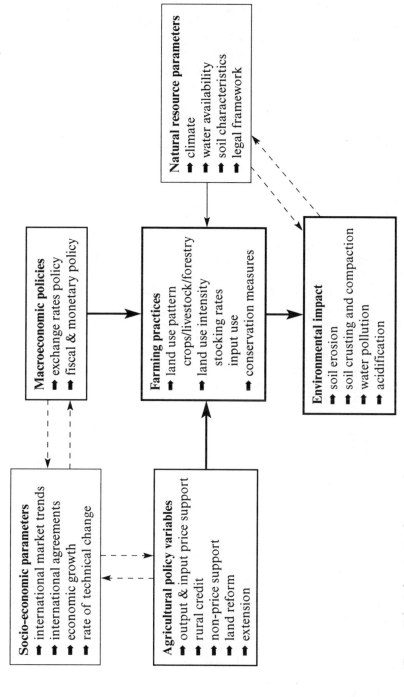

Figure 5.1 A descriptive framework

farming practices, and the consequent influence of the latter on the natural resource environment. Obviously the diagram is a simplification, and there are feedback effects and influential factors affecting environmental status which are not included. The intention here is to encapsulate those interactions which are pertinent to the chapter.

5.3 The dynamic context

The framework outlined above provides some insight into how researchers and policy makers might approach the links between economic policy variables and the status of the natural resource environment, but in key respects it describes a static context: the dynamic variables with which we might be most concerned are either absent or subsumed as parameters. At the same time, sustainable development by definition requires that the assessment of any impact of a policy decision take account of the dynamic context.

In most developing countries, a key dynamic variable that impacts upon the natural resource environment is the population growth rate (PGR). The relationship between the PGR and environmental degradation, which may be positive in some cases, is often extremely complex. In many contexts, population growth exerts a transforming effect on technology which leads to changes in how agriculture is practised. Boserup (1965) used this relationship to explain the transition from shifting cultivation with long fallow periods to short fallow farming and then to intensive monoculture. More recently, Pearce and Warford (1993) have suggested that the relationship between population growth and food output might be reduced to a balance of two opposing forces:

- the role of population pressure in inducing production-increasing technical change,
- the latter's role in wider resource degradation that eventually reduces agricultural growth.

This provides the principal focus for this chapter. We pose two central hypotheses:

1. *Changes in the policy context impact on the natural resource environment through their effect on the type of technology practised by farmers.*
2. *The speed of evolution of technical change, as governed by population pressure and the policy environment, determines the likely magnitude and significance of the resulting impacts on the natural resource environment.*

Thus technological change creates the potential for farmers to increase production within ecological constraints by shifting the production function upwards (Bumb, 1995). Putting this observation in the context of the sequence described by Pearce and Warford (1993), this implies that population growth might lead to a reduced fallow period and increased land use intensity, which in turn decreases soil productivity. The latter leads to a shift in the type of technology used to raise the productivity per unit of land in order, as a minimum, to maintain the level of output per capita.

At the same time, the policy context often presents a constraint to the adoption of the new technologies. For example, in many countries of sub-Saharan Africa, a combination of exchange rate, trade and agricultural price polices has eroded incentives to increase agricultural production, that is, the mechanisms for transmitting changes in agricultural technology have become severely inadequate (Cleaver and Schreiber, 1994).

5.4 A methodology for tracing the impacts of policy decisions

We begin by assuming that policies can be categorized as those that

1. directly affect relative prices of agricultural inputs and outputs, such as input subsidies and taxes, export subsidies, exchange rate policies; and
2. place/ease constraints on resource access such as land reform, credit/interest rate policies and so on.

We are concerned to detail a methodology which incorporates the often contradictory nature of policy change and which allows the decision maker in a particular location or country to determine, for example, the likely impact of an exchange rate devaluation on the natural resource environment. We describe a two-stage indirect link between these two sets of variables.

- In the first stage, farmer behaviour as depicted by the farming practice adopted is central to the discussion. In a static analysis this is constrained by, and contingent upon, the incumbent state of technology. If we could assume some standard and static technology we could hypothesize as to the likely response of the farmer to a policy change, in terms of any increase or decrease in input levels (both capital and land), and therefore in changes in the proportion of land under annual crops as opposed to some other use. The nature of production technology at farm level thus plays a pivotal role in determining the way in which policy influences input use (Fox, 1993).
- In the second stage, we are interested in a more dynamic scenario. The extent to which technological evolution is driven by population growth and constrained by the policy context becomes an important

focus: we need to know, therefore, the rate of technical change in order to consider the potential impacts on a range of environmental indicators that are likely to be changed as a result.

However, farming practices are varied, and are often constrained by the current technology. This impinges not only on the likely response in terms of changes in farming practice, but also upon the magnitude and significance of any resulting increase or decrease in the status of the environmental indicator.

As we shall demonstrate, these impacts are likely to be ambiguous due to

1. the initial starting point of the agriculture sector in terms of the current level of intensification and/or extensification of the production system, and
2. the likely direction of change towards the extensive or intensive margins.

These are in turn dynamically related to the policy environment, and provide important points of departure when considering how to mitigate any adverse implications of the policy change, or what complementary measures might be appropriate to implement with the change.

5.5 Analysing the impacts of price policy

Consider a policy that alters the relative price ratio in favour of annual crops. The supply response literature[2] suggests that the supply elasticity in developing countries is positive; thus we would expect an aggregate increase in the production of annual crops as presented in Figure 5.2.

However, this type of analysis tells us nothing about the way in which the additional output is produced. Clearly, this depends upon the farming practice that is adopted, and the latter will determine the likely implications of the policy change. For example, there could be increased environmental damage through increased input use, resulting in deteriorating water quality; or there could be natural resource degradation in the form of soil erosion or deforestation as a result of the opening up of frontier land for crop production.

One approach designed to bridge this predictive gap involves constructing an archetypal household based on household-level data to assess the economic response to policy, and to link this response to environmental degradation through a quantification of changes in input use. Typical of this approach is Freeman *et al.* (1995), in a study using data from a high-performance zone in northern Nigeria. The main problem with this approach is that the data requirement is high, and that the scope for using secondary data sources is often limited.

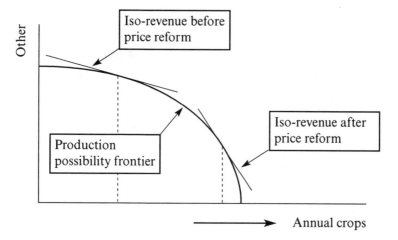

Figure 5.2 Production possibility frontier

5.6 The central role of farming practice

How, therefore, can farming, practices be depicted in a manner that will allow us to determine which environmental indicators are likely to be affected and, more importantly, to what degree? An appropriate way forward is to classify responses in terms of an extensification or intensification of farming practices.

In referring to farming practice we imply the particular set of activities for which land is used, in combination with the technical parameters describing production methods. The centrality of the concept to our concerns can be illustrated through a simple diagram such as Figure 5.3. This juxtaposes different technical systems with land use patterns as described by the ratio of crop production to pasture. Thus the south-west quadrant, as illustrated by point A, describes a land use system characterized by a small proportion of cropping but where most land is devoted to pasture or forest. It would typically involve mixed farming systems with a long crop rotation or fallow. In contrast, the north-west quadrant, exemplified by point B, contains arable systems which could be described as low-capital or 'traditional', while the south-east and north-east quadrants represent more intensive production systems.

The south-west quadrant represents the type of farming practice likely to be the most benign with regard to the natural resource environment. However, the circumstances in which a farming system characterized by such practices is sustainable are not widespread. Such practices are generally static in terms of output per unit of resource and, when subject to the twin pressures of population expansion and income growth, both of

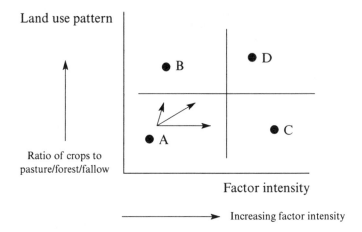

Figure 5.3 Hypothetical scatter plot of farm practices

which increase the demand for agricultural output, shifts in one or more of the directions indicated by the arrows are likely to occur.

This simple diagram is useful in highlighting the influence of both the socio-economic parameters and the agricultural policy variables with which we are concerned in this chapter. The long-term effect of changes in the socio-economic environment will bring continuing pressure for production activity to move away from that typified by the south-west quadrant of Figure 5.3. Within certain constraints, agricultural policy may then have a substantial influence on the direction and speed of these movements.

5.7 The relationship between farming practice and environmental indicators

We can extend the diagram to capture, in principle, the relationships between changes in farming practice and changes in natural resource conditions. We can assume the following:

1. Any form of cropping exposes the land to the risk of soil erosion through the combined influence of wind and water. Within certain limits it is probably the case that the more intensive these cropping practices become, the greater is the risk of erosion, with consequent on-site and off-site costs.
2. The more intensive the land use activities, the greater the risk of environmental degradation from a number of other causes, including salinization, chemical pollution, soil compaction and erosion as a consequence of overgrazing.

These two channels of environmental degradation are not entirely distinct, but are sufficiently different to illustrate that agricultural policy can influence the direction of agricultural change and therefore the environmental costs of change. However, these relationships describe the *propensity* for natural resource degradation, rather than its inevitability. There are conservation measures and better management practices which, within limits, can reduce this risk, but these in turn have an associated cost.

Figure 5.4 shows the environmental implications of a change in farming practices in a given direction, that is, towards both an increase in the cropping percentage and in the intensity of production. The shapes of the two environmental cost functions C_1 and C_2 will vary with the particular context, especially according to patterns of temperature, rainfall and soil structure. The shape of the curves could also vary with the type of crop, since any variation in cultivation technique, due to a change in the crop produced, may change the environmental impact. Nevertheless, in general, it can be expected that environmental costs will increase more than proportionately with increases in cropping or land use intensity.[3] The costs represented by these functions include both the value attributed to environmental damage caused by agricultural activity, and/or the costs of reducing or eliminating that damage.

Separating the two functions facilitates the separate consideration of the two underlying features of agricultural change: extending the extensive margin of cultivation (ploughing of virgin pasture, shortening of fallows and so on) and extending the intensive margin of cultivation (typically through the use of improved varieties and agricultural chemicals).

To a degree environmental degradation associated with agricultural production can be reduced or eliminated through the application of conservation measures and improved farming practices. The costs associated with such measures will be borne directly through the expenses incurred in undertaking conservation measures, or indirectly through any productivity loss associated with different farming practices.[4] In either case the environmental costs are borne, in the absence of government subsidy, by the producer. Of course, in the great majority of countries, these external costs, even when considerable, are not fully internalized in this way, but are borne by society as a whole.

Policy interventions can influence environmental costs and the direction of change from the initial position in Figure 5.4, through their influence on the incentive structure and, through this, on the type and range of crops produced. An intervention which changes relative output prices, will also influence the relative profitability of individual crops. This could change the slope of the cost function C_1 in Figure 5.4.

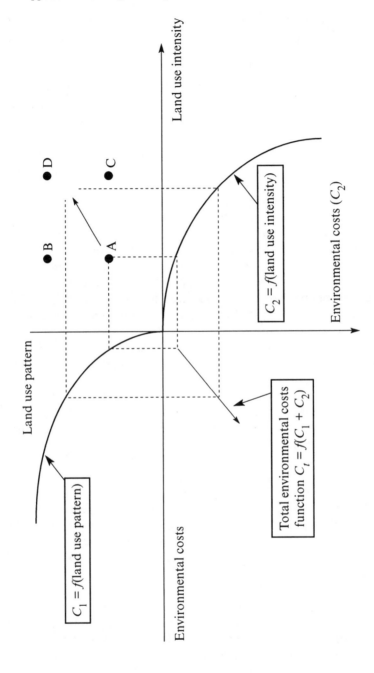

Figure 5.4 Farming practices and environmental implications

Similarly, policy interventions can influence environmental costs through changing the extent and form of the intensification of agricultural production. This would be reflected in the shape of cost function C_2. The total cost function (C_1 plus C_2) can shift in either direction, illustrating that a policy change can reverse, exacerbate or leave unchanged previous trends in natural resource degradation.

5.8 The effect of policy changes

It is apparent that the movement from A to B can engender a variety of very different environmental impacts. Economic policy, for the reasons described above, can not only influence the way in which increased agricultural activity occurs, as demonstrated by the movement for A to B, but also the way in which a given volume of output is produced, demonstrated by a variety of outcomes at, for example, point B. This can be explained as follows.

If we assume that the starting point for a typical farm is A, and that policy changes imply that the typical farmer is presented with an incentive to increase crop production, the question arises as to whether an increase in crop production will be achieved by a move to B, where intensity remains constant but land in annual cropping increases, or C, where land under crops remains constant, but input use increases. The response will be determined by the technology or production system currently employed, which in turn will depend upon the relative prices of land to capital, as characterized by land availability.

Farmers are unlikely to have the incentive to intensify agricultural production unless there are constraints on their access to land. If there are no land constraints it makes sense to extend the use of land and minimize the use of other inputs, that is, capital and labour (Cleaver and Schreiber, 1994). Thus a movement towards B is likely to be the preferred response. In this case we could hypothesize, for example, that there would be an increase in the risk of natural resource degradation from soil erosion rather than an increase in pollution or acidification.

Technology is not standard, however, and the relative prices faced by different sectors of the farming community also vary. *In consequence, we do not know where to position point A for the farming community as a whole, nor whether the long-term direction of responses to a policy change will be horizontal or vertical.* Thus, while production economics enables a qualitative assessment to be made of the individual effects of different types of policy on input use and output levels (Fox, 1993), the net effect often cannot be determined without empirical investigation.

5.9 Incorporating the existing state of technology

We continue to develop the framework qualitatively, indicating later more specific requirements for quantitative data. Figure 5.5 is a simple representation of the widely divergent responses that might be observed under differing levels of capital intensity of the system employed.

Following Boserup (1965), we might expect to see farming practice evolving from one characterized by Figure 5.5(a) to one characterized by Figure 5.5(c). However, with rapidly increasing population pressure traditional systems may be overwhelmed, leading to increased environmental degradation (Cleaver and Schreiber, 1994).

In the absence of sufficiently rapid and widespread technical change, farmers might be constrained to using existing technology, represented by Figure 5.5(a), and population growth would then lead to a rapid expansion of area under cultivation, frequently involving the conversion of marginal lands and the loss of forests, wetlands, river valleys and savannah. This is depicted in the movement from A to B in Figures 5.3 and 5.4.

Of course, land scarcity is not a problem in all areas. While there is a common perception that there is little scope for increased production through the expansion of cultivated area, in some countries there are still large tracts of uncultivated land with productive potential. For example, one estimate suggests that out of the total area of 2.5 billion ha with rainfed crop production potential of varying quality, developing countries (excluding China) have about 760 million ha currently under cultivation (Alexandratos, 1995).

In other countries, however, for example Bangladesh, there is now no alternative but to continue to intensify agricultural production (Pagiola, 1995). At the same time, it should be noted that natural resource degradation is not an inevitable consequence of intensification: some modern technologies such as high-yielding varieties, which require less pesticide application, can have the reverse effect if correctly applied. In these circumstances, the most appropriate policy intervention might be to invest more in farmer education than in modifying polices affecting prices or resource access.

Figure 5.6 combines elements of Figures 5.4 and 5.5. Hypothetical technology 'zones' have been mapped in the north-east quadrant of the diagram. It is assumed that farming practices characterized by so-called 'traditional' technologies, typically with low levels of capital and labour input per unit of land (Figure 5.5(a)), will be located in Zone I. At point **a** agricultural activity is also characterized by a relatively small proportion of annual crop production: that is, there has been little pressure on either the extensive or intensive margins of cultivation. Points **b** and **e** represent farming practices where the response to population pressure or

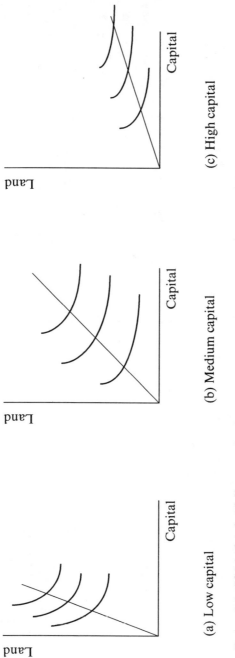

(a) Low capital   (b) Medium capital   (c) High capital

Figure 5.5 Change under different technologies

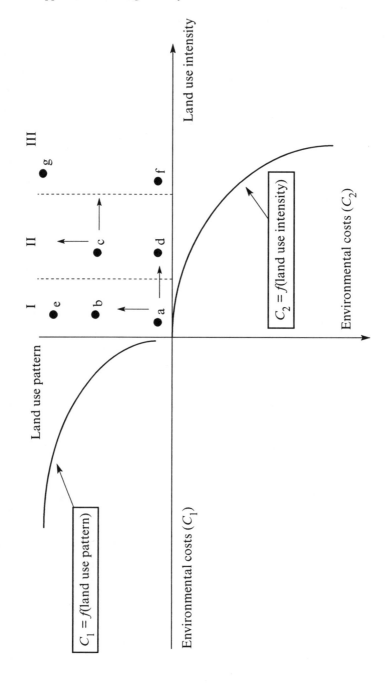

Figure 5.6 Technology-specific zones

increased incomes has led to an expansion of area under annual crops. Zone II, typically point **d**, depicts a zone of limited technical change characteristic of many developing country situations where there is limited use of chemical inputs, and where labour inputs per ha may be high compared to Zone I (Figure 5.5(b)). Zone III is more typical of so-called 'modern' agriculture (Figure 5.5(c)), where both the intensive and extensive margins of cultivation (point **g**) have been extended as far as modern technology will allow. Point **f** is observed in some developing countries' agriculture where there is a dual system of ownership.

With environmental costs increasing more than proportionately with the degree of extensification or intensification, as depicted in the cost functions, the marginal unit of environmental cost (in terms of, for example, soil loss or nitrate pollution) associated with any shift from that starting point, is greater, the more extensive or intensive the existing system.

Of course, local contexts will vary considerably in these respects, and ideally the functions for each such context would be calculated. As suggested above, however, this would be an extremely data intensive exercise, and in most cases the more practical solution would be to use the 'typical' farm context and generalize from this.

Nevertheless, the significance of the 'starting point' should not be underestimated. As noted above, farming practices in most developing countries are likely to be characterized by a technology 'set' and degree of extensification typical of Zone II although, where communications are poor, there may be areas characteristic of points **a** and **b** in Zone I. Most developed countries' agriculture would fall into Zone III, with a tendency to shift towards point **g**.

This implies that the type of environmental cost typically experienced at the margin in developed countries is often different to that experienced in developing countries. In the latter case the main concern may be with costs associated with the C_1 function, as a response, for example, to shifts towards point **e**, while for the former, farming practices are more likely to be subject to C_2 type costs:[5] that is, the key natural resource issues in developing countries are likely to stem from attempts to raise production through extending the extensive margin of cultivation, whereas in developed countries the issues are those associated with the intensive margin. As a simplification it is possible to argue that the main concerns are with soil erosion, on the one hand, and soil pollution and degradation, on the other. There are of course exceptions to the rule. In South and South-East Asia, in particular, the extensive margin has already been encroached and, as noted above, the only option for increasing food production could be an intensification of agriculture from **e** to **g**.

The key point here, however, is that agricultural policy which brings about changes in farming practice will have different implications for the natural resource environment, depending on the point of departure. As far as developing countries are concerned, if farming practices are located in Zone I, then the environmental costs associated with increased production are likely to be relatively small, as suggested by a shift from **a** to **c** in Figure 5.6, and the concomitant movements along the two cost functions. Similarly, a shift from **d** towards **c** would imply some increase in external costs, but proportionately less than for farmers already using practices located in Zone III. Given that most farmers in developing countries are likely to be operating close to point **b** in Zone I or point **c** in Zone II, agricultural policies designed to raise food production, for example, could extend input subsidies to encourage a higher uptake of fertilizer and pesticide use without having a major effect on environmental costs.

5.10 Implications of non-price policies

So far we have studied policy that affects output directly via changes in price. Policies such as land reform, infrastructure improvement and targeted credit schemes will also potentially lead to increased output. We can use the same descriptive framework to describe this process. In Figure 5.7, the north-east quadrant of Figure 5.6 has been reproduced and constraint lines introduced to demonstrate how barriers to resource access may result, in the context of population growth and/or rising incomes, in the diversion of farming practices towards more costly solutions in terms of natural resource degradation than would otherwise be the case. If the starting point was at point **d**, for example, and land distribution was highly skewed, the bulk of farmers would be forced, in response to rising population and incomes, to adopt practices typical of point **f** rather than point **c**. From the perspective of the natural resource environment, this may be the higher-cost solution. If so, a redistributive land reform could produce environmental benefits. Production function analysis could be used to demonstrate where such a reduction in the intensity of farming could be a rational response.

An analogous case can be made with regard to non-price policies which improve the access of farmers to capital inputs. In many developing countries, so-called 'modern' inputs are simply not available to large numbers of farmers, for example, as a consequence of poor physical infrastructure, inadequate marketing infrastructures or lack of purchasing power during crucial time periods. If the starting point is at point **b**, this can 'force' the adoption of practices more typical of point **e** rather than the lower-cost (in terms of natural resource degradation) point **c**. Policies to improve access, such as investment in physical and marketing

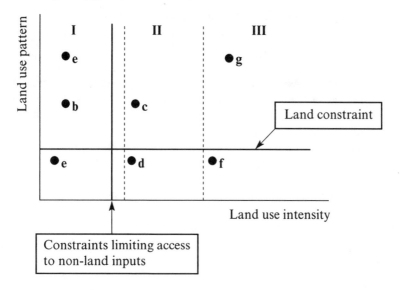

Figure 5.7 Effects of barriers to resource access

infrastructures, and the provision of low-cost credit can overcome this constraint and achieve environmental benefits.

5.11 A framework for the analysis of potential impacts of alternative policies

From the discussion above it is apparent that the static, or short-term, response to a policy change will depend upon the technology currently employed by farmers. In addition, the dynamic or longer-term response will depend upon how conducive the policy context is to the adoption of technologies which impart lower overall costs on the natural resource environment.

In order to simplify the difficulty of specifying one technology from a range, it may be reasonable to use a categorization of farm types similar to that employed by an FAO study (1982). In that study three levels of technology were defined which could be hypothesized as being similar to those represented in Figure 5.5.

- Low level: no fertilizer, pesticide or herbicides. Traditional crop varieties, simple tools and techniques. This could include farming practices **a**, **b** and **e** in Figure 5.6 or as characterized by Figure 5.5(a).
- Intermediate level: basic fertilizers and biocides, some improved crop varieties, limited use of machinery. As represented by practices **d** and **c** in Figure 5.6, or by Figure 5.5(b).

- High level: heavy use of fertilizers and biocides, using most recently bred seed mixes and highly mechanized. As seen in practices **f** or **g** in Figure 5.6 or in Figure 5.5(c).

This typology allows the development of a simplified flow diagram that could provide a framework for both qualitative and quantitative assessment of the likely type and degree of impact that, given the technology adopted, individual policy changes might have on the natural resource environment. In addition, the framework can provide a guide to estimating a probable dynamic path according to different policy environments.

Figures 5.8(a) and 5.8(b) demonstrate how such a flow diagram might be used. They give examples of how, once the initial starting point, and therefore the prevailing technology, is determined, it is possible to trace the natural resource indicators which are most likely to be affected by a specific policy change, as well as the likely degree of change in these indicators.

In Figure 5.8(a), we assume a supply response to a policy shift which leads to an increase in the relative output price of the principal annual crops. This occurs under the further assumptions of an equitable land holding structure where land area is not constrained until the extensive margin is reached (that is, no policy-induced land constraints), but where access to additional non-land inputs is limited (the non-land constraint shown in Figure 5.7).

In Figure 5.8(b), the same policy shift occurs, but in this scenario land distribution is highly skewed, resulting in the land constraint as depicted in Figure 5.7, while access to additional inputs is not limited until the intensive margin is reached, that is, when negative marginal returns to input use occur.

In each diagram the arrowed lines refer to the direction of change in farming practice in response to a change in the policy context. In addition, the environmental indicators most affected are shown. The weight of the lines is intended to convey the degree of likely impact on these indicators. The fact that some arrows continue beyond the boundaries of the diagram conveys the likely irreversibility of the impact on the natural resource environment.

In both scenarios the static response is constrained by the technology currently employed. Thus in Figure 5.8(a), a shift in the policy context would be likely to lead to the following types of change depending on the starting point: from **a** we would see more land employed and the direction of change in farming practice would be towards **b**.

In the longer term, however, we would expect a greater supply response as farming systems are further modified, especially if the increased level of incentives were maintained, or if population growth increased the

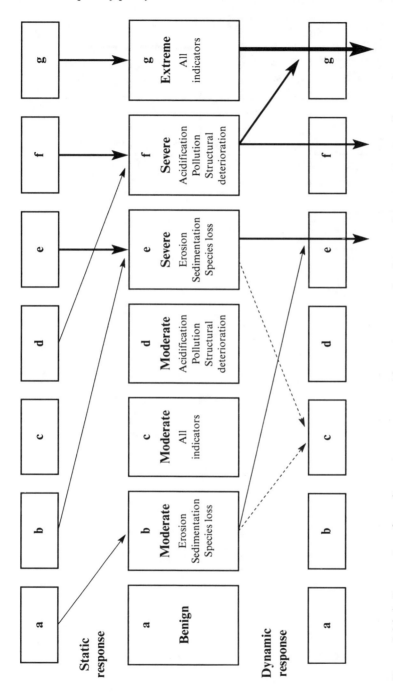

Figure 5.8(a) Propensity of a policy to impact on specific environmental indicators (output price increase, in the context of a uniform land distribution, with limited access to non-land inputs)

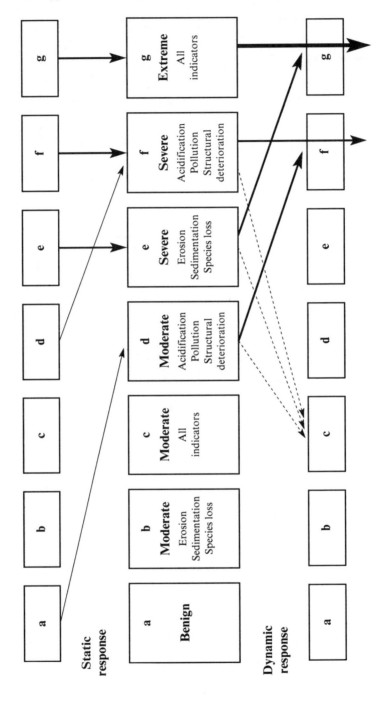

Figure 5.8(b) Propensity of a policy to impact on specific environmental indicators (output price increase with skewed land distribution, and access to non-land inputs)

pressure on output prices. In a conducive policy environment, indicated by the broken lines, we might see a movement from **b** towards **c**. However, if access to non-land inputs is constrained by, for example, poor infra-structure or inadequate credit supplies, or if input prices rose substantially in response to an exchange rate devaluation or other policy intervention, a further shift towards **e** might occur.

A similar analysis is given in the case of a policy environment where access to land is severely limited. Again the starting point is crucial, and the influence of the policy context, in so far as it determines the con-straints on farmer choice of farming practice, governs the likely short- and long-term responses.

5.12 Conclusions

It is important for policy makers to realize that a specific policy change (such as an exchange rate devaluation) can have a wide array of potential impacts on the natural resource environment, depending on the wider policy context and the type of technology currently employed. Using flow charts such as Figures 5.8(a) and 5.8(b), it should be possible, in a limited information scenario, to trace the likely response of farmers in terms of their farming practices, in order to determine which natural resource indi-cators should be monitored, and what complementary measures are likely to be necessary in order to offset any unacceptable environmental costs.

Flow diagrams such as Figures 5.8(a) and 5.8(b) can be drawn for each type of policy shift conjectured, and the interaction of price and non-price factors in determining farmers' response could be followed through before policy implementation. By comparing the different scenarios which would be likely to emanate from each policy context, and the natural resource indicators which would be most affected under each scenario, prior judge-ments can be made, and further investigations conducted.

It should be stressed, however, that the approach outlined in this chap-ter is merely designed to preface more detailed research before policy implementation. In particular, more empirical investigation would be required to:

1. Classify farming practices in terms of (a) the technology employed and (b) how close existing systems are to the margin.
2. The extent and trajectory of the environmental costs as represented by the shape of the cost curves.

Point 2 refers to the fact that the degree of impact of agricultural activity of any kind on the natural resource environment will vary considerably with the technical parameters described by, *inter alia*, the soil structure, topography, climate, and periodicity of rainfall. As suggested in this chapter, these can vary enormously even at the local level. Nevertheless, use of 'typical' farms as proxies for what would otherwise be an impossible level of disaggregation provides a way forward.

It is apparent that in this analysis we have not attempted to incorporate the effects of conservation measures and the effects which extension and other environmental policy interventions might have in terms of the adoption of more sustainable farming practices. An extension of the above analysis to incorporate such interventions in a similar manner to those describing alternative economic policies should, however, be relatively straightforward.

Notes

1. The so-called global food debate. See, for example, Brown (1994), McCalla (1994).
2. Although there is no real consensus as to the magnitude of supply response – see, for example, Bond (1983) who estimates long-run elasticities of 0.15 for nine African countries as compared to Peterson (1979) who estimates elasticities in the range 1.25 to 1.66 – there is a positive response. Streeten (1987) suggests that the divergence in estimates depends upon the assumptions made about labour supply constraints, the ability to adopt new technologies and therefore to alter cropping patterns.
3. Note that the total cost function, C_t, cannot be represented graphically in two-dimensional space.
4. In valuing environmental costs, the first implies use of the preventive expenditure method, and the second can be viewed as a variant of the effect on production method. See Winpenny (1991), ch. 3, The Techniques of Economic Valuation'.
5. In fact, in developed countries' agriculture, marginal external costs are likely in many cases to emerge from movements along both functions, although problems associated with chemical pollution tend to outweigh those arising from soil erosion.

References

Alexandratos, N. (1995), 'The outlook for world food and agriculture to year 2010', in Nurul Islam (ed.), *Population and Food in the Early Twenty-first Century: Meeting Future Food Demand of an Increasing Population*, Washington, DC: International Food Policy Research Institute.

Binswanger, H., Y. Mundlak, M.-C. Yang and A. Bowers (1983), *Estimation of Aggregate Agricultural Supply Response*, mimeo, Washington, DC: World Bank.

Bond, M. (1983), 'Agricultural response to price in sub-Saharan countries', *IMF Staff Papers,* **30** (4), Washington, DC.

Boserup, E. (1965), *The Conditions of Agricultural Growth: The Economics of Agrarian Change under Population Pressure*, London: Allen and Unwin.

Brown, L. (1994), 'Facing food insecurity', in L. Brown (ed.), *State of the World 1994*, New York: Worldwatch Institute.

Bumb, B. (1995), 'Growth potential of existing technology is insufficiently tapped', in Nurul Islam (ed.), *Population and Food in the Early Twenty-first Century: Meeting Future Food Demand of an Increasing Population*, Washington, DC: International Food Policy Research Institute.

Cleaver, K. and G. Schreiber (1994), *Reversing the Spiral: The Population, Agriculture and Environment Nexus in Sub-Saharan Africa*, Washington, DC: World Bank.

FAO (1982), *Potential Population Supporting Capacities of Lands in the Developing World*, Report FPA/INT/513, Rome. Cited in Pearce and Warford (1993).

Fox, G. (1993), 'The environmental assessment of agricultural policies: a Canadian perspective', Background paper for *Crop Insurance Environmental Assessment Literature Review*, published by Agriculture Canada, Ottawa.

Freeman, A., T. Roe and J. Smith (1995), 'The effects of policies on environmental degradation in Northern Nigeria', paper presented at the Environment and Development Conference, Stockholm, 9–11 September.

Lutz, E. and M. Young (1992), 'Integration of environmental concerns into agricultural policies of industrial and developing countries', *World Development,* **20** (2), 241–53.

McCalla, A. (1994), 'Agriculture and food needs to 2025: why should we be concerned?' Sir John Crawford Memorial Lecture, International Centres Week, 27 October 1994, Washington, DC.

Ministry of Agriculture and Food, New Zealand (1993), 'Impacts on the environment of reduced agricultural subsidies: a case study of New Zealand', *MAF Policy Technical Paper 93/12*.

Munasinghe, M. and W. Cruz (1994), *Economywide Policies and the Environment*, Washington, DC: World Bank.

OECD (1995), *Developing a Set of OECD Agri-Environmental Indicators*, mimeo, Food, Agriculture and Environment Directorate, Paris, December.

Pagiola, S. (1995), 'Environmental and natural resource degradation in intensive agriculture in Bangladesh', *Environmental Economic Series Paper No. 15*, Washington, DC: World Bank.

Pearce, D. and J. Warford (1993), *World Without End*, Oxford: Oxford University Press.

Peterson, W. L. (1979), 'International farm prices and the social costs of cheap food prices', *American Journal of Agricultural Economics*, **61** (1): 12–21.

Streeten, P. (1987), *What Price Food?* Basingstoke, UK: Macmillan Press.

Winpenny, J. (1991), *Values for the Environment*, London: HMSO.

6 Economic valuation of environmental impacts: the temptations of EVE

James Winpenny

6.1 Introduction

EVE (economic valuation of the environment) is growing up. We no longer ask, why do it? Its theoretical rationale has been rehearsed at length (in, amongst many others, Pearce and Turner, 1989; Freeman, 1993; OECD, 1994; Oates and Cropper, 1992). We need no longer ask how to do it, since plenty of practical guidance is now available (for example Dixon *et al.*, 1994; OECD, 1995; Winpenny, 1991). We are now at the stage when a variety of applications of EVE are being explored. However, the higher public profile of EVE has stoked even greater controversy about this subject.

This chapter starts by considering EVE's current application to environmental policy issues, drawing attention to some obvious gaps. The second section considers some of the issues which continue to inspire controversy. The chapter ends by making some suggestions for improving the general acceptability of EVE to policy makers and the general public.

6.2 Applications

EVE is proving useful in a number of areas: project appraisal and environmental impact assessment, the planning of nature conservation programmes, assessment of the seriousness of global climatic effects, as basic data for national resource accounting, for the appraisal of environmental policies, in the regulation of public utilities and in litigation. These uses will be briefly discussed below.

Project appraisal and EIA

EVE's most common application is still probably in the appraisal of individual projects, especially where formal appraisal of environmental impact is required. In the latter case EVE can complement the use of environmental impact assessment (EIA). A number of international aid agencies, to take one example, support the use of EVE on their own programmes (though it should be added that practice lags well behind the theory in almost all cases). Sometimes EVE is incorporated into *ex-post* evaluation, to indicate how projects would have fared if they had been subjected to EVE at the time of appraisal (for example Abelson, 1996).

Nature conservation programmes

Much of the literature of contingent valuation (CV) and the travel cost method is devoted to the appraisal of individual natural sites and conservation features, especially in North America and Western Europe (OECD, 1994). This application is rapidly gaining ground in developing countries, too, thanks to the availability of international funds for nature conservation through the Global Environment Facility and environmental non-governmental organizations (NGOs) such as WWF and IUCN. The sponsors of such projects have grasped that economic arguments provide cogent justification for the use of scarce national resources on conservation, compared to orthodox 'bricks and mortar' investments.

Global climatic effects

A number of studies purport to measure the costs of global warming and chlorofluorocarbon CFC emissions, using an eclectic variety of methods (see Winpenny, 1994), with a wide range of resulting values (Brown and Pearce, 1994). As regards global warming, economic valuation is hampered by scientific uncertainty about the existence, the force, and even the direction of the trend. The phenomenon of ozone depletion is better established and its impact on human receptors somewhat clearer. Estimates have been made of the costs of increased ultraviolet radiation on human health (malignant melanoma, suppression of immunity and damage to eyes), materials damage (faster deterioration of paint, plastic and rubber), damage to biological food chains (reduced crop growth and yields, decreased ocean plankton and fish production) and photochemical smog (damage to humans, plants and animals) (SEI, 1996).

In a related mode, there are several estimates of the value of storing atmospheric carbon in trees, either in terms of the avoided damage costs (Brown and Pearce, 1994) or the avoided costs of alternative policies (Anderson and Bird, 1992).

As data for natural resource accounting

A few countries (for example, France and Norway) regularly produce environmental indicators to complement their conventional national accounts ('satellite' accounts). Studies have been done of other countries (for example, Indonesia, the Philippines, Mexico and Costa Rica) illustrating the impact on conventional estimates of national income of the inclusion of environmental 'depreciation', such as mineral depletion, reduced soil fertility or deforestation (Steer and Lutz, 1993). Some of these studies make adjustments for a particular sector, such as agriculture (Mackenzie, 1994). EVE furnishes the building blocks for these accounting exercises.

For the appraisal of policies

There is no reason why EVE should not apply to policies and programmes, just as to individual projects, provided their environmental costs and benefits can be clearly identified and valued. Cost–benefit studies have been produced for US air and water quality legislation (for example Portney, 1990; Howe, 1991), the benefits of which are based on EVE methods. Indeed, in the USA cost–benefit analysis must now be carried out for all major regulations, including environmental ones (under Executive Orders 12291 and 12866).

The UK's Department of the Environment has produced guidance on the environmental appraisal of public policies (DOE, 1991). Nevertheless, many UK environmental policies have been adopted without close analysis of their benefits, at major cost to industry, utilities and, ultimately, consumers. Examples include measures to counter acid rain emissions by large power stations and standards for river water. Other measures, on the contrary, are not implemented as fully as they might be if decisions were based on cost–benefit analysis (for example, certain traffic safety measures) (Newbery, 1995).

In the regulation of utilities

Starting in the USA, the environmental externalities caused by the generation of electric power are becoming factors used by regulators of private utilities. 'Electricity adders', produced by standardized EVE methods, are used in approving different options for new investment, and in authorizing the merit order for running existing plant (Woolf and Mickle, 1993; Palmer and Krupnick, 1991). EVE is not yet used in the UK for this purpose, though there is clear potential for its use by the new Environment Agency in approving new investments by the water companies, and in the comparison of supply schemes with demand management.

One obvious application of EVE would be in connection with the rising level of underground water in London (POST, 1995): private companies claim it is not cost-effective for them to extract it, yet a consideration of the environmental benefits accruing to property owners and the London Underground might tip the balance in favour of its exploitation. In this case, some scheme for compensating the private water companies for pumping the water could be in the wider national interest.

In litigation
In the USA, evidence of damage to the non-use values of natural resources is admissible in the award of damages to trustees and others. EVE, and specifically contingent valuation, is the only method of estimating these values. The American environmental economics profession received a major fillip from the litigation following the Exxon Valdez oil spillage in 1989. It should, however, be pointed out that virtually all the damage settlement by the oil company to date has been based on the loss of *use* values by fishermen, property owners and other victims.

6.3 Outstanding issues

Despite this chronicle of progress made in the application of EVE, certain of its features remain controversial both within the profession and in relations between economists, other environmental professionals and the general public. The four issues highlighted here are contingent valuation, the value of health and life, the treatment of future events and the role of benefit transfers.

Contingent valuation
The use of contingent valuation (CV) continues to be a matter of controversy and contention. The National Oceanic and Atmospheric Administration (NOAA) Report, commissioned in the aftermath of the Exxon Valdez accident in Alaska, was intended to provide guidance for the use of CV, and an authoritative pronouncement on its relevance to the estimation of non-use values. The guidelines it produced have not been universally welcomed and accepted (Willis, 1995; Portney, 1994), though they are likely to have a major influence on future work. It is worth emphasizing that they have been developed with US circumstances in view – namely, where ample resources are usually available for the study, and where CV is increasingly part of the process of litigation.

The NOAA Report failed to stem controversy over the use of CV. In the USA, the increasing use of CV in litigation has drawn environmental economists in on both sides of the debate (although a boon for the income of environmental economists, this tendency is practically guaranteed to widen the rift in the profession over CV!).

It is widely acknowledged, even by the champions of CV, that survey results are often anomalous and internally inconsistent. Answers to willingness-to-pay (WTP) questions are shown to depend on the order in which the questions are asked. WTP for specific individual goods is frequently greater than that for the whole generic environmental good which includes that individual! (Willis, 1995). WTP for a specific environmental action, or good, is often practically the same as for an action or good of the same kind, but which is very much smaller. When individuals are asked simultaneously about many projects, WTP is usually well below the sum of WTP from asking about the projects separately (Diamond and Hausman, 1994). WTP for a good is heavily influenced by the context or 'theatre' in which it is presented to the respondent (Willis, 1995).

Some of these anomalies are related to the 'embedding problem' (or 'part–whole bias', where WTP responses are very similar across different surveys, whereas we would expect them to be very different, because a specific good is 'embedded' in a more inclusive good). To some extent WTP responses can be made more consistent by more careful survey design. But one of the most damning criticisms of CV is that the embedding problem merely illustrates the fact that people lack preferences for the environmental goods, sites or measures that they are questioned about:

> [W]e do not think that people generally hold views about individual environmental sites (many of which they have never heard of) or that, within the confines of the time available for survey instruments, people will focus successfully on the identification of preferences, to the exclusion of other bases for answering survey questions. (Diamond and Hausman, 1994, p. 63)

If valid, this is a fundamental flaw of CV, which no amount of tinkering with methodology will eradicate. In a similar vein, comparisons of hypothetical WTP and actual offers for private goods and charitable donations indicate large discrepancies. This is an uncomfortable reminder that CV measures what people say, rather than what they do.

It is no defence against these criticisms to say that 'some number is better than no number' (if the 'real' value is 5, taking zero will be less misleading than taking a figure of 20). Likewise the argument that CV is the only methodology available for estimating existence values is a hollow defence if CV contains deep and irremediable flaws. Or again, to defend CV by adducing weaknesses in other methods such as revealed preference approaches (for example Hanemann, 1995) hardly amounts to a ringing endorsement!

I shall have a modest proposal to make in the final section that might make survey methods more acceptable and realistic in the context of environmental policy. But before leaving the subject of CV, I would like to note an interesting, and potentially subversive, idea. Much of the controversy over CV arises precisely because of its use in estimating existence value. Hitherto, the concept of existence value has been discussed almost entirely in an environmental context. But there is no reason why it should not have wider application.

Most people hold non-use values, in the sense that they value, and in certain cases are 'willing to pay for' the survival of objects, buildings, sites and works of art that they do not enjoy directly. These objects of desire do not have to be 'environmental' in the usual sense – they could include human artefacts, factories, refineries, motorways, and so on, the very existence of which gives satisfaction to someone. Or people may attach value to the existence of laws, regulations and policies which are of public benefit, even though they themselves do not directly benefit. To extend the logic of the argument, there could be existence losses as well as benefits from environmental actions, if valued artefacts or institutions were affected:

> If I derive some utility from the mere existence of certain natural environments I never intend to see . . . , might I not also derive some satisfaction from knowing that refineries provide well-paying jobs for hard-working people, even though neither I nor anyone I know will ever have such a job?. . . Since regulatory programs will always impose costs on someone . . . lost existence values may figure every bit as prominently on the cost side of the analytic ledger as the benefit side. (Portney, 1994, p. 13)

The implications of this line of thought for the use of CV in cost–benefit analysis are truly radical! To anticipate the discussion in the next section, altruistic people may hold existence values for the lives and health of others they may never meet. They may be willing to pay (and sometimes actually do, through donations to medical programmes and emergency relief) for the survival and improved health of these others. This line of reasoning is a further subversion of international comparisons of the value of life and health, to which we now turn.

Health and the value of life
Economists argue that the key to discovering people's preferences about their health and life span is to examine what they are willing to pay to reduce the risk of ill-health or accident. The valuation can be based on what they say they are willing to pay, what they actually pay, or by inferring their views from extra costs they incur to reduce their exposure to disease or mishap.

In the case of health, the values obtained by any of the above-mentioned methods can be grossed up (by a factor given by the reduction in the probability of illness or non-fatal accident) to produce an implied value of the illness or accident in question. In this context, bednets impregnated with insecticide have been shown to be effective in reducing the risk of catching malaria, and surveys have been carried out of villagers' WTP for insecticide (Mills *et al.*, 1994). Even in this apparently concrete and clear-cut example, respondents gave low WTP values, reflecting their income constraints (and also possible 'strategic bias', in anticipation of getting the bednets free!).

In another survey, respondents are told of a course of treatment which would greatly reduce the risk of catching malaria, and asked what they would be WTP for them (Whittington, Pinheiro and Cropper, 1995). In this scenario, a great deal depends on the respondent recognizing the symptoms of the disease in question and separating them from related symptoms, accepting the credibility of the treatment, and being able to assess (and value) probabilities – the reduced risk of catching the disease. Each of these steps is hazardous.

People's information about changes in risk, and their reaction to it, is especially problematic:

> It is clear in CV studies that people's ability to process small probability event changes is limited . . . Many changes to policy in the environment typically result in small changes in the probability of a certain event occurring. In such cases great care is required in interpreting WTP estimates of the benefits of such policy changes. (Willis, 1995, p. 133)

For such reasons, the 'cost of illness' approach is still used in the valuation of health measures, despite its theoretical inferiority to WTP.

Much the same procedure applies to the valuation of the risk of fatal accidents and death. In casual parlance, the 'value of a statistical life' soon becomes 'the value of life' and the tissue of assumptions that lies behind these figures is soon overlooked. The punishment for economists who are careless in their language is to be portrayed as unethical monsters who 'place a monetary value on human life'!

Sometimes governments face the same charge: a safety programme costing £x million, with a probability of saving y lives can be presented as 'implying' that a human life is valued at £z. In reality, of course, government departments are inconsistent, irrational and budget-constrained, with the consequence that their 'revealed preferences' are scarcely reliable in this area.

However, by far the greatest misunderstandings, and obloquy, arise from attempts to make international comparisons of the value of health and life, and to transfer values arrived at in one country to the circumstances of another. Since all the common economic approaches to valuing health, safety or death rely on either monetary WTP, the value of working time lost, or proxies, and since these are highly correlated with the level of development and income per head, it is inevitable that these will differ between rich and poor countries. This is not to argue that these methods are invalid for a particular country; merely to point out that it is dangerous to make international comparisons and data transfers.

Much valuation of, say, pollution costs is still based on transferring US data on health costs, deflated by a factor reflecting the dividend of the local income per head and that of the USA. The result is that original US estimates, drawn from local preferences expressed in a market for health care that is distorted by insurance and legal practices, are transferred to other countries, typically divided by a factor of 20 or more.

Back to the future

The use of discounting in the estimation of future environmental costs and benefits continues to generate controversy. Devising new 'solutions' to the problem has become a bravura exercise of academic ingenuity; but few if any proposals are of practical use in routine appraisal.

The environmental critique of discounting has a number of arguments. It is argued that many environmental risks are only likely to materialize in the long term, when they will be discounted to an insignificant level. For the same reason, projects yielding environmental benefits in the more distant future would not receive a fair weight compared to those with short-term benefits. In sum, discounting overlooks environmental 'bads' and penalizes environmental 'goods'.

The use of high discount rates also hastens the rate of exploitation of renewable natural resources, such as forests, fisheries and game. This lends an 'exploitative' rather than a 'conservationist' bias to the exploitation of concessions. In extreme cases, where the discount rate exceeds the rate of natural regeneration, it is rational to harvest a resource to extinction. For these reasons, the interests of future generations are not properly safeguarded. Investment decisions are myopic and 'anti-future'.

Various solutions have been proposed: low or zero discount rates; the application of lower discount rates to environmental projects or specific environmental effects; applying distributional weights to costs and benefits accruing to future generations; using a declining discount rate; applying a separate discount rate for each year's streams.

Some of these are impractical. They all require a clear distinction to be drawn between 'environmental' and other projects, or between 'environmental' and other effects within the same project. Using distributional weights to benefit future generations is a highly subjective and arbitrary process, fraught with philosophical, moral, economic and practical problems. Introducing differential discount rates could also distort capital markets where government and private investors are active in the same sectors.

In their attempt to remove one perceived distortion – against the environment – some proposals would create undesirable distortions of their own. It is a bad idea, as a matter of principal, to apply low discount rates in poor countries that are short of capital. This would encourage the use of capital-intensive schemes and allow more unproductive schemes to proceed, which would increase the use of natural resources and encroachment on hitherto undeveloped areas. More generally, it would result in the wasteful use of capital.

A satisfactory solution to discounting will continue to be the environmental economists' El Dorado. Meanwhile, the least unsatisfactory course is to continue to use conventional discount rates, subject to the 'sustainability constraint' (Markandya and Pearce, 1988) and incorporating full environmental valuation. On this approach, environmental costs and benefits should be valued to the full extent, 'preservation values' may be allowed to increase over time, encroachment on critical capital should be avoided, and the use of resources in excess of their sustainable yield should be treated as depletion (OECD, 1995).

Benefit transfer
In the last few years, there has been much discussion of benefit transfers (BTs) (for example WRR, 1992). BTs apply a data set developed for one particular use to a quite distinct alternative situation. In a very general sense, where data on environmental values in a specific project and/or locality are absent, it is common to borrow unit values developed elsewhere to illustrate orders of magnitude. The non-timber values of tropical rain forest, estimated from detailed surveys in a few parts of the Amazon, West Africa and South-East Asia, have been widely quoted to illustrate the potential values of other tracts of forest. A number of studies use empirical relationships on afforestation and soil fertility, or soil erosion and crop yield, developed in specific areas, more widely to 'slot into' exercises where local empirical data are not available.

However, BT has come to mean something more specific. It usually applies to non-market values (for example, of air and water quality, or recreation), since these are not so easy to obtain as market values. The location where the data were generated is known as the *study site*, and the project or area that the benefits are transferred to is the *policy site*. In some cases the methodology developed at the study site can be transferred to the policy site, using empirical data at the latter. In other cases, the methodology, data and values are transferred wholesale.

BT is appropriate when certain conditions are present: there are insufficient funds, time, or personnel to undertake a satisfactory new study; the study is similar to the policy site; the issues (for example, proposed policy change, or nature of project) are similar in the two cases; and the original valuation procedures were sound and the exercise was done conscientiously.

A large number of travel cost studies of recreational values has been performed in the USA, and these studies are often used in BT. Outside the USA and Western Europe there is much less scope for using BT since original studies are very much fewer, and cross-country BTs are problematic. Contingent valuations studies, for instance, are dominated by US literature, with Western Europe a poor second, and are concentrated on air quality, recreational fishing, forestry, health risks, recreational hunting, parks, nature reserves and wildlife, water quality and water supply. Travel cost studies are mainly to be found in recreational fishing, parks, nature reserves and wildlife, and water supply and quality. Hedonic property studies have been done mainly for air quality, noise and parks, nature reserves and wildlife (OECD, 1994).

In the typical situation, a policy maker or analyst is confronted with poor local data, and inadequate time and resources to carry out a fully satisfactory study. The choice is often between using BT, on the one hand, and carrying out a short-cut, rapid appraisal using whatever local information is available at the time, on the other. The conscientious environmental economist may, in these circumstances, feel trapped between the Devil and the Deep Blue Sea. However, such are the problems attending BT, especially internationally, that recourse to local data, even of a rough and ready kind, is not automatically an inferior option. The ideal is, of course, to generate more relevant local data, which is starting to happen in, for example, the health impact of urban air pollution (Cropper, ongoing).

6.4 Suggestions for better integration

How can EVE be made more credible and acceptable? The first obvious route is to increase the penetration of EVE into relatively uncontroversial cases where its use would clearly improve the quality of decisions. The exploitation of underground water in London would be one such example. Note that this example would involve using the simpler and more robust techniques based on the market valuation of physical effects (MVPE). This leads to the second sugestion, that practitioners of EVE do not lose sight of the usefulness of such methods as MVPE, which are often more immediately appealing and comprehensible to the decision maker.

Third, the credibility of CV might be improved through the use of more fully detailed and realistic scenarios. Thus, instead of enquiring about WTP for preserving a forest about to be destroyed in the construction of a road by-pass, the exercise would consist of describing alternative options with and without the proposed development, each of which would have its financial, economic and environmental implications fully spelled out. If the respondent voted 'yes' to the by-pass, it would be in full awareness of its environmental and financial costs, as well as the presumed economic benefits of the road. If the vote was 'no', this would also be taken in full possession of the facts, including the economic costs of not proceeding. In this case, the CV exercise would be tantamount to a pilot local referendum on the issue.

Fourth, the problems with using international benefit transfers, especially where health and life values are involved, would be avoided by the increased generation of local values. This is easily said, and it should be recognized that international value transfers arise precisely because of the scarcity of local data. However, where there is a choice between a benefit transfer, involving crude and arbitrary adjustments to suspect original data, on the one hand, and the collection of rough and ready local data by rapid appraisal and short-cut methods, the latter is not automatically inferior.

Finally, it is vital to take account of the distribution of the costs and benefits of environmental chance. At a deeper level, this invokes the question, whose environment is it? (Bromley, 1995). Just as market-based economic values and prices reflect the distribution of power and property in society, so EVE is influenced by our assumptions about rights and ownership of the environment, for example, the well-known discrepancy between WTP and WTA (willingness to accept compensation). Every environmental appraisal should probe who gains, who loses, and by how much.

References

Abelson, Peter (1996), *Project Appraisal and Valuation Methods for the Environment with Special Reference to Developing Countries*, London: Macmillan.

Adams, John (1996), 'Cost–benefit analysis: the problem, not the solution,' *The Ecologist*, **26** (1), January/February.

Anderson, Dennis and Catherine Bird (1992), 'Carbon accumulations and technical progress: a simulation study of costs', *Oxford Bulletin of Economics and Statistics*, **54** (1).

Bromley, Daniel W. (1995), 'Natural resource issues in environmental policy in South Africa', Land and Agriculture Policy Centre, Johannesburg.

Brown, Katrina and David Pearce (1994), 'The economic value of non-market benefits of tropical forests: carbon storage', in J. Weiss (ed.), *The Economics of Project Appraisal and the Environment*, Aldershot, UK: Edward Elgar.

Cropper, Maureen, *et al.*, (ongoing), 'Measuring the health effects of air pollution in developing countries', Research project in World Bank's Policy Research Department, Washington, DC.

Department of the Environment (DOE) (1991), *Policy Appraisal and the Environment*, London: HMSO.

Diamond, Peter A. and Jerry A. Hausman (1994), 'Contingent valuation: is some number better than no number?' *Journal of Economic Perspectives*, **8** (4), Fall.

Dixon, J.A., L.F. Scura, R.A. Carpenter and P.B. Sherman (1994), *Economic Analysis of Environmental Impacts*, new edition, London: Earthscan.

Freeman, A. Myrick III (1993), *The Measurement of Environmental and Resource Values: Theory and Methods*, Washington, DC: Resources for the Future.

Hanemann, W. Michael (1995), 'Contingent valuation and economics', in K.G. Willis and J.T. Corkindale (eds), *Environmental Valuation: New Perspectives*, Wallingford, UK: CAB International.

Howe, Charles W. (1991), 'An evaluation of US air and water policies', *Environment*, September.

Mackenzie, Craig (1994), 'Degradation of arable land resources: policy options and considerations within the context of rural restructuring in South Africa', Land and Agriculture Policy Centre, Johannesburg,

Markandya, Anil and David Pearce (1988), 'Environmental considerations and the choice of the discount rate in developing countries', *World Bank Environment Department Working Paper* No. 9, Washington, DC.

Mills, A., J. Fox-Rushby, M. Aikins, U. D'Allessandro, K. Cham and B. Greenwood (1994), 'Financing mechanisms for village activities in The Gambia and their implications for financing insecticide for bednet impregnation', *Journal of Tropical Medicine and Hygiene*, **97**.

Newbery, David (1995), 'Establishing, priorities for valuation research in government, in K.G. Willis and J.T. Corkindale (eds), *Environmental Valuation: New Perspectives*, Wallingford, UK: CAB International.

Oates, Wallace and Maureen Cropper (1992), 'Environmental economics: a survey', *Journal of Economic Literature*, **XXX**, June.

OECD (1994), *Project and Policy Appraisal: Integrating Economics and Environment* (authors D. Pearce, D. Whittington, S. Georgiou and D. James) Paris: OECD.

OECD (1995), *The Economic Appraisal of Environmental Projects and Policies: a Practical Guide* (author J. Winpenny), Paris: OECD.

Palmer, Karen N. and Alan J. Krupnick (1991), 'Environmental costing and electric utilities' planning and investment', *Resources,* Resources for the Future, No. 105, Fall, Washington, DC.

Pearce, D.W. and R.K. Turner (1989), *Economics of Natural Resources and the Environment*, London: Harvester Wheatsheaf.

Portney, Paul R. (ed.) (1990), *Public Policies for Environmental Protection*, Washington DC: Resources for the Future.

Portney, Paul R. (1994) 'The contingent valuation debate: why economists should care', *Journal of Economic Perspectives*, **8** (4), Fall.

POST (Parliamentary Office of Science and Technology) (1995), 'The 1995 drought', *Technical Report* No. 71.

Steer, Andrew and Ernst Lutz (1993), 'Measuring environmentally sustainable development', *Finance and Development*, December, Washinaton, DC.

Stockholm Environment Institute (SEI) (1996), 'Tracking the cost of environmental degradation: the Earth Audit', *Bulletin*, **2** (3–4), February.

Water Resources Research (WRR) (1992) **28** (3), March. The whole issue is devoted to benefit transfer.

Weiss, John (ed.) (1994), *The Economics of Project Appraisal and the Environment*, Aldershot, UK: Edward Elgar.

Whittington, Dale, A.C. Pinheiro and M. Cropper (1995), 'The economic benefits of malaria control: a contingent valuation study in Marracuene, Mozambique', unpublished, October.

Willis, Ken (1995), 'Contingent valuation in a policy context: the National Oceanic and Atmospheric Administration Report and its implications for the use of contingent valuation methods in policy analysis in Britain', in K.G. Willis and J.T. Corkindale (eds), *Environmental Valuation: New Perspectives*, Wallingford, UK: CAB International..

Willis, K.G. and J.T. Corkindale (eds) (1995), *Environmental Valuation: New Perspectives*, Wallingford, UK: CAB International.

Winpenny, J.T. (1991), *Values for the Environment: A Guide to Economic Appraisal*, London: HMSO.

Winpenny, J.T. (1994), 'The relevance of global climatic effects to project appraisal', in J. Weiss (ed.), *The Economics of Project Appraisal and the Environment*, Aldershot, UK: Edward Elgar.

Woolf, Tim and Craig Mickle (1993), *Integrated Resource Planning: Making Electricity Efficiency Work in Europe*, London: Association for the Conservation of Energy (for Greenpeace International).

7 The relevance and consistency of EIA and CBA in project appraisal

Norman Lee and Colin Kirkpatrick

7.1 Introduction

This chapter examines the relationship between environmental impact assessment (EIA) and cost–benefit analysis (CBA) as inputs to project appraisal and decision making. It focuses, in particular, on issues relating to their respective *relevance* to appraisal and decision making, and to the *consistency* of their procedures and methods where they are used in combination. The chapter suggests, at the theoretical level, that there should be no problems of relevance and consistency when EIA and CBA are jointly used within certain appraisal and decision-making contexts. However, in practice, problems of both relevance and consistency do occur, particularly in other appraisal and decision-making situations. Some of these problems can be reduced or eliminated, and the means by which this might be achieved are briefly examined at the end of the chapter.

7.2 Relevance and consistency in specified theoretical contexts

There are two theoretical situations where EIA and CBA should be mutually relevant and consistent. First, there is the situation where projects are being appraised (and decisions made) according to economic efficiency criteria and all components of social cost and social benefit are measurable in economic/monetary terms. In this case, the EIA provides the physical measures of the expected environmental benefits and disbenefits of the project which are then converted into economic measures for inclusion in a standard social cost–benefit analysis for subsequent use in appraisal and decision making.[1] This perception of the role of EIA in project appraisal is to be found in some of the environmental economics literature.[2] Second, there is the situation where projects are being appraised according to commercial (that is profit-maximizing) criteria and all externalities are internalized. In this case, the internalization of environmental externalities may be achieved through a system of charges/taxes (for negative environmental impacts) and grants/subsidies (for positive environmental impacts).[3] In these circumstances, EIA provides the physical measures of the expected environmental disbenefits and benefits which developers recognize will (if they allow those impacts to occur) eventually be reflected, following their valuation, in environmental charges and receipts to them. Therefore, estimates of these charges and receipts are incorporated into their project appraisals (that is, through the calculation of their expected net present values) and these are consistent with the CBA criterion, given that all externalities are assumed to be internalized. In this context, EIA is supportive of a system of economic instruments which is regarded by many economists as central to any efficient system of environmental controls.[4]

7.3 Relevance and consistency in practice

In practice, there is a variety of other circumstances where the relevance and mutual consistency of EIA and CBA in project appraisal and decision making are less obvious. A number of these are identified and briefly discussed below. They are grouped, for purposes of presentation, into the following categories:

1. Valuation of environmental impacts and use of economic instruments.
2. Variations in appraisal and decision-making contexts and in regulatory/procedural requirements for EIA and CBA.
3. Consistency issues, concerning content and methodology, relating to the combined use of EIA and CBA.

Valuation of environmental impacts and use of economic instruments

Valuation of environmental impacts This is a topic on which a number of papers were presented at the Conference[5] (including Hearne, 1996; and Winpenny, 1996, Chapter 6, this volume). In summary, we conclude that, despite considerable advances in research, the extent to which environmental impacts are valued in monetary terms, and then used as the sole measure of those impacts in project appraisal and decision making, remains fairly limited. The reasons for this are a complex mixture of methodological difficulties, data shortages, relatively low political and public acceptability and inappropriateness of certain of the regulatory and institutional situations (see below) in which they might otherwise be used.[6] The practical consequence, both now and in the foreseeable future, is that those environmental impacts which cannot be valued in monetary units must *either* be excluded from appraisal and decision making *or* be incorporated in a different way (that is, other than within a CBA framework, as conventionally understood). Hence, the relationship between EIA and CBA, as defined in Section 7.2, is unavoidably modified (in what ways, such as through the use of some form of multi-criteria analysis (MCA), are explored later).

Use of economic instruments Limitations on the monetary valuation of environmental impacts necessarily reduce the extent to which economic instruments can be used to internalize environmental impacts. However, even in their more modest role of promoting, cost-effective compliance with environmental quality standards, economic instruments currently make only a limited contribution. For example, OECD and other surveys of the use of economic instruments show that, despite their apparent wider use over time, they are still only applied to a small proportion of wastes and pollutants and, more importantly, are often set at too low a level to achieve efficiency or cost-effectiveness objectives.[7] Hence, in practice, the relationship between EIA, economic instruments and conventional investment appraisal (where externalities are internalized) is tenuous at best. This situation is unlikely to change radically in the short or medium term.

Almost certainly, the conclusions drawn apply equally, if not more forcefully, in developing countries as in the developed economies. In both cases, EIA is more likely to coexist alongside other forms of appraisal, rather than just be an input in an all-embracing economic appraisal.

Variations in appraisal and decision-making contexts and in regulatory requirements for EIA and CBA
EIA and CBA are not applied in a legal and institutional vacuum but in differing regulatory and procedural circumstances which greatly influence their respective statuses, the processes through which appraisals and decision making are conducted, and the appraisal criteria and methods which are used. Since EIA and CBA may be undertaken in differing contexts and involve different institutions, their relevance to project appraisal may also differ and their mutual consistency (in terms of appraisal criteria, coverage, methods, and so on) cannot be guaranteed. This is elaborated below.

First, appraisal and decision-making criteria differ between public- and private-sector projects, especially where externalities (including environmental externalities) are not internalized. From the private developer's standpoint, the most appropriate investment criteria may be derived from the objective of maximizing profits subject to the constraint of complying with a set of environmental quality or emission standards. CBA is not an appropriate method of investment appraisal in these circumstances. However, EIA still has a potential role to play, from the standpoint of the developer, and possibly the competent authority, in helping, to identify the least-cost method of securing compliance with statutory environmental requirements. In those countries where there is a policy trend towards privatization, CBA becomes less relevant; the EIA role is maintained but its orientation may change.[8]

Second, in practice, the role of appraising and approving projects and their associated activities, both in the private and public sectors, may be shared between different institutions, authorities and regulatory systems. As a consequence, the areas of competence of each, and their appraisal and decision-making criteria and procedures, may differ. The private developer, as indicated above, may appraise his project on a constrained, profit-maximizing basis. However, a UK planning authority would be expected to appraise a project subject to development control according to different and broader planning considerations whilst the pollution control authorities would each appraise according to their own pollution control objectives. Additionally, equity as well as efficiency considerations may be reflected in the appraisal and decision-making criteria used by certain of the authorities.

In some of the above situations, neither CBA nor EIA (used separately or in combination) may be relevant; in other situations, the appraisal criteria may need to be modified to make either or both of them relevant. Additionally, given the fragmentation of the appraisal and decision-making role between different institutions and regulatory systems, the risks of the inconsistent application of EIA and CBA, even in circumstances where both are relevant, may be considerable.

Third, differences between EIA and CBA, in their regulatory status and procedural characteristics, can result in significant differences between them in the *manner* in which each is involved in appraisal and decision making.

In a large, and increasing, number of countries EIA has become a statutory requirement which (through more specific regulations, circulars, and so on) may establish, in some detail, the *process* through which EIA is to be undertaken and integrated into project appraisal, decision making and implementation.[9] Additionally, in the case of a number of developing countries and countries in transition, the EIA requirements of the aid agencies and development banks have to be taken into consideration. In certain bilateral aid agencies, these requirements are specified in the national legislation of the donor countries; in other cases they form part of the internal procedural requirements of the agency or bank concerned.[10] These various requirements will often relate to a number of the following components of the process: the selection of projects to be subject to EIA, and the determination of the scope of the assessment and the assessment methods to be used; the documentation of the assessment and the involvement of statutory authorities and the public in its evaluation; the use of that documentation, and the comments received from those who have been consulted, in the decision-making process; and monitoring/environmental management plans to help in securing effective implementation.

In contrast, CBA (and economic appraisal more generally) is less likely to be subject to statutory regulation and external scrutiny. Formal procedures relating to screening scoping, production of appraisal documentation, consultation and the monitoring of implementation are *sometimes* less systemized and *often* less transparent.

Since the *processes* of EIA and CBA are very different, their evaluation *outcomes* are more likely to be different (and possibly inconsistent), because of their different approaches to information gathering, its interpretation and use. Achieving consistency between EIA and CBA will always be more difficult to achieve where two distinct appraisal processes are in operation, each with very different procedural characteristics.

The conclusions drawn here are likely to apply in both developed and developing countries. However, if anything, the variation in, and complexity of, appraisal/decision-making contexts and regulatory/procedural requirements is likely to be greater in the developing countries, due to the additional involvement of bilateral and multilateral aid agencies and development banks.

Consistency issues, concerning content and methodology, relating to the combined use of EIA and CBA

Problems of consistency, relating both to the coverage of appraisals and the assessment methods used, can arise both *within* EIA and CBA and *between* them when they are used in combination. In this chapter we concentrate more on the latter. In part, these problems stem from circumstances which have already been described in Section 7.2 but, additionally, they arise from uncertainties and shortcomings of a more fundamental, methodological nature. Certain of these are identified and briefly examined below.

Coverage of EIA and CBA EIA, according to some procedures and certain practitioners, should cover not only the environmental impacts which directly result from the project being appraised (for example, a new power station) but also those from any ancillary infrastructure which may be required or other developments which may be stimulated, as a result of the initial project. However, the scope of the CBA for the same project may be different (and sometimes narrower), especially where the induced developments are owned and financed by different institutions.[11]

There is also a number of double-counting problems (that is, duplicating the assessment of the same impacts within the appraisal) which may occur both within and between EIA and CBA. The double-counting problem has long been recognized in economic appraisal and many of those involved are sensitized to its detection.[12] However, this is not yet as widely recognized in EIA or in the combined use of EIA and CBA. Two illustrations of this potential problem are given below:

- In EIA, appraisers may assess a project's impact on the quality of the receiving environment (for example, changes in river quality measured according to the river's ability to support different species of fish) *and* include impacts on fresh-water flora and fauna (including the above-mentioned fish species) as an additional impact. Similarly, an appraiser may include, within an EIA, *both* a measure of noise impacts (based upon the expected change in noise levels for different residential properties) *and*, as a socio-economic impact, the depreciation in house prices which results from the same increase in noise levels.
- Socio-economic impacts, possibly of different scope and evaluated in different ways, may be recorded in both EIA and CBA findings. Problems of both duplication and consistency can then arise if the two assessments are combined in an overall appraisal. Part of this problem stems from uncertainty over the extent to which socio-economic impacts should be covered within EIA; this issue is examined separately in the annex to this chapter.

Consistency between EIA and CBA evaluation methods The methodological differences between EIA and CBA in the evaluation of impacts extend well beyond the much publicized issue of using monetary units of measurement, as illustrated below.

First, CBA mainly relies on values derived from actual or simulated market situations; EIA *may* use market values to some extent but mainly relies on values derived from the combined use of scientific evidence, consultations and the judgements of decision makers. The valuation methodology, in the former case, is reasonably well defined whereas in the latter case (for example, when defining and measuring the significance of an impact, or when aggregating different impacts) is much less well defined. Increasingly, in EIA, some form of multi-criteria analysis (MCA) is being recommended – but a generally agreed form and methodology has not yet emerged.[13]

Second, the timing and duration of impacts are usually systematically taken into account in CBA through the use of discounting procedures.[14] However, in EIA, the duration of impacts (for example, those related to the duration of the construction and operating phases) may be indicated but their timing is not usually taken into account. Hence, the difference in treatment of time between CBA and EIA extends beyond the choice of appropriate time preference rates and discount factors.

Third, uncertainties in impact predictions are often handled inadequately within both CBA and EIA; but, additionally, they may be handled differently. In EIA, issues of uncertainty may be ignored (for example, by only providing single-point predictions which imply certainty) or be circumvented by providing qualitative rather than quantitative predictions.[15] An important exception to these types of practice is where the EIA incorporates a risk assessment (for example, relating to potential accidents associated with the project) where a more probabilistic approach to impact assessment may be used.[16] The treatment of uncertainty within CBA also varies: the existence of uncertainty may be ignored, a probabilistic approach may be used, discount factors may be adjusted to incorporate a risk premium or some form of alternative scenario/sensitivity analysis may be applied.[17] Given this situation, consistency in the handling of uncertainty between the EIA and CBA is unlikely to occur in the majority of cases.

Finally, distributional issues may also be handled differently both within and between EIA and CBA. Distributional issues have been examined at considerable length in the CBA literature.[18] Various approaches have been identified, including the presentation of information relating to the distribution of benefits and costs by socio-economic group; the use of differential weightings of benefits and costs for different groups, before the calculation of the net present value; and the use of different shadow prices when valuing impacts on different groups. In practice, however, distributional considerations are often ignored or played down in CBA studies where the primary focus is usually on efficiency criteria. In the EIA literature, no clearly defined methodology has yet emerged for incorporating distributional considerations into project appraisal and decision making. Indeed, as in CBA, such issues often receive little explicit and systematic examination in practice. Nevertheless, there is some use of methods borrowed from the planning literature (for example, planning balance sheet, goals-achievement matrix) or from the MCA literature, to make the socio-economic and geographic distribution of environmental impacts more explicit within the appraisal process and to check these against any planning and distributional goals for the projects concerned.[19]

In summary, there are content and method inconsistencies both within and between EIA and CBA arising, from:

- differences in the scope of EIA and CBA and from double-counting, problems;
- conflicts between the market valuation methods used in CBA and the methods used for determining the significance of environmental impacts within EIA;

- differences between the single criterion (net present value, NPV) appraisal approach of CBA and the more disaggregated and multi-criteria approaches commonly used in EIA;
- differences between EIA and CBA in approaches to time preference and discounting, the handling of uncertainty and the treatment of distributional issues.

Deficiencies in these areas create problems of internal consistency both *within* EIA and CBA (especially in the former case, since they have received less consideration than in CBA) and, of particular concern in this chapter, *between* EIA and CBA (and other forms of economic appraisal). These deficiencies are believed to occur in both developed and developing country situations and to be fairly pervasive in both.

7.4 Improving relevance and consistency in the use of EIA and CBA in project appraisal

There seems little doubt that relevance and consistency need to be improved within and between EIA and CBA. The remaining, question is how this might be best achieved. Here, three types of investigation are proposed which should help in clarifying this.

Checking for relevance
A useful first step would be to check the relevance of both EIA and CBA to project appraisals *taking into account the specific regulatory and procedural context in which different appraisals are to take place.* This should clarify the circumstances where either one, both or neither approaches are applicable. It might also serve to sharpen the focus of the assessment criteria and procedures used in project appraisals, and to indicate those adjustments to regulatory and procedural frameworks which would enable the combined use of EIA and economic appraisal to be carried out more satisfactorily.

Evaluate fully integrated approaches to project appraisal
Two fully integrated frameworks might be investigated: first, where all types of impacts (economic, social and environmental) are appraised within a single, cost–benefit framework and where EIA is treated as an input to the cost–benefit analysis; and second, where all types of impacts (as above) are appraised within a single, planning framework and where EIA is treated as one of a number of inputs in a multi-criteria analysis. Whilst such studies could yield valuable insights for a future strategy, it is suspected that, *to be widely applied,* they would require considerable insti-

tutional and regulatory change to take place, which might not be feasible in the short or medium term.

Evaluate approaches to greater consistency in project appraisal requiring minimal institutional and regulatory change
This investigation might deliver surer benefits in the short and medium term without overcoming all the consistency problems identified earlier. The questions it might address are:

- What kinds of developments in the valuation of environmental damage and in the use of economic instruments would be helpful in improving the consistency of environmental and economic methods of project appraisal?
- What are the minimal regulatory, procedural and institutional changes that would increase the relevance and consistency of environmental and economic methods of project appraisal?
- What are the main ways in which EIA and economic appraisal methods can be made more consistent with each other and with the overall assessment criteria by which projects are to be appraised?
- For such investigations to succeed, they will require the assistance of specialists and practitioners using different approaches (EIA, CBA, MCA and so on) to project appraisal who will need to work together within a broader paradigm than can be provided by a single discipline. Similar investigations should also be carried out at the policy, plan and programme (PPP) level where comparable problems of relevance and consistency may be emerging between strategic environmental assessment (SEA) and other forms (for example, economic, social) of PPP appraisal.[20]

Annex: the treatment of socio-economic impacts within EIA
Some confusion exists over the extent to which socio-economic impacts (that is, impacts of a social and/or economic nature) should be included within an environmental impact assessment. In the context of the USA, CEQ regulations (1978) have attempted to clarify the situation in the following terms:

> 'Human environment' shall be interpreted comprehensively to include the natural and physical environment *and the relationship of people with that environment* [our emphasis]. This means that economic or social effects are not intended by themselves to require preparation of an environmental impact statement. [However] when an environmental impact statement is prepared *and economic or social and natural or physical environmental effects are inter-related* [our emphasis], then the environmental impact statement will discuss all of these effects on the human environment. (Quoted in Canter, 1996, p.500)

A similar interpretation may be placed on Directive 85/337/EEC which applies in the European Union (Council of the European Communities, 1985). According to its provisions, the EIA should include effects on human beings (both directly and indirectly through changes in their environment) which result from the physical characteristics of the project, the natural resources it uses and the residuals which it generates.

In brief, some (but not necessarily all) of the social and economic effects resulting from a project should be covered within the EIA; and this may leave some other social and economic effects to be covered in other ways for inclusion, together with the EIA findings, within *overall* project appraisal and decision making. Inevitably any lack of clarity of the dividing line between the two could lead to duplication or total omission of particular socio-economic impacts from project appraisal. These issues are examined in greater detail in Newton (1995).

Notes

1. There is a burgeoning literature on the economic valuation of environmental effects for use within cost–benefit analysis. Recent contributions include OECD (1995a), OECD (1994a), Dixon *et al.* (1994), Pearce (1993), Turner *et al.* (1994), Hearne (1996), Winpenny (1996; also Chapter 6, this volume).
2. For example, the aim of the OECD (1995a) manual 'is not to supplant the criterion of economic efficiency but to incorporate environmental factors into it. There is no need for a separate "environmental" criterion if environmental effects can be valued in economic terms. If that is the case, using a modified economic criterion would suffice' (p. 12).
3. See OECD (1996a, 1994b), Panayotou (1991, 1994), and Moldan (1995) as examples drawn from a substantial literature on this topic.
4. See, in the context of developing countries, Eskeland and Jimenez (1992), World Bank (1992), as well as the references cited in note 3.
5. See, for example, Blore and Nunan, Hearne, Moran and Moraes, Wattage, Lovell, Waughray and Moran, and Winpenny in *Integrating Environmental Assessment and Socio-Economic Appraisal in the Development Process: Conference Papers*, Development and Project Planning Centre, University of Bradford, 1996. The paper by Blore and Nunan also appears as Chapter 13, this volume; that by Lovell *et al.* as Chapter 12; and that by Winpenny as Chapter 6.
6. The limitations of monetary valuation methods are, to varying degrees, recognized by environmental economists. OECD (1995a) states explicitly that it is 'evidently not true' that all environmental effects can be reduced to 'economic coinage' (p. 12). Munasinghe (1990) refers to attempts to incorporate all environmental impacts into a single economic cost–benefit analysis as 'seeking for the holy grail' (p. 136) See the literature cited in notes 1 and 5 for further details.
7. See OECD (1996b, 1995b, 1994a, 1994b, 1993, 1991), Commission of the European Communities (1996) as well as the references cited in notes 3 and 4.
8. See, for further details, Kirkpatrick and Lee (1997a, 1997b, forthcoming).
9. See Lee (1995) for a review of the growth in the number of countries in which EIA is a statutory requirement and Wood (1995) for a comparative analysis of EIA procedures and processes in different countries.
10. For a review of national aid agency requirements see OECD (1996c). The EIA procedures of a number of multilateral development banks are described in World Bank, (1993). Brew and Lee (1996) provide a comparative evaluation of certain development agencies' EIA procedures.

11. The issue of the scope of both EIA and CBA is a complex one. Assessment should, according to many EIA regulations, cover direct and indirect impacts and, in the view of many practitioners, the indirect impacts should include those resulting from secondary developments. However, this will be constrained, in particular cases, by restrictions in the project authorization regulations on the scope of the assessment that is permitted in practice. The scope of a CBA may, in principle, cover all social benefits and social costs but its ability to consider secondary developments may also be seriously limited in practice.
12. Most basic textbooks in cost–benefit analysis (for example, Curry and Weiss, 1993) and a number of investment appraisal manuals (for example, H.M. Treasury, 1991) discuss the double-counting problem.
13. See Nijkamp *et al.* (1990), van Pelt (1993) and Rogers and Bruen (1995) for further information on certain MCA approaches to project appraisal and decision making where environmental impacts are to be taken into consideration.
14. These are fully described in the CBA literature already cited in this chapter. However, it is worth noting that, though the concept of time preference is widely accepted, there is disagreement among economists on the choice of appropriate discount rates, especially as applied to environmental projects; see, for example, Knetsch (1995), Markandya and Pearce (1991), Price (1996), Livingstone and Tribe (1995).
15. Reviews of the handling of uncertainty within EIA can be found in de Jongh (1988) and Carpenter (1995).
16. Further details on the use of risk assessment within EIA can be found in Carpenter (1995), Grima *et al.* (1989) and Petts and Eduljee (1994).
17. See, for example, Little and Mirrlees (1990), Curry and Weiss (1993, ch. 8), and Asian Development Bank (1990).
18. See Curry and Weiss (1993, ch. 6). For the practitioner's view of the applicability of distributional weighting in CBA, see Devarajan et al. (1996).
19. For the planning, balance sheet approach, see Lichfield (1992); for the goals achievement matrix, see Hill (1968); for the MCA approach, see references in note 13.
20. See Boothroyd (1995), Department of the Environment (1991, 1994), EIA Centre (1995) and Sadler and Verheem (1996) for further information and references on SEA and policy/plan appraisal. Also see papers by Abaza, Grainger, Morrison and Pearce, Niekerk and Arts, and Potier in *Integrating Environmental Assessment and Socio-Economic Appraisal in the Development Process: Conference Papers*, Development and Project Planning Centre, University of Bradford, some of which are included in this volume as Chapter 2 (Abaza), Chapter 4 (Grainger), Chapter 5 (Morrison and Pearce) and Chapter 3 (Potier).

References

Abaza, H. (1996), 'Integration of sustainability objectives in structural adjustment programmes through the use of strategic environmental assessment', *Project Appraisal*, December; Chapter 2, this volume.

Asian Development Bank (1990), 'Environmental risk assessment: dealing with uncertainty', *ADB Environmental Paper No.7*, Manila: ADB.

Boothroyd, P. (1995), 'Policy appraisal', in F. Vanclay and D.A. Bronstein, (eds), *Environmental and Social Impact Assessment*, Chichester, UK: Wiley.

Brew, D. and N. Lee, (1996), 'Reviewing the quality of donor agency environmental assessment guidelines', *Project Appraisal*, 11 (2), 79–84.

Canter, L.W. (1996), *Environmental Impact Assessment*, second edition, New York: McGraw-Hill.

Carpenter, R.A. (1995), 'Risk assessment', in F. Vanclay and D.A. Bronstein (eds) *Environmental and Social Impact Assessment*, Chichester, UK: Wiley.

Commission of the European Communities (1996), *Progress Report from the Commission on the Implementation of the European Community Programme of Policy and Action in Relation to the Environment and Sustainable Development*, (COM (95) 624 final), Brussels: CEC.

Council of the European Communities (1985), Directive 85/337/EEC on the Assessment of the Effects of Certain Public and Private Projects on the Environment *Official Journal of the European Communities* L175/40 (5.7.1985).

Curry, S. and J. Weiss (1993), *Project Analysis in Developing Countries*, London. Macmillan.

Department of the Environment (1991), *Policy Appraisal and the Environment: A Guide for Government Departments*, London: HMSO.

Department of the Environment (1994), *Environmental Appraisal in Government Departments*. London: HMSO.

Devarajan, N., L. Squire and S. Suthiwait-Narueput (1996), 'Project appraisal at the World Bank', in C. Kirkpatrick and J. Weiss (eds), *Cost–Benefit Analysis and Project Appraisal in Developing Countries*, Cheltenham, UK and Brookfield, US: Edward Elgar.

Dixon, J.A., L. Fallon-Scura, R.A. Carpenter and P.B. Sherman (1994), *Economic Analysis of Environmental Impacts*, London: Earthscan.

EIA Centre (1995), 'Strategic environmental assessment,' EIA Leaflet Series No. 13, Department of Planning, University of Manchester.

Eskeland, G. S. and E. Jimenez, (1992), 'Policy instruments for pollution control in developing countries,' *World Bank Research Observer*, 7 (2), July.

Grima, A.P. et al. (eds) (1989), *Risk Perspectives on Environmental Impact Assessment*, Institute for Environmental Studies, University of Toronto.

Hearne, R. (1996), 'Economic valuation of use and non-use values of environmental goods and services in developing countries', *Project Appraisal*, December.

Hill, M. (1968), 'A goals–achievement matrix for evaluating alternative plans', *Journal of the American Institute of Planners*, 34, 19–29.

H.M. Treasury (1991) *Economic Appraisal in Central Government: A Technical Guide for Government Departments*, London: HMSO.

de Jongh, P. (1988), 'Uncertainty in EIA', in P. Wathern (ed.), *Environmental Impact Assessment: Theory and Practice*, London: Unwin Hyman.

Kirkpatrick, C. and N. Lee (1997a, forthcoming) 'Market liberalisation and environmental assessment in developing and transitional economies', *Journal of Environmental Management*, 50 (3), July.

Kirkpatrick, C. and N. Lee (1997b, forthcoming), 'Market liberalization and environmental assessment', in F. Wilson (ed.), *Towards Sustainable Project Development*, Cheltenham, UK and Lyme, US: Edward Elgar.

Knetsch, J. (1995), 'Assumptions, behavioural findings and policy analysis', *Journal of Policy Analysis and Management*, 14 (1).

Lee, N. (1995), 'Environmental assessment in the European Union: a tenth anniversary', *Project Appraisal*, 10 (2), 77–90.

Lichfield, N. (1992), 'The integration of environmental assessment into development planning: part 1, some principles', *Project Appraisal*, 7 (2), 55–66.

Little, I.M.D. and J. Mirrlees (1990), 'Project appraisal and planning twenty years on', *Proceedings of the World Bank Annual Conference on Development Economics*, Washington DC: World Bank.

Livingstone, I. and M. Tribe (1995), 'The discount rate and the economic appraisal of projects with long time horizons', *Project Appraisal*, 10 (4).

Markandya, A. and D.W. Pearce (1991), 'Development, the environment and the social rate of discount', *World Bank Research Observer*, **6** (2).

Moldan, B. (ed.) (1995), *Economic Instruments for Sustainable Development: Workshop Proceedings*, Prague: Ministry of the Environment of the Czech Republic.

Moran, D. and A.S. Moraes (1996), 'The contingent valuation of uncertain environmental change: an estimation of pollution damage in the Pantanel', in C. Kirkpatrick and N. Lee (eds), *Integrating Environmental Assessment and Socio-Economic Appraisal in the Development Process*, Conference Papers, Bradford.

Munasinghe, M. (1990), 'Comment on "the environment and emerging developing issues by Desgupta and Mäler"'. *Proceedings of the World Bank Annual Conference on Development Economies 1990*, Washington DC: World Bank.

Munasinghe, M. and W. Cruz (1995), 'Economywide policies and the environment', *World Bank Environment Paper No. 10*.

Newton, J.A. (1995), 'The integration of socio-economic impacts in environmental impact assessment and project appraisal', M.Sc. dissertation, University of Manchester (UMIST), Manchester (mimeo).

Niekerk, F. and J. Arts (1996), 'Impact assessment in Dutch infrastructure planning: towards a better timing and integration', *Project Appraisal*, December.

Nijkamp P., P. Riebveld and H. Voogd (1990), *Multicriteria Evaluation in Physical Planning*, Amsterdam: North-Holland.

OECD (1991), *The State of the Environment*, Paris: OECD.

OECD (1993), *Environmental Taxes in OECD Countries: A Survey*, Paris: OECD.

OECD (1994a), *Project and Policy Appraisal: Integrating Economics and Environment*, Paris: OECD.

OECD (1994b), *Managing the Environment: The Role of Economic Instruments*, Paris: OECD.

OECD (1995a), *The Economic Appraisal of Environmental Projects and Policies: A Practical Guide*, Paris: OECD.

OECD (1995b), *Environmental Taxes in OECD Countries*, Paris: OECD.

OECD (1996a), *Integrating Environment and Economy: Progress in the 1990s*, Paris: OECD.

OECD (1996b), *Implementation Strategies of Environmental Taxes*, Paris: OECD.

OECD (1996c), *Coherence in Environmental Assessment: Practical Guidance on Development Co-operation Projects*, Paris: OECD.

Panayotou, T. (1991), 'Economic incentives in environmental management and their relevance to developing countries', in D. Erocal (ed.), *Environmental Management in Developing Countries*, Paris: OECD.

Panayotou, T. (1994), 'Economic instruments for environmental management and sustainable development', paper prepared for the UN Environment Programme, Nairobi.

Pearce, D. (1993), *Economic Values and the Natural World*, London: Earthscan.

van Pelt, M.J.F. (1993), *Ecological Sustainability and Project Appraisal*, Aldershot, UK: Avebury.

Petts, J. and G. Eduljee (1994), *Environmental Impact Assessment for Waste Treatment and Disposal Facilities*, Chichester, UK: Wiley.

Price, C. (1996), 'Discounting and project appraisal: from the bizarre to the ridiculous', in C. Kirkpatrick and J. Weiss (eds), *Cost–Benefit Analysis and Project Appraisal in Developing Countries*, Cheltenham, UK and Brookfield, US: Edward Elgar.

Rogers, M.G. and M.P. Bruen (1995), 'Non-monetary based decision-aid techniques in EIA – an overview', *Proc. Inst. Civil Engineers, Municipal Engineer*, **109**, 98–103.

Sadler, B. and R. Verheem (1996), *Strategic Environmental Assessment: Status, Challenges and Future Directions*, No. 53, Ministry of Housing, Spatial Planning and the Environment, The Hague, Netherlands.

Turner R.K., D. Pearce and I. Bateman (1994), *Environmental Economics*, London: Harvester Wheatsheaf.

Wattage, P.M. (1996), 'Contingent valuation: estimation of benefits of water quality improvement', in *Integrating Environmental Assessment and Socio-Economic Appraisal in the Development Process: Conference Papers*, Development and Project Planning Centre, University of Bradford.

Winpenny, J. (1996), 'Economic valuation of environmental impacts: the temptations of EVE', *Project Appraisal*, December, Chapter 6, this volume.

Wood, C. (1995), *Environment Impact Assessment: A Comparative Review*. Harlow, UK: Longman.

World Bank (1992), *World Development Report*, London: OUP for the World Bank.

World Bank (1993), *Proceedings of EA Technical Workshop for Multilateral Financial Institutions*, Washington DC: World Bank.

8 Community impact evaluation in the development process

Nathaniel Lichfield and Dalia Lichfield

8.1 Some reasons for the lack of integration

Environmental assessment (EA) in its modern dress was born in 1969 in the US National Environmental Policy Act (NEPA). A lusty child, it rapidly spawned EA practice in countries around the world and in international organizations. Socio-economic appraisal of development projects is older. As cost–benefit analysis it took off, again in the USA, in the Flood Control Act of 1936 which authorized federal participation in flood control schemes 'if the benefits to whom so ever they accrue are in excess of the estimated costs'. Again a lusty child, it spawned the practice around the world, with a widened scope. For one thing the application was extended to cover a great many additional kinds of public-sector development (Prest and Turvey, 1965; Peters, 1971; Schofield, 1987; Lichfield, 1988). During this period the assessment has widened over the years in scope, from narrowly economic to socio-economic impacts (Schofield, 1987). More recently it has acquired a new set of clothes, comprising social and economic impact assessment as part of environmental assessment (Vanclay and Bronstein, 1995).

Why then did we, as late as 1996, find it necessary and useful to have an international conference on the integration of the two approaches in development projects? The answer would appear to be in the different origins of the two topics, with each being supported in theory and practice by quite different academic and professional skills. Environmental assessment has given rise to a growth industry of environmental scientists, each tending to specialize in a particular aspect of the environment, without much cross-fertilization or integration between the specialisms, or between those specialisms and the land use planning profession and practice (Lichfield and Marinov, 1977). Furthermore, while Section 102 of NEPA 1969 made it clear that the term environment 'is meant to be interpreted broadly and includes the physical, social, cultural, economic dimension . . .' (Rau and Wooten, 1980), the world has been slow to include the social and economic impacts within the typical EA (Glasson and Heaney, 1993).

This lack of integration can also be seen *within* the application of the economics discipline to development appraisal. While cost–benefit analysis has matured enormously over the whole of the public sector since the 1930s, moving more recently into the environment (Pearce *et al.*, 1989), it shows little integration with other methods of appraisal within what we have come to see as a 'cost–benefit family' (Lichfield, 1996, ch. 4.2). This

Table 8.1 Methods of project appraisal used by different decision takers and stakeholders

Kind of cost and benefits/disbenefits	Developer/ entrepreneur/ financier		Business or industrial		Government		Planning authority	
	Private	Public	Private	Public	Municipal	Central	Central	Local
1	2	3	4	5	6	7	8	9
Costs/resources								
Financial	x	x	x	x	x	x	x	x
Economic					x	x	x	x
Benefits/disbenefits								
Financial	x	x	x	x	x	x	x	x
Fiscal					x	x	x	x
Economic					x	x	x	x
Social						x	x	x
Health						x	x	x
Cultural							x	x
Natural environment					x		x	x
Traffic					x		x	x
Possible method of project appraisal	FA SFA	FA SFA	FA SFA IA	FA SFA IA	FA SFA IA CBA SCBA CRA PPB	FA SFA IA CBA SCBA CRA PPB	CIA as nest for others	CIA as nest for others

Notes: FA = financial appraisal, SFA = social financial appraisal, CBA = cost–benefit analysis, SCBA = social cost–benefit analysis, CRA = cost–revenue analysis, CIA = community impact analysis, IA = impact assessment, PPB = planning programming budgeting.

Source: Lichfield (1996), Table 4.1.

comprises the methods which can be introduced alongside each other on any particular development project, in all cases being concerned with the relationship between the output and input, which is the hallmark of the economics approach. Table 8.1 gives a general impression of the differentiation. The rows show the kind of costs and benefits/disbenefits that can arise in relation to a typical project, and the columns which of these a particular kind of stakeholder in the project would take into consideration in pursuing his choice amongst options.

At the foot of the table is shown the member of the cost–benefit family that the stakeholder could typically use to make his analysis. For example, the developer/entrepreneur/financier (private or public) would not be concerned with externalities of the project but only those financial costs he has to bear and financial benefits for which he can charge. He would ask for financial analysis (FA). A municipal government would, on the contrary, be concerned with the financial costs that would fall upon itself as an authority, and the financial benefits which it could obtain through increases in local taxes. For this reason it could employ cost–revenue analysis (CRA). In this, by definition, it would be concerned with such costs and benefits which fall *off-site* to the project and not only those within it.

In brief, not only is there a lack of integration between the EA and CBA, but also the lack is felt within cost–benefit analysis. In essence the reasons would again appear to lie in the diverse and distinct origins of methodology or assessment/appraisal which have grown up, accompanied by what would appear to be inadequate attempts to rationalize and simplify the connections between the various methods, in the educational processes of the disciplines and professions involved.

Against this background the remainder of this chapter concerns itself directly with its title: how community impact evaluation (CIE) (which we consider also to be a member of the cost–benefit family) can be used as a means of integrating environmental assessment and socio-economic appraisal.

8.2 Origins of CIE

As with the other methodologies just described, it is useful to trace the origins of CIE as a preliminary to judging its role today. Unlike the other methods, the concept originated primarily in relation to the discipline of urban and regional planning. It was presented in the mid-1950s as part of a study of economics in development and planning (Lichfield, 1956, chs 18, 19). In essence the argument was as follows. Development was seen as the prime engine of urban and regional growth, with planning as a mechanism for social control (regulation, stimulation, coordination) on behalf of the community. This necessitated 'planned development', with 'development' (as in the rest of this chapter) being 'physical development for socio-economic functions'. In pursuing a development project, the land owner/developer/financier and his advisers draw up a 'development balance sheet' (DBS) that, as indicated above, would be concerned only with the direct costs and benefits (largely on site) to the project promoter. For this reason the development balance sheet would not take into account the costs and benefits falling on the remainder of the community as a result of the project. Accordingly, in making his/her own assessment on the same project, and offering advice to his/her authority, the planning officer should have regard not only to the direct costs and benefits of concern to the developers but also to the indirect costs and benefits (externalities) falling on others. S/he would prepare a 'planning balance sheet analysis' (PBSA). Since the community is not homogenous, the benefits and costs will not be uniform for different groups. The PBSA would accordingly distinguish between the impacts on the different sectors. On this foundation, the method was progressed in two ways: in theory (Lichfield, 1960, 1964, 1968) and also by application of the evolving method in case studies (Lichfield, 1996, appendix 1).

Since PBSA is concerned with both direct and indirect benefits and costs on the community as a whole, it could constitute a socio-economic appraisal of the project's contribution to the overall welfare of the community itself (Lichfield, 1960). This implied the adoption of the cost–benefit approach to the appraisal of welfare. However, cost–benefit analysis, as then put forward (for example, Eckstein, 1958), was designed primarily for non-market public-sector projects and was not readily usable for the wider purpose of urban and regional planning. Accordingly, trademark cost–benefit analysis needed adaptation. For example, in the planning decision consideration needed to be given not only to *efficiency* (total benefit less total cost) but also to *distribution* in terms of equity (whose benefit and whose cost?).

We later introduced two other features into PBSA. First, as evaluation is embedded in planning theory and practice, it was necessary to show how it should not be a discrete step in the planning process but should be integrated within it. So the analyst should be, in effect, a member of the planning team from the outset (Lichfield *et al.*, 1975). One result is that the analyst could provide the planning/design team with the approach and parameters of the evaluation which could be used judgementally for increments in the design that were not subject to formal evaluation. Second, in the work undertaken before the National Environmental Policy Act, PBSA practice mirrored cost–benefit analysis in failing to emphasize that it was not the costs and benefits from a project *per se* that were being predicted, but rather the costs and benefits from the *impacts* of that project (physical, social, economic, cultural and so on) (Lichfield, 1985). However, PBSA was ready to take on board the explosion in the understanding and handling of environmental impacts which burst upon the world in the 1970s. As a result, it was re-christened 'community impact evaluation' (CIE). From being somewhat buried in the 'black box' of the PBSA, the evaluation of *impacts* was now brought into the open, with considerable back-up from the rich accumulating work on impact assessment.

8.3 Integrating environmental assessment within CIE

In 1988 the UK introduced the Town and Country Planning (Assessment of Environmental Effects) Regulations 1988, in response to the 1985 EEC Directive on environmental impact assessment. Schedule 3 of the Regulations requires that regard should be had to the impact of develop-ment on a range of aspects, including the natural environment (fauna and flora, and so on) as well as some aspects of the man-made environment (material assets and cultural heritage) and, last on the list, the impact on human beings. The Regulations require that the applicants' Statement, providing environmental information, should be assessed by the planning authorities and fed into their planning decision.

In 1989 we acted as consultants to one of the first projects for which an EA was required – British Airways' new HQ development of some 50 000 m^2 near Heathrow, in the Green Belt. General planning negotia-tions between BA and the London Borough of Hillingdon, as local planning authority, had been going on for some time. There was a clear overlap between subject matters being generally considered for town plan-ning assessments and those included in the environmental assessment.

While the processes required by the government for environmental analysis and assessment are fairly rigorous and precise, those required for planning are not. Yet if the two sets of information are to be assessed together as part of a planning decision, their degree of rigour and credi-bility should be comparable. Furthermore, there is need for a common denominator between 'planning impacts' and 'environmental impacts' for the purpose of trade-off which is inevitable in most planning decisions. Hence a new, integrated, method of assessment was required. This should avoid duplication and enable all concerned to share a recognizable approach and comparable information. However, for this no standard practice had yet been developed.

There is, indeed, a clear common denominator between EA and gen-eral planning, in that the ultimate concern of both is the well-being of *people*. Schedule 3 of the Regulations puts impacts on 'human beings' in its list of matters of concern, since 'The purpose of the planning system is to control the development and use of land in the public interest'; what is the 'public' if not the aggregate of many different groups of people?

But how can both planning and environmental information be used to portray the interests of the public and its constituent human beings? Rather than consider scientific or economic data on effects alone, consultants are asked to consider *who* will experience the effects of the proposals. Clearly, different groups or sectors of the community will experience different effects – some beneficial, some detrimental. Moreover, the same effect could have a different impact on different groups. The scientific effects are thus viewed as one link in a chain which culminates in the impacts on people. This can be illustrated by the effect of a bullet being shot (noise, movement, and so on) and what really matters, namely, *who* suffers the impact of the bullet.

This led us to suggest that an integrated planning and environmental assessment within a community impact evaluation (CIE) (D. Lichfield, 1992) should serve as the common framework for analysis of all those matters with which both planning and EA were concerned. The proposed method was presented to a joint meeting of the local authority officers and the British Airways team and was accepted with enthusiasm, leading to a very fruitful collaboration. The planning officer commented that he 'wished this would be a role model for submission of all applications' (N. Lichfield, 1992; Lichfield and Lichfield, 1992).

8.4 The CIE method in outline
CIE, as a method of evaluation, is applicable to plan making and to policies, programmes and projects. But, as with all the methods in the cost–benefit family, the application is simplest in relation to projects, whose content is most easily capable of precise definition. We therefore show the application here in relation to projects. Since the application varies according to project type (road or airport or new town); scale (local to regional); and resources available for the study (time, skills and money), we refer here to a *generic method*. With this as a basis, the method can then be simplified for studies which are constrained by lack of resources, time or data; or adapted for non-project elements of plan making (for example, policies, proposals) (Lichfield, 1996, ch. 13).

We now enumerate the main steps in the generic method; these are organized into three groups (Lichfield, 1996, chs 7–10).

(a) Description of the project

1. It is important at the outset to identify the nature of the planning process involved in the particular instance: in plan making, construction, implementation and operation (which includes management) and/or post completion.

2. The description of the project should reflect: the physical features of the development and its associated prospective activities; any new or additional activities which do not include new development (such as an increase in cultural tourism for the same cultural stock); a new linkage (such as the introduction of a new road); or a decommissioning activity (such as the demolition of a power station).

3. We next need to compare the alternative ways of carrying out the project. Some options are on site (affecting the working population, physical fabric and activities/uses); and some are off site (for example, affecting road linkages). In relation to the options, it is the *differences between them* which is pertinent, (since the evaluation relates to those differences) and not the absolute measures *per se.*

4. Since the project and each of its options will, when completed, introduce changes into the regional system of which they are a part, it is important to visualize what the changes will be, in relation to the system elements which were introduced under point 3. These changes can be categorized into those from blight, displacement, retention, construction, completion and operation. Each should be traced through in relation to the current situation and, where practicable, to the situation which would prevail if the project were not carried out.

5. Having in this way become fully familiar with the nature of the project, we then pose the questions which the analyst seeks to answer in the next part of the process. These questions can relate simply to the standard ones in economic evaluation, such as relation of benefits to costs and thereby to socio-economic welfare, or also to others which are particularly pertinent to the project itself.

(b) Analysis and evaluation

6. *Effect assessment* The starting point is the summary of the *effects* of the injection by the development/project into the system. These effects can relate to any of the system elements mentioned above, both on site and off site. The prediction and measurement of these effects are made using well-established methods of 'effect assessment' or 'impact assessment' which have entered the environmental assessment field since the 1970s (for example, Morris and Therivel, 1995; Canter, 1996). Using the techniques now available, it is possible to predict, subject to margins of error, the size of many of the effects (for example, the number of jobs and the amount of income which are generated, or the amount of congestion which results from traffic on the roads) and also indicate their characteristics, such as kind, type, timing, probability, reversibility and likely significance.

7. *Impact evaluation* Having made an *effects assessment*, it is now practicable to go beyond this to *impact evaluation*. This is done using the *impact chain* (Figure 8.1) which aims to show how the particular community sectors which experience the *effects* are affected in their *way of life* (in physical, social, economic, environmental and cultural terms). In other words they receive an *impact* which is a contributory factor to their welfare. As Figure 8.1 shows, the initial effect could be the starting point for other effects and impacts on the same or other community sectors, which in turn produce second-round impacts, and so on. This, then, is the basis for the socio-economic appraisal of the project, in terms of the total costs and benefits to the affected community, and their distribution between the different sectors.

(c) Conclusions and recommendations drawn from the analysis and evaluation

8. From the preceding description it can be seen that there is unavoidable complexity in the analysis and evaluation, for the process itself is inherently complex. Furthermore, the display of effects and impacts under (b) will inevitably contain many items that are not readily measured or valued, and therefore cannot be directly compared. Thus, in order to assist in reaching conclusions, it is helpful to summarize the impact evaluation for each of the options. An example of such a summary is given in Table 8.2, which relates to the Manchester Airport Second Runway project. This, and the textual description which would accompany it, provides the basis for reaching a conclusion on the community's overall preference between the options, based on the assumptions, data and so on which are provided (Lichfield 1996, ch. 8).

9. The conclusions reached are then incorporated into a comprehensive report to the decision takers, and the community at large, on the evaluation process which has been carried out, including any recommendations for decision.

10. This leads to the final step of decision making by those authorized to do so, as a preliminary to implementation.

8.5 Nesting of stakeholders within the CIE

Socio-economic appraisal via CIE needs to probe more exhaustively into the results of the appraisal than is the tendency of its parent, orthodox cost–benefit analysis. This can be seen by referring to Table 8.1, which shows the different interests of the various stakeholders in a project, and

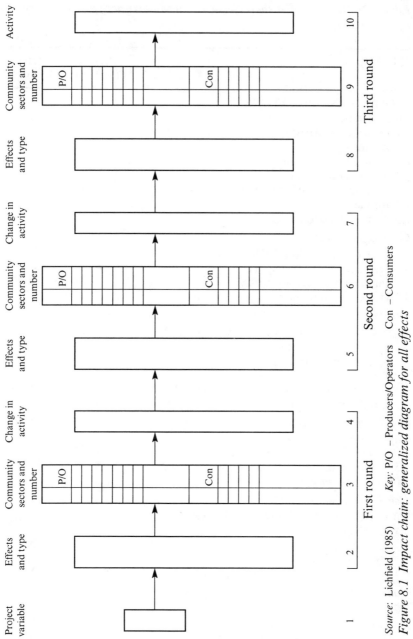

Source: Lichfield (1985)   *Key:* P/O – Producers/Operators   Con – Consumers

Figure 8.1 Impact chain: generalized diagram for all effects

Table 8.2 Manchester Airport Second Runway: extract from summary of sectoral preferences

SECTOR	Prefer Option A	Prefer Option B
PRODUCERS/OPERATORS		
1.0 AIRPORT		
1.1 Manchester Airport	X	
1.2 Airline operators		
(officers, crew, engineering)	X	
1.3 Services operators		
(catering, car parking, maintenance)	X	
1.4 Builders	X	
1.5 Airport-related companies		
Conclusion of sector	X	
3.0 SURFACE TRANSPORT		
3.1 Department of Transport	=	=
3.2 Public Transport Authority	=	=
3.3 Haulage companies	X	
Conclusion of sector	X	
5.0 ASSOCIATED URBAN DEVELOPMENT		
5.1 Central government		
(community services)		X
5.2 Local government		
(service provider, housing, tax collector)		X
5.3 Utility undertakers	=	=
Conclusion of sub-sectors		X
5.4 Private developers		
(commercial, housing)	X	
5.5 Commercial company operators	X	
5.6 Leisure operators	X	
Conclusion of sub-sectors	X	
7.0 CURRENT LANDOWNERS, FARMERS		
7.1 Displaced by		
(a) Airport		X
(b) Access links		X
(c) Associated urban development		X
Conclusion of sub-sectors		X
7.2 Not displaced		
(a) Development sites	X	
(b) Sites blighted by the airport		X
(c) Farmland		X
Conclusion of sub-sectors	N/C	

Table 8.2 continued

SECTOR	Prefer Option A	Prefer Option B
9.0 LABOUR FORCE		
9.1 Local		
(i) Unemployed	X	
(ii) Employed	X	
9.2 Non-local		
(i) Unemployed	X	
(ii) Employed	X	
Conclusion of sector	X	
11.0 REGIONAL ECONOMY	X	
Conclusion of sector	X	
13.0 THE REST OF THE BRITISH ECONOMY	N/C	
Conclusion of sector	X	
CONSUMERS		
2.0 AIR TRAVELLERS AND FREIGHT SHIPPERS		
2.1 Passengers	N/C	
2.2 Freight shippers	X	
Conclusion of sector	N/C	
4.0 SURFACE TRANSPORT USERS		
4.1 Car users		
(i) Local road users		X
(ii) Motorway users		X
4.2 Public transport users	N/C	
4.3 Cyclists		X
Conclusion of sector	N/C	

Notes:
1. Option A adds a second runway (RI + R2) whereas Option B rejects the second runway (RI only).
2. The sector column relates to a part of the total array of producers/operators sectors, which is followed by an array relating to consumers.
3. 'X' shows the preferred options for the sectors. '=' shows that the sector has no preference for either. 'N/C' is used where this is no clear balance of preference in the sub-sector or sector as a whole.

the different members of the cost–benefit family from which they would seek help in appraisal from their standpoint. Since as stakeholders they are important voices in securing agreement on the project (the disinclination of the financier to invest money can completely undermine a project, even though the net socio-economic benefits are shown to be high), it is understandable and desirable that they should wish to pursue one or other form of analysis to explore the projects feasibility and viability from their viewpoint.

However, for the reasons indicated above (Section 8.2), each of the existing appraisal methods has evolved independently of others, so that there may not be complete consistency between them. If so, the conclusions of the individual stakeholders could be at variance simply because of inconsistencies in the interpretation of data or in the methods of appraisal they use.

It is here that CIE has a particular contribution to make. The possibility of reconciliation is provided in the preparation of the community impact evaluation, since each of the distinct methods in the cost–benefit family can be seen as *nesting* within an overall evaluation, as illustrated in Table 8.3. For this purpose there would need to be a reconciliation of the different forms of data used in the different methods (for example, the financial based on accountancy and the economic on economics) (Sugden and Williams, 1978). This would enable stakeholders to have a clear basis for discussion and negotiation. Provided the pertinent stakeholders find their individual answers satisfactory (or, by negotiation among themselves, can achieve satisfactory answers), a partnership can be formed between the stakeholders concerned for the realization of the project.

8.6 Summary
This chapter has highlighted the current weakness in integrating environmental assessment with socio-economic appraisal in the development process. After suggesting reasons for this, it has presented a method for integrating both forms of appraisal within community impact evaluation. The main steps in CIE have been described and it has been shown how the decision taker could be helped form its own conclusions and how the different stakeholders can use the findings to negotiate mutually acceptable outcomes to the development proposals under consideration.

Table 8.3 The nesting principle in CIE

| Community sector | Evaluation method | | | |
No. Description	FA	CRA	CBA	CIE
PRODUCERS/OPERATORS				
1 Current landowner on site	✔			✔
3 Developer/financier	✔			✔
5 Municipality on site	✔	✔	✔	✔
7 Government on site	✔	✔	✔	✔
• National heritage				
9 Municipality off site	✔	✔	✔	✔
11 Other landowners			✔	✔
(1) Adjoining				
(2) Elsewhere				
13 Local economy	✔	✔	✔	✔
(1) Employers/firms				
(2) Urban services				
15 Government budget				✔
CONSUMERS				
2 Current occupiers of site	✔			✔
4 Residents in flats	✔			✔
6 Users of site			✔	✔
(1) Traffic on site				
(2) Visitors to NHM				
(3) Visitors to Grove				
(4) Visitors to open space				
(5) Passers-by				
8 Tourists and visitors		✔	✔	✔
10 Traffic			✔	✔
(1) To site				
(2) General				
12 Other occupiers	✔			✔
(1) Adjoining				
(2) Elsewhere				
14 Local economy		✔	✔	✔
(1) Workforce				
(2) Nearby residents – air/visual				
(3) Downtown users				
(4) Users of urban services				

Source: Adapted from Lichfield (1988), Part IV.

References

Canter, L.W. (1996), *Environmental Impact Assessment*, second edition, New York: McGraw-Hill.

Eckstein, O. (1958), *Water Resource Development: The Economics of Project Evaluation*, Cambridge, MA: Harvard University Press.

Glasson, J. and D. Heaney (1993), 'Socio-Economics Impacts: The Poor Relations in British Environmental Impact Statements', *Journal of Environmental Planning and Management,* **36**.

Glasson, J., R. Therivel and A. Chadwick (1994), *Introduction to Environmental Impact Assessment*, London: University College London Press.

Lichfield, D. (1992), 'Making the Assessment Link', *Planning* (975), 4–5.

Lichfield, D. (1994), *Manchester Airport Second Runway: Proof of Evidence.*

Lichfield, N. (1956), *Economics of Planned Development*, London: The Estates Gazette.

Lichfield, N. (1960), 'Cost Benefit Analysis in City Planning', *Journal of the American Institute of Planners*, **26** (4), 273–9.

Lichfield, N. (1964), 'Cost Benefit Analysis in Plan Evaluation', *Town Planning Review*, **35** (2), 159–69.

Lichfield, N. (1968), 'Economics in Town Planning: A Basis for Decision Making', *Town Planning Review* , **39** (1), 5–20.

Lichfield, N. (1985), 'From Impact Assessment to Impact Evaluation', in A Faludi and H. Voogd (eds), *Evaluation of Complex Policy Problems*, Delft: Delftsche Uitgers Maatschappij BV.

Lichfield, N. (1988), *Economics in Urban Conservation*, Cambridge: Cambridge University Press.

Lichfield, N. (1992), 'The Integration of Environmental Assessment into Development Planning, Part 1, Some Principles', *Project Appraisal*, **7** (2), 58–66.

Lichfield, N. (1994), *Manchester Airport Second Runway: Proof of Evidence.*

Lichfield, N. (1996), *Community Impact Evaluation*, London: UCL Press.

Lichfield, N. and D. Lichfield (1992), 'The Integration of Environmental Assessment and Development Planning, Part 2: Prospect Park, Hillingdon', *Project Appraisal*, **7** (3), 175–85.

Lichfield, N., P. Kettle and M. Whitbread (1975), *Evaluation in the Planning Process*, Oxford: Pergamon.

Lichfield, N. and U. Marinov (1977), 'Land Use Planning and Environmental Protection: Convergence or Divergence', *Environment and Planning,* A **9** (8), 985–1002.

Morris, P. and R. Therivel (eds) (1995), *Methods of Environmental Impact Assessment*, London: UCL Press.

Pearce, D., A. Markandya and E.B. Barbier (1989), *Blueprint for a Green Economy*, London: Earthscan.

Peters, G.H. (1971), *Cost Benefit Analysis in Public Expenditure*, London: Institute of Economic Affairs.

Prest, A.R. and R. Turvey (1965), 'Cost Benefit Analysis: A Survey', *The Economic Journal* **75** (300), 683–735.

Rau, J.G. and D.C. Wooten (eds) (1980), *Environmental Impact Assessment Handbook*, New York: McGraw-Hill.

Schofield, J.A. (1987), *Cost Benefit Analysis in Urban and Regional Planning,* London: Allen & Unwin.

Sugden, R. and A. Williams (1978), *The Principles and Practice of Cost Benefit Analysis*, Oxford: Oxford University Press.

Vanclay, F. and D. Bronstein (eds) (1995), *Environmental and Social Impact Assessment.* Chichester, UK: Wiley.

PART III

APPRAISAL AND INTEGRATION: CASE STUDIES

9 Environmental assessment and economic valuation of ground water remediation projects (U.S.)

Larry W. Canter

9.1 Introduction

Environmental impact studies on proposed development or remediation projects have been conducted for over 25 years. Ground water remediation projects can cause undesirable impacts even though their basic thrust is toward restoring the quality and available quantity of the ground water system. Such projects have comprised a major programme in the USA since the Comprehensive Environmental Response, Compensation, and Liability Act (CERCLA) of 1980, also known as the 'Superfund' law; and the Superfund Amendments and Reauthorization Act (SARA) of 1986. Environmental impacts studies, often including components on risk reductions to both human populations and ecological resources, are required as one element in remediation technology selection.

The application of the environmental impact assessment (EIA) process to remediation projects which are anticipated to have beneficial and/or detrimental impacts on ground water resources is explored below. Emphasis will also be given to the potential opportunities for enhancing decision making by using economic valuation and cost–benefit analysis (CBA) as integrating tools within the EIA process. The basic thesis is that more informed decision making is desirable within the context of ground water remediation projects. Accordingly, the traditional EIA process will be combined with a ground water valuation framework to develop an integrative approach for remediation projects.

9.2 Traditional methodology for assessing ground water impacts

Six steps can be utilized in predicting and assessing ground water impacts of proposed development projects. The six steps, shown in Figure 9.1, include (Canter, 1996): (1) identification of the types and quantities of ground water pollutants to be introduced or ground water quantities to be withdrawn, or other impact-causing factors, as a result of the project; (2) description of the environmental setting in terms of ground water flows and quality; hydrogeological characteristics; relationships to existing surface water resources; ground water classifications and/or wellhead

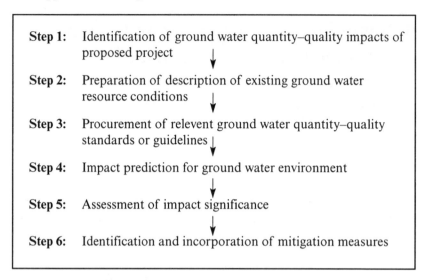

Step 1: Identification of ground water quantity–quality impacts of proposed project

Step 2: Preparation of description of existing ground water resource conditions

Step 3: Procurement of relevent ground water quantity–quality standards or guidelines

Step 4: Impact prediction for ground water environment

Step 5: Assessment of impact significance

Step 6: Identification and incorporation of mitigation measures

Source: based on Canter (1996).

Figure 9.1 Conceptual approach for a traditional study focused on ground water impacts

protection areas; existing point and non-point sources of pollution; and pollution loadings and ground water withdrawals for usage; (3) procurement of relevant laws, regulations, or criteria related to ground water quality and/or usage, and any relevant compacts (agreements) between states, countries, or other entities; (4) conducting of impact prediction activities, including the use of qualitative approaches based on analogues and professional judgement, simple mass-balance calculations, empirical index methods, and/or quantitative ground water flow and solute transport modelling; (5) use of pertinent information from step 3, along with professional judgement and public input, to assess the significance of anticipated beneficial and detrimental impacts; and (6) identification, development, and incorporation of appropriate mitigation measures for the adverse impacts.

The following should be noted relative to the traditional methodology for addressing potential ground water impacts:

1. The methodology (which is primarily based on hydrogeological features, pollution conditions and ground water usage) as described has typically been applied to development projects; application to remediation projects would necessitate refinement of some of the generic steps, such refinements will be addressed in a subsequent section.

2. Other than the implied value (or service) of ground water usage as a water supply, systematic recognition of other extractive, ecological, and *in situ* values is not included; thus the total economic value (TEV) of the affected ground water resource is not recognized.
3. Environmental cost–benefit analysis (ECBA) concepts are not incorporated in the methodology.

9.3 Economic concepts basic to ground water valuation

Several concepts or methods are fundamental to the economic valuation of ground water, including TEV, ground water services (or functions) and a framework for their valuation, and specific techniques for valuation. The TEV of ground water resources can be defined as:

$$TEV = \text{extractive value} + \text{ecological value} + \textit{in situ} \text{ value}$$

Extractive value includes the use of ground water for domestic, industrial, and/or agricultural purposes. Ecological value recognizes the provision of stream base flows from ground water systems, and numerous hydrological relationships between wetland areas and their functions and local ground water resources. *In situ* value incorporates both option and existence value; in addition, the 'buffer value' of ground water as an alternative to surface water supplies during drought, and as a deterrent to land subsidence, can be included. It is important to recognize TEV even though it may not be possible to develop specific quantitative separations of the various components. Descriptive information or surrogate quantitative measures that are not monetized may be the only information available for some TEV components. However, delineations of what can be and cannot be quantified can be useful to decision makers for either development or remediation projects.

One key requirement is an appropriate framework for linking hydrogeological, pollution, and usage information with TEV or components thereof. Such a framework has been developed by Boyle and Bergstrom (1994) for use by the US Environmental Protection Agency in valuing ground water in conjunction with regulatory impact analyses (RIAs). The framework can also be used for impact studies on ground water development, protection, or remediation projects.

Figure 9.2 summarizes the technical data required to define ground water services and their economic value (Boyle and Bergstrom, 1994). Monitoring (Box 1) is required to assess the current or baseline aquifer condition in both quantity and quality dimensions (Box 2). Boxes 1 and 2 are analogous to Steps 2 and 3 in Figure 9.1. The next step is to assess

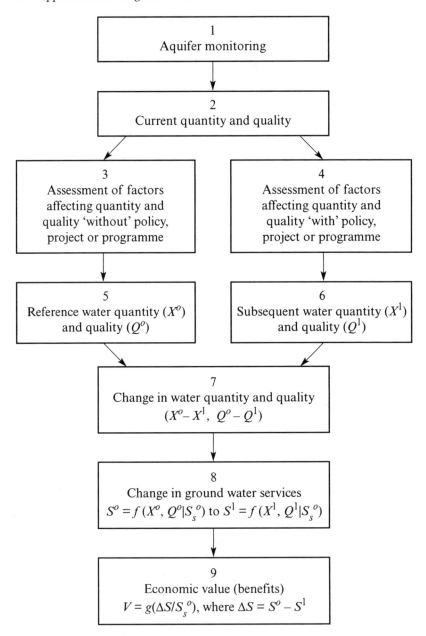

Source: based on Boyle and Bergstrom (1994).

Figure 9.2 Framework for valuation of ground water

how the current quantity and quality of ground water will change 'with' and 'without' the proposed policy, project or programme (Boxes 3 and 4). Influencing factors include extraction rates, natural recharge and discharge, natural and human-induced contamination, and public policies regarding the use and protection of ground water. The approach suggested by Boxes 3 and 4 could be used for decisions related to increases in ground water uses, development of resource protection programmes, and/or planning for pollution source control and/or remediation projects. Boxes 3 and 4 are analogous to impact prediction based on Steps 1 and 4 in Figure 9.1.

As shown in Boxes 5 and 6, the assessments from Boxes 3 and 4 can be used to estimate the reference (without policy, project or programme) ground water quantity (X^o) and quality (Q^o), and the subsequent (with policy, project, or programme) ground water quantity (X^1) and quality (Q^1). Resultant changes in quantity and quality ($X^o - X^1$, $Q^o - Q^1$) are delineated in Box 7. Reference services (S^o) are determined by the 'without condition' quantity (X^o) and quality (Q^o); and subsequent services (S^1) are determined by the 'with condition' quantity (X^1) and quality (Q^1). The reference and subsequent services are conditional upon given levels of substitute and complementary service flows depicted as S^o_s, in Box 8. Steps 5 and 6 in Figure 9.1 are related to Box 8. Finally, the economic value of the ground water resource as a function of the changes in services is shown in Box 9 (Boyle and Bergstrom, 1994). Boxes 5 to 9 in Figure 9.2 are delineated economics-related aspects of information suggested for inclusion in Steps 4 to 6 in Figure 9.1.

Hydrogeologists, biophysical scientists and engineers are most intensively involved in the work associated with Boxes 1 to 7 in Figure 9.2; and they should also be involved in a cooperative fashion in planning and conducting the activities related to Boxes 8 and 9. Economists are most heavily associated with Boxes 8 and 9; and they can also participate in work on Boxes 1 to 7. Accordingly, an interdisciplinary approach is needed. Economists must begin to play a greater role in interdisciplinary impact studies related to ground water development or remediation projects, and ground water professionals must be involved in related valuation studies.

There are numerous uncertainties associated with the application of the valuation framework in Figure 9.2; likewise, uncertainties exist for the six steps in Figure 9.1. The uncertainties may be related to biophysical, geological and engineering information; uncertainties also exist in delineating and valuing ground water services. Such uncertainties should be recognized in both impact and ground water valuation studies.

A pragmatic issue relates to appropriate techniques to use for evaluating various extractive, ecological and *in situ* services of TEV (Boxes 8 and 9 in

Figure 9.2). Examples of such techniques for various services are shown in Table 9.1 (after Boyle and Bergstrom, 1994). The listed techniques represent both direct and/or indirect methods of valuation, and they each have advantages and limitations. Their review is beyond the scope of this discussion; however, it can be noted that key techniques include avoided costs, contingent valuation, benefits transfer and hedonic pricing.

Table 9.1 Examples of valuation techniques for several ground water services

Services	Effects	Valuation techniques
Provision of drinking water	Change in welfare from increase or decrease in availability of drinking water	Market price/demand function Supply or cost function Producer/consumer cost savings Contingent valuation Hedonic price/property value Benefits transfer
	Change in human health or health risks	Market price/demand function Supply or cost function Consumer/producer cost savings Contingent valuation Hedonic price/wage Averting behaviour Benefits transfer
Provision of water for crop irrigation	Change in value of crops or production costs	Market price/demand function Supply or cost function Consumer/producer cost savings Contingent valuation Hedonic price/property value Benefits transfer
	Change in human health or health risks	Market price/demand function Supply or cost function Consumer/producer cost savings Contingent valuation Hedonic price/wage Averting behaviour Benefits transfer
Provision of water for manufacturing processes	Change in value of manufactured goods or production costs	Market price/demand function Supply or cost function Consumer/producer cost savings Contingent valuation Benefits transfer
Provision of water/ soil support system for preventing land subsidence	Change in cost of maintaining public or private property	Market price/demand function Supply or cost function Consumer/producer cost savings Contingent valuation Benefits transfer
Provision of passive or non-use services (e.g., existence or bequest motivations)	Change in personal utility	Contingent valuation Benefits transfer

Table 9.1 continued

Services	Effects	Valuation techniques
Provision of erosion, flood, and storm protection	Change in cost of maintaining public or private property	Market price/demand function Supply or cost function Consumer/producer cost savings Contingent valuation Benefits transfer
	Change in human health or or health risks through personal injury protection	Market price/demand function Supply or cost function Consumer/producer cost savings Contingent valuation Hedonic price/wage Averting behaviour Benefits transfer
	Change in economic output attributable to use of surface water supplies for disposing wastes	Market price/demand function Supply or cost function Consumer/producer cost savings Contingent valuation Benefits transfer
Support of recreational swimming, boating, fishing, hunting, trapping and plant gathering	Change in quantity or quality of recreational activities	Market price/demand function Supply or cost function Consumer/producer cost savings Contingent valuation Travel cost method Benefits transfer
	Change in human health or health risks	Market price/demand function Supply or cost function Consumer/producer cost savings Contingent valuation Hedonic price/wage Averting behaviour Benefits transfer
Support of commercial fishing, hunting, trapping and plant gathering	Change in value of commercial harvest or costs	Market price/demand function Supply or cost function Consumer/producer cost savings Contingent valuation Benefits transfer
Support of on-site observation or study of fish, wildlife and plants for leisure, educational or scientific purposes	Change in quantity or quality of on-site observation or study activities	Market price/demand function Supply or cost function Consumer/producer cost savings Contingent valuation Travel cost method Benefits transfer
Provision of non-use services (e.g., existence services) associated with surface water body or wetlands environments or ecosystems supported by ground water	Change in personal utility or satisfaction	Contingent valuation Benefits transfer

Source: based on Boyle and Bergstrom (1994).

9.4 Ground water valuation studies

A chronological listing of 27 examples of economic or related valuation studies conducted on ground water issues is contained in Table 9.2. The majority of the studies are from the USA and are based on ground water quantity protection from over-usage, quality protection from contamination, or damage assessments from previous pollution. Based on a review of these studies the following two observations can be made: (1) the focus was typically on the valuation of limited services provided by ground water, and not on the TEV; and (2) numerous limitations and uncertainties were identified. In addition, even though 27 studies have been identified, the resultant information base is less than complete. For example, Smith (1993) noted that there is limited evidence available on the comparative features of indirect and direct methods for valuing ground water resources; and Crutchfield, Feather and Hellerstein (1995) observed that with respect to ground water valuation, the available literature upon which to draw conclusions is much thinner than it is for surface water valuation.

Table 9.2 Chronological listing of examples of economic or other valuation studies conducted on ground water related issues

Description of study	Reference
An integrated hydrological and economic model for analysing agricultural usage of ground water in semi-arid areas with declining water tables	Gisser and Mercado (1973)
Economic study of the Ogallala aquifer in Oklahoma in relation to agricultural uses of ground water for various crops and operational scenarios	Mapp (1984)
Economic analysis of the utilization of a ground water storage programme in the Chino Ground Water Basin in southern California	Tom (1984)
Discussion of economic considerations associated with waste water recharge of ground water systems in California	Vaux (1985)
Use of hydrologic and economic modelling to analyse several institutional alternatives for managing the South Platte River (an interrelated stream–aquifer system) in north-eastern Colorado	Young, Daubert and Morel-Seytoux (1986)
Case study of the costs and benefits of a ground water protection programme for Suffolk County (eastern two-thirds of Long Island), New York	Suffolk County Department of Health and Human Services (1987)
Description of a contingent valuation study of option prices (or household's willingness to pay to keep the option of further uses of ground water) to prevent uncertain, future nitrate contamination of a potable supply of ground water in Cape Cod, Massachusetts	Edwards (1988)
Description of econonic framework for assessing ground water pollution, protection of ground water resources, and potential remediation programmes.	Foster and Foster (1989)
Survey of the direct and indirect costs of ground water contamination based on queries to representatives of Minnesota cities, utilities and industries, and one state agency; all the respondees had been affected by ground water contamination	Freshwater Foundation (1989)

Table 9.2 continued

Description of study	Reference
Simulation of the economic consequences of banning the use of certain highly soluble active ingredients (pesticides) for crops grown in counties in the south-eastern USA with high ground water vulnerability	Gianessi, Kopp and Puffer (1989)
Use of risk and costs of risk reduction in decision making related to pesticide contamination of ground water in Fresno County, California	Lichtenberg, Zilberman and Bogen (1989)
Central Pennsylvania case study related to measuring economic losses from ground water contamination through the usage of the averting expenditures (avoidance costs) method	Abdalla (1990)
Economic analysis of farm management practices for reducing nitrate ground water pollution from irrigated agriculture	Oh (1991)
Determination of the buffer value of a stock of ground water when used in association with a stochastic source of surface water for agricultural irrigation purposes. Buffer value is defined as the difference between the maximal value of a stock of ground water under uncertainty and its maximal value under certainty where the supply of surface water is stabilized at its mean	Tsur and Graham-Tomasi (1991)
Description of the design and pre-testing of a survey instrument to be used in a national contingent valuation study of the non-use values of ground water	Lazo (1992)
Description of a two-stage contingent valuation study, conducted in Portage County, Wisconsin, of the benefits of ground water protection from agricultural nitrates	Poe and Bishop (1992)
Description of a contingent valuation study to measure the benefits of ground water contamination control (via an option price or individual's maximum willingness-to-pay to secure the option of using the ground water resource in the future) in an agricultural area in south-western Georgia	Sun, Bergstrom and Dorfman (1992)
Two case studies on the use of avoidance costs (averting expenditures) for estimating conertain ground water values	Abdalla (1993)
Discussion of issues related to the measurement of non-use values of ground water	Crutchfield (1993)
Use of contingent valuation method to determine the benefits of management measures to reduce nitrate pollution from agricultural practices in the Abbotsford aquifer in British Columia, Canada	Hauser (1993)
Connectivity between river and ground water systems in relation to ecological benefits (services) of ground water	Holland (1993)
Use of residential property sales (property value studies) as an indication of the economic value of ground water contamination; and the influence of public perception on such sales	Michaels (1993)
Use of bid-rent approach to the hedonic price model to determine the willingness of households in the rural Philippines to pay for different types of water sources	North and Grffin (1993)
Contingent valuation study of the effects of information on risk perceptions, and the nature of the damage function for risks, in relation to nitrates in ground water in Portage County, Wisconsin	Poe (1993)
Discussion of externalities associated with ground water extraction under a common property arrangement; the externalities included a pumping cost externality and a stock externality	Provencher and Burt (1993)
General discussion of a conceptual approach for ground water valuation	Smith (1993)
Benefits transfer study related to ground water valuation in four agricultural regions in the USA	Crutchfield, Feather and Hellerstien (1995)

9.5 Ground water remediation projects – an opportunity to integrate impact assessment and economic valuation

As alluded to earlier, the environmental impacts of remediation projects at Superfund sites can be both beneficial and adverse. Beneficial impacts may include improved ground water duality, reduced health risks to ground water users, enhanced surface water quality during stream base-flow periods, and the minimization of ecological damage to wetlands fed by ground water flow. Adverse impacts related to remediation efforts can include terrestrial habitat disturbances, atmospheric emissions from air stripping towers used for removing volatile organic compounds (VOCs), and ground water flow disruptions due to added nutrients and excessive microbial growth in the subsurface environment. These impacts can be identified and assessed via appropriate specific delineation of the steps in Figure 9.1. Further, CBA (or ECBA) can be included as a means of integrating impact study findings with economic valuation concepts (Paulson, Portney and Krupnick, 1989). Such integration is important for two reasons: (1) large expenditures are required for remediation efforts; and (2) current decision-making policy focuses only on cost comparisons of alternative remediation technologies.

Due to the enormous potential expenditures, ground water remediation at all designated Superfund sites can be questioned based on economic grounds. To support this point, Anderson (1990) noted the following situations which might preclude remediation: (1) the costs of clean-up far exceed the expected benefits of clean-up in terms of human health and ecological stability; (2) the contaminated resource is not used and has a low potential for future use; (3) there are inexpensive water supply substitutes; (4) the resource will probably not be used after remediation, because users will take permanent averting action; and (5) finally, the contamination does not degrade ground water quality to an unsafe level. Accordingly, depending upon the site-specific conditions, it might be appropriate to choose 'no action' as the recommended alternative based on an economic valuation of the remediation project. Further, such studies could also be used in the prioritization of expenditures for multiple remediation sites in an overall programme.

An integrative methodology

Based on a case study from east Woburn, Massachusetts (Spofford, Krupnick and Wood, 1989), the mandated decision-making process used for remediation action selection for Superfund sites, and the related EIA process information described above, Table 9.3 has been developed to demonstrate how ECBA can be included in site-specific decision making. Some of the information needed in the seven-step methodology can be obtained from the remedial investigation/feasibility study (RI/FS) conducted for the site, including related impact and risk assessments. Table

Table 9.3 Suggested steps for incorporating environmental cost–benefit analysis into site-specific decision making regarding Superfund sites

---

Step 1: Characterize the ground water resource(s) at the designated Superfund site (focus should be on resource without the presence of the Superfund site; that is, the background conditions)

    (a) Define boundaries of study area.

    (b) Sumarize biophysical and hydrogeological characteristics as related to ground water quantity and quality; interrelationships with surface water supplies.

    (c) Delineate historical patterns and current trends related to ground water usage (municipal, industrial, and agricultural) in the area.

    (d) Identify the multiple 'services' of the ground water resource in the study area (e.g., extractive, ecological, and non-use services); aggregate any relevant information related to such uses.

    (e) Discuss uncertainties related to any information items or interpretations associated with Step 1.

Step 2: Describe the ground water contamination and/or usage problem(s) which caused the site to be included on the National Priority List (NPL) for non-governmental sites, or a prioritized list for governmental sites

    (a) Describe site history in terms of land usage and/or waste disposal practices.

    (b) Identify source (or sources) of site contamination and expected contaminants.

    (c) Depict the spatial and temporal patterns of current contaminant concentrations at the site.

    (d) Summarize any ground water flow and solute transport simulation modelling studies which depict future contaminant plume characteristics at the site.

    (e) Summarize information from the risk assessment (also called endangerment assessment) conducted for the site and study area.

    (f) Qualitatively address the implications of site ground water contamination on the multiple services of the ground water resource in the study area (could use a simple interaction matrix to identify the implications).

    (g) Discuss uncertainties related to any information items or interpretations associated with Step 2.

Table 9.3 continued

Step 3: Delineate institutional requirements, constraints and/or policies

 (a) Identify clean-up standards for various ground water contaminants.

 (b) Summarize relevant constraints and decision criteria from federal, state and local laws or regulations.

 (c) Define any secondary requirements which might limit the usage of any remediation technology; for example, air pollutant emission concerns related to air stripping.

 (d) Define institutional requirements, policies or constraints in relation to ground water services; examples include usage restrictions, maintenance of base flows in rivers, and wetlands maintenance and preservation.

 (e) Specify funding sources and related requirements in association with remediation technologies.

 (f) Discuss uncertainties related to any information items or interpretations associated with Step 3.

Step 4: Define potential remediation alternatives and summarize cost and effectiveness information for each

 (a) Identify individual alternatives and appropriate combinations thereof to meet clean-up requirements as defined in Step 3. As appropriate, group the alternatives into those related to alternative water supplies, source control, plume management, and ground water treatment and disposal.

 (b) Characterize each of the identified alternatives in terms of technical feasibility, development status and other pertinent features.

 (c) Summarize cost information related to each alternative (initial costs, operation and maintenance costs, and present value of costs over the remediation project life cycle).

 (d) Define the effectiveness features of each alternative; examples of such features include compliance with clean-up standards, reductions in human health risk, and reductions in contaminant plume size and concentration levels.

 (e) Discuss uncertainties related to any information items or interpretations associated with Step 4.

Step 5: Delineate potential benefits of remediation alternatives

 (a) Qualitatively identify the potential benefits of each alternative in relation to the ground water services affected by the contamination (see Step 2f).

Table 9.3 continued

(b) Economically quantify the benefits of each alternative for each ground water service through the use of engineering and hydrogeological information and other techniques as appropriate. Examples of techniques which could be used include:
- (1) for benefits related to avoided costs in relation to extractive services – engineering feasibility studies and ground water usage studies;
- (2) for benefits related to reductions in health risks – risk assessment information and generic information on the value of a statistical life (cancer risk) or the health costs of non-cancer illnesses;
- (3) for ecological benefits related to wetlands – wetland habitat evaluation methods and generic information on the economic valuation of stream habitat units;
- (4) for ecological benefits related to the provision of base flows in rivers – aquatic habitat evaluation methods coupled with in-stream flow incremental methodology, and generic information on the economic valuation of stream habitat units;
- (5) for non-use benefits – carefully planned contingent valuation surveys (or possibly hedonic pricing techniques).
(c) Determine the present value of the benefits over the remediation project life cycle.
(d) Discuss uncertainties related to any information items or interpretations associated with Step 5.

Step 6: Develop and summarize economic information (costs and benefits) on each remediation alternative

(a) For each alternative, cost information from Step 4c and benefits information from Steps 5b and 5c in terms of net benefits and benefit/cost ratios.
(b) For costs of benefits which have been identified but not included in the analysis, develop a table which qualitatively displays the influence of each non-included item on net benefits and benefit/cost ratios.
(c) Display cost effectiveness information for each alternative, with measures of effectiveness (Step 4d) displayed versus various economic measures (costs, benefits, net benefits and benefit/cost ratio).
(d) Based upon the results of Steps 6a to 6c, adjust or combine remediation alternatives as appropriate.
(e) Discuss uncertainties related to any information items or interpretations associated with Step 6.

Table 9.3 continued

Step 7: Display the decision factors related to the remediation alternatives and choose the alternative to become the recommended action

   (a) List the key decision factors; examples include the decision criteria specified by SARA, and the cost and benefits information as developed in Step 6.
   (b) Develop a decision matrix table wherein the decision factors are displayed versus the remediation alternatives; complete the table by including summary quantitative or qualitative (descriptive) information for each alternative relative to each decision factor.
   (c) Utilize systematic decision support systems (multi-criteria decision making) to conduct a trade-off analysis; based on the results, identify the alternative which will become the recommended action.
   (d) Discuss uncertainties related to any information items or interpretations associated with Step 7.

9.4 summarizes the relationships between the seven steps in Table 9.3, the six traditional steps for EIA in Figure 9.1, and the nine boxes in the valuation framework in Figure 9.2. As can be seen, the three schemes are related to each other.

Table 9.5 (p. 170) summarizes where RI/FS information could be used in the seven steps in Table 9.3 along with necessary specific economic analyses or other work needed for the inclusion of ECBA in decision making. The seven-step methodology provides a general framework which can be modified for specific applications; it is presented as a means of integrating hydrogeological studies, contaminant removal studies, environmental impact and risk assessment studies, and valuation techniques. However, it should be recognized that quantification of all benefits and costs may not be possible. Accordingly, their qualitative inclusion in a tabular format showing whether they would increase the overall costs, benefits, or net benefits can be beneficial to the decision-making process.

Costs and benefits information
Remediation cost information is relatively easy to develop at both general and refined levels, and six examples will be cited. First, a compendium of costs of remedial technologies was developed based on 31 case studies (Yang *et al.*, 1987). Second, a manual has been prepared by the US Environmental Protection Agency to delineate remedial action costing

Table 9.4 Relationships between the proposed integrative methodology, the traditional EIA process and the valuation framework

Step in integrative methodology (from Table 9.3)	Related step(s) in traditional EIA Process (from Figure 9.1)	Related box(es) in valuation framework (from Figure 9.2)
1	2	1, 2
2	2, 3	1, 2, 3
3	3	3
4	1, 4	3, 4, 5, 6, 7
5	–	8, 9
6	5, 6	8, 9
7	5, 6	–

procedures (Burgher, Culpepper and Zieger, 1987). Some specific cost manuals have also been developed; one example is a US Air Force manual which can be used to develop cost information on VOC removal from ground water contaminated with jet fuel (Counce, Wilson and Thomas, 1992). The Superfund CASHOUT computer model, a user-friendly model, enables calculation of the present value of clean-up costs at Superfund sites (Industrial Economics, Inc., 1992). A guidebook for cost information on hazardous waste site remediation projects has been developed by a 'roundtable' of federal agencies consisting of the US Environmental Protection Agency, the US Department of Defense, the US Department of Energy, and the US Department of the Interior (Federal Remediation Technologies Roundtable, 1995). Finally, a cost-effectiveness methodology exists for prioritization of mitigation projects across several hazardous waste sites (Thompson, 1993). Performance criteria allow the ranking of projects based on the most lives saved per dollar of mitigation project expenditures.

McClelland *et al.* (1992) conducted a comprehensive nationwide contingent valuation study in the USA to determine the total benefits (including use, altruistic, bequest and existence values) of cleaning up contaminated ground water; the resultant information can be used in a 'benefits transfer' context for programmes or projects related to Superfund or the requirements of the Resource Conservation and Recovery Act (RCRA). The four identified components of value were defined (McClelland *et al.*, 1992) as: (1) use value – the direct value to each household for the clean water they consume themselves (including any adjustment for uncertainty which has been termed option value); (2) altruistic value – the value that households

Table 9.5 Information sources for the seven-step method for incorporating cost–benefit analysis into Superfund site decision making

Step from Table 9.3	RI/FS[a]	Information sources Valuation studies[b]	Integrative studies[c]
Step 1a	x		x
1b	x		
1c	x		x
1d		x	
1e			x
2a	x		
2b	x		
2c	x		
2d	x		x
2e	x		
2f		x	
2g			x
3a	x		
3b	x		x
3c	x		x
3d		x	
3e	x		x
3f			x
4a	x		
4b	x		
4c	x		x
4d	x		x
4e			x
5a		x	
5b		x	
5c		x	
5d		x	x
6a	x	x	
6b		x	
6c		x	
6d			x
6e			x
7a			x
7b			x
7c			x
7d			x

Notes:
[a] RI/FS denotes remedial investigation/feasibility study; it is assumed that any health risk assessments, impact assessments or ecological risk assessments would also be included in the RI/FS.
[b] Valuation studies denote specific economics-related studies conducted to determine the benefits of ground water services and related economic features.
[c] Integrative studies refer either to additions to the RI/FS or valuation studies, or special efforts needed to address the listed step.

place on other households having clean ground water today; (3) bequest value – the value that the current generation places on the availability of clean ground water to future generations; and (4) existence value – the value that individuals place on simply knowing that ground water is clean independent of any use, that is, the value that would remain for clean-up even if people never used the water.

The national study gave emphasis to the non-use value of ground water; this value is defined as all value over and above use value and includes bequest value and existence value (McClelland *et al.*, 1992). The mean non-use values were approximately US$3.00 per household/per month (McClelland *et al.*, 1992). While these values are not exceptionally large, they are significantly larger than zero, thus indicating that non-use values are likely to be a valid component in studies related to the valuation of ground water services (McClelland *et al.*, 1992). The study also determined that several sociodemographic and regional variables were found to be significant in explaining willingness to pay, including income, age and education.

The US Environmental Protection Agency (1993) has developed a methodology which can be used to estimate the specific costs and benefits of site clean-up at hazardous waste treatment, storage and disposal facilities regulated under RCRA. The methodology can also be used in conjunction with Superfund sites. Cost estimates in the methodology are based on the capital, operation and maintenance, and investigatory components of each remedial activity. The total costs are adjusted to include design, oversight and contingency assumptions, and then discounted using a mandated 7 per cent discount rate (US Environmental Protection Agency, 1993). Benefits measures include human health risk reduction, averted water use costs, non-use benefits and increases in land values. In addition, ecological risk under baseline conditions can be estimated along with the effects of facilities on nearby residential property values (US Environmental Protection Agency, 1993).

9.6 Summary
Integration of EIA process requirements with economic valuation of ground water can facilitate decision making relative to Superfund remediation projects. The seven-step generic methodology described herein represents the integration of several types of studies associated with Superfund remediation efforts. In this regard, the following specific issues for Superfund remediation projects should be noted:

1. Economic valuation of ground water for specific hazardous waste sites can enrich the availability of information for use in decision making. The information, when expressed in an ECBA context, can be used as

a screening tool to determine sites requiring clean-up, and also to prioritize multiple sites in an overall remediation programme.

2. Technical and economic uncertainties must be recognized; therefore, stochastic modelling of the contamination problem and potential effectiveness of clean-up measures should be used to develop ranges of resultant information which can be viewed as a type of 'sensitivity analysis'. The possible influences of uncertainties and non-delineated costs and benefits should also be considered in a qualitative manner in information interpretation.

3. Planning and implementation of economic valuation studies requires the interdisciplinary efforts of hydrogeological, engineering, environmental and economics professionals. Such individuals must provide contributions from their respective disciplines along with a willingness to interact with and learn from related disciplines.

4. Due to the paucity of site-specific examples of the use of ECBA in remediation decision making, it would be useful to conduct research on a range of site contamination problems and the costs and benefits of remediation. The resultant information could then be used to develop criteria for the broad application of ECBA in remediation programmes.

References

Abdalla, C.W. (1993), 'Avoidance Costs and Ground Water Values: Results of Two Empirical Applications', *Proceedings of Conference on Clean Water and the American Economy Vol. 2, Ground Water (October 19–21, 1992)*, EPA 800-R-93-001b, March, Office of Water, US Environmental Protection Agency, Washington DC, pp. GW 2–17 to GW 2–23.

Abdalla, C.W. (1990), 'Measuring Economic Losses from Ground Water Contamination: An Investigation of Household Avoidance Costs', *Water Resources Bulletin,* **26** (3), June, 451–63.

Anderson, G.D. (1990), 'What Needs To Be Done: A Policy Perspective on Ground Water and Soil Remediation,' *Ground Water and Soil Remediation. Toward Compatible Science, Policy, and Public Perception,* Washington, DC: National Academy Press, pp. 53–69.

Boyle, K.J. and J.C. Bergstrom (1994), 'A Framework for Measuring the Economic Benefits of Ground Water', Rep. 459, August, Maine Agricultural Experiment Station, University of Maine, Orono, Maine.

Burgher, B., M. Culpepper, and W. Zieger (1987), 'Remedial Action Costing Procedures Manual', EPA/600/S8-87/049, December, Hazardous Waste Engineering Research Laboratory, US Environmental Protection Agency, Cincinnati, OH.

Canter, L.W. (1996) *Environmental Impact Assessment,* second edition, New York: McGraw-Hill, pp. 248–303.

Counce, R.M., J.H. Wilson and C.O. Thomas (1992), 'Manual for Estimating the Cost of VOC Removal from Groundwater Contaminated with Jet Fuel', AFESC/ESL-TR-90-50, May, Martin Marietta Energy Systems, Inc., Oak Ridge, TN.

Crutchfield, S.R. (1993), 'Issues in Measurement of the Non-Use Value of Ground Water', *Proceedings of Conference on Clean Water and the American Economy Vol. 2, Ground Water (October 19–21, 1992)*, EPA 800-R-93-001b, March, Office of Water, US Environmental Protection Agency, Washington, DC, pp. GW 4–17 to GW 4–27.

Crutchfield, S.R., P.M. Feather and D.R. Hellerstein (1995), 'The Benefits of Protecting Rural Water Quality: An Empirical Analysis', Agricultural Economic Report No. 701, January, Economic Research Service, US Department of Agriculture, Washington, DC.

Edwards, S.F. (1988) 'Option Prices for Groundwater Protection,' *Journal of Environmental Economics and Management*, **15**, 475–87.

Federal Remediation Technologies Roundtable (1995), 'Guide to Documenting Cost and Performance for Remediation Projects,' EPA-542-B-95-002, March, US Environmental Protection Agency, Washington, DC.

Foster, S.S.D. and V. Foster (1989), 'The Economic Dimension of Aquifer Protection – Or Putting a Price on Ground Water Pollution', in E. Custodio and A. Gurgui (eds), *Groundwater Economics – Selected Papers from a United Nations Symposium held in Barcelona, Spain*, Elsevier, Amsterdam: pp. 201–11.

Freshwater Foundation (1989), 'Economic Implications of Groundwater Contamination to Companies and Cities', St Paul, MN.

Gianessi, L.P., R.J. Kopp and C.A Puffer (1989), 'The Economic Effects of Policies to Prevent Groundwater Contamination from Pesticides: Application to the Southeast', *Proceedings of National Pesticide Conference*, Virginia Water Resources Research Center, Virginia Polytechnic Institute and State University, Blacksburg, VA, pp. 517–26.

Gisser, M. and A. Mercado (1973), 'Economic Aspects of Ground Water Resources and Replacement Flows in Semiarid Agricultural Areas', *American Journal of Agricultural Economics,* August, 461–66.

Hauser, A. (1993) 'Benefits of Improving Water Quality in the Abbotsford Aquifer: An Application of Contingent Valuation Methods', Environment Canada, Ottawa, Ontario, Canada.

Holland, M.M. (1993), 'Issues and Research Needs in Valuing Ground Water: An Ecosystem Perspective', *Proceedings of Conference on Clean Water and the American Economy – Vol. 2, Ground Water (October 19–21, 1992)*, EPA 800-R-93-001b, March, Office of Water, US Environmental Protection Agency, Washington, DC, pp. GW 4-2 to GW 4-5.

Industrial Economics, Inc. (1992), 'Superfund CASHOUT User's Manual', PB 94-141678, September, National Technical Information Service, US Department of Commerce, Springfield, VA.

Lazo, J.K. (1992), 'Non-Use Values and Intertemporal Choice: Essays in Environmental Economics', PhD dissertation, University of Colorado, Boulder, CO, pp. 5–30.

Lichtenberg, E., D. Zilberman and K.T. Bogen (1989), 'Regulating Environmental Health Risks Under Uncertainty: Groundwater Contamination in California', *Journal of Environmental Economics and Management*, **17**, 22–34.

Mapp, H.P. (1984), 'Economic Evaluation of the Ogallala Aquifer in Oklahoma: What does the Future Hold', *Proceedings of the Ogallala Aquifer Symposium II, Lubbock, Texas, June 1984*, pp. 83–97.

McClelland, G.H., W.D. Schulze, J.K. Lazo, D.M. Waldman, J.K. Doyle, S.R. Elliott, and J.R. Irwin (1992), 'Methods for Measuring Non-Use Values: A Contingent Valuation Study of Groundwater Cleanup', October, University of Colorado, Boulder, CO.

Michaels, R.G. (1993), 'When the Home is No Longer a Castle: Inferring the Economic Value of Ground Water Contamination from Residential Property Sales', *Proceedings of Conference on Clean Water and the American Economy – Vol. 2, Ground Water (October 19–21, 1992)*, EPA 800-R-93-001b, March, Office of Water, US Environmental Protection Agency, Washington, DC, pp. GW 2-34 to GW 2-41.

North, J.H. and C.C. Griffin (1993), 'Water Source as a Housing Characteristic: Hedonic Property Valuation and Willingness to Pay for Water', *Water Resources Research*, **29** (7), July, 1923–9.

Oh, S.I. (1991), 'Managing Nitrate Groundwater Pollution from Irrigated Agriculture: An Economic Analysis', Ph.D. dissertation, Washington State University, Pullman, WA.

Paulson, G., P.R. Portney and A.J. Krupnick (1989), 'The Benefits and Costs of Superfund Cleanups: An Information Assessment', September, The Center for Hazardous Waste Management, Illinois Institute of Technology, Chicago, IL.

Poe, G.L. (1993), 'Information, Risk Perceptions and Contingent Values: The Case of Nitrates in Groundwater', Ph.D. dissertation, University of Wisconsin-Madison, Madison, WI.

Poe, G.L. and R.C. Bishop (1992), 'Measuring the Benefits of Groundwater Protection from Agricultural Contamination: Results from a Two-Stage Contingent Valuation Study', Staff Paper No. 341, May, Department of Agricultural Economics, University of Wisconsin-Madison, Madison, WI.

Provencher, B. and O. Burt (1993), 'The Externalities Associated with the Common Property Exploitation of Groundwater', *Journal of Environmental Economics and Management*, **24**, 139–58.

Smith, V.K. (1993), 'Valuing Ground Water Resources: A Conceptual Overview', *Proceedings of Conference on Clean Water and the American Economy – Vol. 2, Ground Water (October 19–21, 1992)*, EPA 800-R-93-001b, March, Office of Water, US Environmental Protection Agency, Washington, DC, pp. GW 1-5 to GW 1-13.

Spofford, W.O., A.J. Krupnick and E.F. Wood (1989), 'Uncertainties in Estimates of the Costs and Benefits of Groundwater Remediation: Results of a Cost-Benefit Analysis', Discussion Paper QE 89-15, April, Resources for the Future, Washington, DC.

Suffolk County Department of Health and Human Services (1987), 'Suffolk County Comprehensive Water Resources Management Plan', Suffolk County, New York.

Sun, H., J.C. Bergstrom and J.H. Dorfman (1992), 'Estimating the Benefits of Groundwater Contamination Control', *Southern Journal of Agricultural Economics*, **24** (2), December, 63–71.

Thompson, R.E. (1993), 'Development of a Cost-Effectiveness Methodology to Prioritize Environmental Mitigation Projects', AFIT/GEE/ENP/93 S-02, September, Air Force Institute of Technology, Wright-Patterson AFB, OH.

Tom, B.J. (1984), 'Groundwater Basin Storage in Southern California', in D. Finlayson (ed.), *Economics and Groundwater – Proceedings of a Session Sponsored by the Irrigation and Drainage Division, American Society of Civil Engineers National Convention, San Francisco, California, October 4, 1984*, American Society of Civil Engineers, New York, pp. 36–49.

Tsur, Y. and T. Graham-Tomasi (1991), 'The Buffer Value of Groundwater with Stochastic Surface Water Supplies', *Journal of Environmental Economics and Management*, **21**, 201–24.

US Environmental Protection Agency (1993), 'Regulatory Impact Analysis for the Final Rulemaking on Corrective Action for Solid Waste Management Units – Proposed Methodology for Analysis', Draft Copy, March, Office of Solid Waste, Washington, DC, pp. 6–1 to 6–12.

Vaux, H.J. (1985), 'Economic Aspects of Groundwater Recharge', ch. 25 in T. Asano (ed.), *Artificial Recharge of Groundwater*, Boston, MA, pp. 703–18.

Yang, E.C. *et al.* (1987), 'Compendium of Costs of Remedial Technologies at Hazardous Waste Sites', EPA/600/2-87/087, October, Hazardous Waste Engineering Research Laboratory, US Environmental Protection Agency, Cincinnati, OH.

Young, R.A., J.T. Daubert, H.J. Morel-Seytoux (1986), 'Evaluating Institutional Alternatives for Managing an Interrelated Stream-Aquifer System', *American Journal of Agricultural Economics*, November, 787–97.

10 Integrated management of the environmental assessment process for projects in the water environment
David Hickie

(UK)   Q25 O22
        Q26

10.1 Introduction

In the UK Midlands Region of the Environment Agency, over £10 million was due to be spent on capital projects to help manage the water environment during 1996/7. Most of this expenditure is on flood defence projects, together with some smaller water resource projects. All such developments require open and integrated assessment processes which clearly take into account all environmental and socio-economic issues. They need a project management system with the ability to deliver the approved projects in an environmentally sensitive manner, with all their associated environmental constraints and mitigation measures. In the past, the failure to manage the assessment process in such an integrated way has led to the implementation of projects which either required excessive additional expenditure when issues had to be dealt with at the 'eleventh hour', or failed to consider some issues, partially or entirely, to the long-term detriment of community and environment. This chapter seeks to explain how the Midlands Region of the Environment Agency has improved the integration of the environmental assessment process for the benefit of the community, the environment and individual project management.

Environmental Assessment (EA) has developed to be a standard project management tool (Morris and Therivel, 1995), which assists in the development of the project in an environmentally sustainable fashion. For some projects, early EA studies clearly indicate that 'do nothing' is the best option and that further expenditure on developing additional options would be futile. Equally, if EA is treated as an 'add on' at the end of the process, there are great dangers that many environmental and socio-economic considerations will not be taken into account in the engineering design process.

The socio-economic effects of flooding are a key consideration for flood and coastal defence projects. The direct effects are flooding of property, land and roads, with indirect effects on property prices and disruption to local economies and quality of life. Whilst the Environment

Agency and its predecessors have discouraged and objected to development in the flood plain, many new developments have been built in such areas. Some house owners have never experienced a flood in their lifetime, and others are quite content to risk being flooded occasionally rather than have flood defences blocking their views or access to the river. Where the majority of the community want to be protected from flooding and a few individuals do not want to be protected, the decision to proceed with constructing a flood defence will be a political decision for the planning authority. It is important to discover the views of the community and relevant individuals and interested parties at the earliest stage possible. Information management can therefore be a key element of the EA process.

10.2 Information management

In the past, the EA process was seen by some practitioners as only a data collecting and analysing procedure, with the environmental statement (ES) as the final output for the process. Such a narrow definition is reflected in environmental statements produced by some developers. The EA process has been defined by many (Munn, 1979; Department of Environment, 1989) to imply that the EA process is mainly about identifying likely consequences to decision makers. Yet it is our experience that the process needs to continue in a proactive manner beyond that point, not just monitoring the effects or the prediction of the impacts, but also assisting in the making of further decisions at the implementation stages, through to the final completion of the project.

Working from first principles, the EA process should:

(a) identify what information inputs and outputs are required;
(b) define who are the interested parties; and,
(c) define who needs to read the ES and understand the EA.

A review of 14 environmental statements, produced between 1989 and 1994 for the Midlands Region of the Environment Agency, revealed a number of shortcomings in communication at different stages in the EA process (Hickie, 1996a). First, not all relevant interested parties were consulted or issues covered. Second, the information obtained was not always used or recorded in the ES. Third, the information provided in the environmental statement was not readily accessible to the average non-technical reader. This has led to the development of a new EA process to be followed by the Midlands Region of the Agency, which is a more open decision-making process, involving the use of scoping, communication and environmental action plans (Hickie, 1996b).

10.3 Management of the EA process in the Midlands Region

In the new EA process the technical, environmental and economic issues involved in the assessment process are integrated from the early stages of project development. This ensures that the project is progressed in a manner which is technically sound, economically justified and environmentally acceptable. It is the responsibility of the project manager (who will be a senior engineer from the Feasibility Section of the Midlands Regional Engineering Services Department) to ensure the integration of all these issues by the project team.

The project team comprises two sections: one dealing with the technical and economic issues, which is managed by the project engineer; and the other managed by the area-based EA officer (from the Fisheries, Recreation, Conservation and Navigation Department), providing the management of the EA process (Table 10.1). However, there will be many overlaps in issues and activities which will be discussed later. Within the Midlands Region of the Agency, the EA staff act in an independent capacity ensuring the compliance with environmental standards and legislation, and the coordination of liaison activities with external bodies on all environmental issues. The independent management of the EA process is felt to be important, as it seeks to ensure the internal and external credibility of the EA process. The coordination of regional consistency and standards, through the management of EA policy, guidelines, audit, research and environmental training is provided by the regional environmental assessment coordinator. From EA project management experience developed over the past five years and a review of best practice worldwide, the Midlands Region has produced, for its own internal use, procedures and guidelines to secure the effective and efficient implementation of the EA process in association with all operational capital works (Hickie, 1996b).

Table 10.1 Project management of issues

Project manager		
Project engineer	(Overlapping responsibilities)	**Project EA officer**
Technical and economics	Socio-economics	Environment

For projects where a potentially significant environmental effect has been identified, an environmental statement is published at the end of the feasibility stage, just before detailed design work begins (see Table 10.2). For flood defence and water resource projects where existing flood defences or structures are being improved, the Land Drainage EA regulations apply, that is, *Statutory Instrument No. 1217 – The Land Drainage Improvement Works (Assessment of Environmental Effects) Regulations 1988*, known as SI No. 1217 (UK Government, 1988a). Under the SI No. 1217 regulations, if the project is predicted to have no significant environmental effects, a written justification for not producing an environmental statement has to be published. In these circumstances the feasibility EA report will be used as the basis for the justification of no predicted significant environmental effects. Such types of output are produced to ensure all the environmental issues are dealt with effectively, and that there is an acceptable environmental audit trail. Even when no significant environmental effects have been predicted, an environmental action plan (EAP) is produced to ensure the delivery of the project in an environmentally sensitive manner. The contents of the EAP are discussed later.

Where completely new works are being proposed, the traditional planning application route is used, and the environmental assessment is undertaken in accordance with *Statutory Instrument No. 1199 – The Town and Country Planning (Assessment of Environmental Effects) Regulations 1988* (UK Government, 1988b). In the Midlands Region, most of the work is undertaken according to Land Drainage SI No. 1217 regulations, because it mostly relates to existing flood defences along many of the rivers and all the estuaries in the region. However, in other regions, such as South-West, which includes the counties of Devon and Cornwall, most projects are assessed using SI No. 1199, because the majority of locations with flood and coastal defence problems have no existing defences.

At the feasibility stage, the environmental issues, including the socio-economic considerations, are investigated in some detail. The output from such investigations tends to be qualitative rather than quantitative in nature. The cost–benefit analysis of the schemes has traditionally been handled separately by the engineering staff and specialist consultants. For flood defence projects, the guidance notes provided by the Ministry of Agriculture Fisheries and Food state that 'all resource costs and benefits ... should be taken into account' (Ministry of Agriculture, Fisheries and Food, 1993, p.4) but add that 'there will often be impacts that cannot be valued, in which case the EA procedure should enable a qualitative appraisal of the options to be made. Impacts not quantified should be set out, and in a way which assists the process of discriminating between options' (Ministry of Agriculture, Fisheries and Food, 1993, p. 14). In practice, because of the nature of flood alleviation schemes, there are a number of direct economic gains to be made, which are reflected in: increased property prices and agricultural yields on land that does not

Table 10.2 Stages in the EA process for projects in the Midlands Region of the Environment Agency, using SI No. 1217 Land Drainage Regulations

Project management stage	EA stage	EA output
Pre-feasibility	– Prepare communications plan – Scoping of environmental issues – Consultation on scoping report – Prepare environmental issues report	– Communications plan – Scoping report – Environmental issues report
Feasibility	– Collate baseline studies – Identify in collaboration with engineering team the viable alternatives to be studied – Assess effects of alternatives – Consult with all relevant internal and external bodies – Prepare feasibility EA report for preferred alternative	– Feasibility EA report
	– Prepare environmental action plan (EAP)	– Draft EAP
	Either: – Prepare feasibility report for publication as environmental statement, or	– Environmental statement, or
	– Publish written justification if no environmental statement	– Written justification
	APPROVAL	
Design	– Review EAP in the light of any conditions in the approval – for inclusion in design brief – Liaison with design engineers on detailed design and specialist environmental and landscape design contracts	– Revised EAP
	– Review final contract drawings and specifications	– Design EA review report
Construction	– Manage implementation of EAP	
Commissioning		
Post-project appraisal	– Review implementation of EAP	– EA review report

flood as frequently; reductions in flood damage frequency to properties and land; and reductions in transport delays due to flooding, most of which can be quantified relatively easily. The indirect costs and benefits of such schemes are more intangible and are rarely taken into account in the actual cost–benefit analysis. This is an area which requires the development of an agreed methodology to allow for the inclusion of environmental values in the decision-making process. A number of approaches have been recommended by the Department of the Environment, including: conventional market prices (market value of the impact); household production function approaches (travel cost methods); hedonic price methods (house price or wage risk analyses); and contingent valuation or ranking methods (willingness to pay) (Department of the Environment, 1991).

The EA process of the Midlands Region makes provision for several further reports at different stages of the process, which are reviewed by internal EA assessors to ensure satisfactory progression as part of the overall EA quality control process. These reports are indicated in Table 10.2. The most important, from a project management point of view, are the communication plan, the scoping report, and the EAP, each of which will be discussed in greater detail below.

10.4 Communication plan

As an environmental protection agency it is important that the Environment Agency is seen to be open and publicly accountable for its actions and activities, and to implement good practice. A key element of the EA process, as has been discussed earlier, is the communication of information within the EA process. The Environment Agency has a legal duty to consult with all parties who may be interested in or affected by a project, and to receive comments and respond to these in an appropriate manner (UK Government, 1988a). In 1995, the Midlands Region examined how it could improve its communication activities, which were considered to be a very important component of the EA and project management process. This led to the development of a communications plan to improve the management of communication with all appropriate parties, internal and external, throughout the project development and implementation stages (Boulton, 1996).

The main objective of the communications plan is to provide the framework for the effective communication of information associated with the project. The recognition and consideration of all those who wish to comment on the development of a project is a key objective of the plan, together with the identification and resolution of as many of the potential issues as possible at the earliest stage. It also seeks to promote an effective explanation of 'how and why' the Environment Agency proposes to implement a project. The project manager is responsible for preparing the communications plan for each project, in consultation with the project EA officer, and the regional public relations manager. Each communications plan includes an internal and external element as part of the overall plan, appropriate to the scale of the project, the range of environmental impacts, and the parties interested in or affected by the project. The plan is initiated, reviewed and updated at the regular project management meetings held for each project.

Consultation with external parties takes place at the very beginning of the project and continues through to the completion of the project and into the operational stage. External consultees include: statutory consultees (English Nature, Countryside Commission and relevant public authorities); landowners, tenants and residents; non-governmental organizations, such as the County Wildlife Trust; other interested parties; and the general public.

Various forms of communication may be used (Canter, 1996; Ministry for the Environment, 1992; Praxis, 1988), and those used by the Midlands Region are listed in Table 10.3. Depending on the issues and range of parties interested in or affected by the project, the most appropriate form of communication will be chosen.

In the case of more complex and sensitive projects, consultative groups may also be used to act as a focus for the exchange of information and the discussion of potentially sensitive issues. The Environment Agency

Table 10.3 Communication plan – forms of communication

Communication of information to include:	Methods to illicit responses from external consultees shall include:
Leaflets	
Booklets	Specific meetings
Reports	Community meetings
Displays	Public meetings
Posters	Open houses
Exhibitions	Questionnaires and surveys
Video	
Local radio interviews	
Press releases	
Advertisements in newspapers	
Telephone information lines	
Site notice boards	
Newsletters	

invites membership of such groups from appropriate elected bodies and interest groups.

Where significant environmental effects are predicted, SI No. 1217 requires that an initial advertisement in two local papers notifies the public that the Environment Agency will be undertaking an EA and intends to publish an ES for the project. It is also made available for inspection at the Environment Agency Area Office and a local library or other suitable location during the consultation period of 28 days. Whilst it is not a legal requirement, the Midlands Region normally prepares a concurrent exhibition in a local library or other suitable venue.

When a planning application is required for new works, and if the local planning authority decides that a project does not require an associated ES to be published under SI No. 1199, the Environment Agency may decide to voluntarily publish an ES for public consultation, before submitting it as supporting environmental information with the planning application. The advantage of such a strategy is that it helps to improve public confidence and, more importantly, identifies potential objectors who have not already been identified in the EA consultation process. Discussions with such objectors at this stage may lead to them withdrawing their objections, either through clarification of the issues, or through design changes, before the planning application is submitted.

In summary, the communications plan is a programme for the internal and external communication of information and liaison with other parties, from initial inception of the project through to post-project appraisal of the completed project, including long-term liaison if necessary. The plan is initially prepared at the project start-up meeting and should evolve as the project develops to accommodate new issues and lines of communication. Table 10.4 summarizes the typical stages and contents of a communication plan.

10.5 Scoping stage
The scoping stage of the process entails the preparation and publication of a scoping report to explain the assessment process and to secure a consensus among the interested parties and other agencies as to the scope of the environmental issues to be addressed in the EA. This report is produced at an early stage in the planning of the project, once its need has been identified, but before feasibility studies have been commenced. Whilst UK legislation and the proposed amendments to Directive 85/337/EEC on environmental assessment do not require the publication of a scoping document, the Midlands Region has started to publish such reports for projects with likely significant environmental effects, as a matter of good practice. This consultation helps clarify the significant issues and their

Table 10.4 Typical communications plan for a flood defence project

Project management stage	Form of consultation
Pre-feasibility	Internal: project start-up meeting Initial contact with appropriate consultees External: SCOPING REPORT Possible mailshot Possible advertisement in the press Possible establishment of consultative group Internal: ENVIRONMENTAL ISSUES REPORT
Feasibility	Ongoing liaison with appropriate consultees identified previously Liaison with riparian owners, tenants and others likely to be affected by the works Continue liaison with consultative group if established Agreement with statutory consultees on preferred scheme and whether ES is required Publication of ENVIRONMENTAL STATEMENT and EAP (if required by SI No. 1217 or 1199) Exhibition in local library or similar venue
APPROVAL	
Design	Liaise with appropriate consultees if there are design changes. Detailed consultation with riparian owners, tenants and others affected by the works Continue liaison with consultative group if established Re-publish ES if there are significant changes
Construction	Provide pre-construction information to landowners and local community via newspaper, mailshot, etc. Provide point of contact for queries from public Organize liaison meetings as appropriate Continue liaison with consultative group if established Provide information updates to local community
Post-construction	Consider permanent information boards Liaise with appropriate consultees as part of any agreed post-project appraisal Continue liaison with consultative group, if established, on any issues that require remedial action.

perceived importance as viewed by the local community and others, in an open and transparent manner. The scoping process objectives have been developed from the New Zealand Ministry for the Environment recommendations for scoping (Ministry for the Environment, 1992), and are to:

(a) Identify the possible effects, both beneficial and detrimental, of the proposal on the environment.
(b) Identify the possible effects on people of potential environmental changes.
(c) Identify possible environmental enhancements, which could be incorporated in the proposal.
(d) Inform potentially affected people of the proposal.
(e) Understand the values held by individuals and groups about the quality of the environment that might be affected by the proposal.
(f) Evaluate concerns expressed and possible environmental effects for the purpose of determining how and whether to pursue them further.
(g) Define the boundaries of any required further assessment in terms of time, space and subject matter.
(h) Determine the nature of any required further assessment, in terms of analytical methods and consultation procedures.
(i) Organize, focus and communicate the potential benefits, impacts and concerns to assist further analysis and decision making.
(j) Provide a mechanism which helps the Environment Agency implement its duty to conserve and enhance the environment in all operational activities.

The more traditional considerations of the effects of project development, such as ecological and landscape issues, are readily identified by EA staff at these early stages. The wider socio-economic issues have been dealt with in a very weak manner to date, but new prescriptive regional procedures for EA (Hickie, 1996b) should ensure that such issues are now more fully taken into account in the EA process, including direct and indirect economic issues, demographic changes, housing, local services and other social issues (Morris and Therivel, 1995; Burdge and Vanclay, 1995). Flood defence projects in the UK tend not to be as potentially socio-economically intrusive as many other projects, such as industrial or commercial developments. As they tend to be projects which upgrade, rather than create new flood defence schemes, most do not lead to major changes in land use. However, there may be potentially significant indirect effects arising from some projects, due to secondary developments taking place once the flood defence scheme has improved the flood defence of an area, but such effects are hard to quantify.

10.6 Environmental action plan

The environmental action plan (EAP) forms the last section in the environmental statement published by the Midlands Region for each project. The plan includes details of how the environmental constraints and mitigation measures will be managed and implemented. It also provides for the management of the integration of all the environmental and social constraints, their monitoring and any remedial action required.

The EAP was developed from the four needs of:

(a) providing details of environmental parameters and constraints for work in Sites of Special Scientific Interest (SSSIs);
(b) summarizing such issues for the design team;
(c) explaining how the environmental constraints and mitigation measures were going to be implemented; and
(d) the need for objectives and targets for successful post-project appraisal.

The need to provide an integrated mechanism which facilitated these needs was the basic requirement for the new EAP. The format was developed by the regional environmental assessment coordinator, in close collaboration with the regional engineering services manager. This ensured that the new procedures had the full support of the senior engineering managers, who have assisted in their implementation as a standard component of all regional operational projects which require capital funding. The provision for the EAP also fitted in well with the internal strategy to improve the management system for external engineering consultants, by the provision of more detailed briefs for consultants, incorporating all the environmental, technical and economic constraints.

The resultant EAP format contains three elements. First, it specifies the management system required for the EA process, from the published ES to the successful completion of the project, that is, once the project is operational and all remedial works have been implemented. Second, it contains the environmental objectives and targets for each of the environmental constraints identified in the ES. Third, it provides a summary list of environmental specifications for inclusion in the engineering contract documents to enable the environmental requirements to become contractual requirements. Table 10.5 summarizes the content of an EAP.

The EAP clarifies the responsibilities for the environmental input and approval systems required for the project. The in-house project EA officer is responsible for managing the overall environmental technical input to the project. However, the engineering consultants are responsible for providing a landscape architect to detail all the non-engineering works, for

Table 10.5 Elements of an environmental action plan

A *Management and monitoring of final design and delivery of the project in accordance with the ES:*

  (i)   Summary of EA process and the environmental constraints to be taken into account, in terms of protection, conservation, mitigation and enhancement measures
  (ii) Management of change in project design and implementation, in relation to environmental impact
  (iii) Communication programme: internal staff; engineering consultants and contractors; residents; landowners; public; user groups; and conservation bodies, etc.
  (iv) Commitment to procedures and staff resourcing, normally a project EA officer (as an independent member of the project team) and an environmental clerk of works (as part of the supervising resident engineering team); environmental protection schedules (EPS) to be checked by the environmental clerk of works on a weekly basis; and environmental incident forms and an associated reporting and follow-up system
  (v)   EA quality assurance system

B *Objectives and targets for each environmental constraint:*
  (This will include environmental monitoring objectives)

  (i)   Objective
  (ii) Implementation statement
  (iii) Target for objective (to be reviewed at post-project appraisal stage and remedial works instigated if necessary)

C *Summary of environmental specifications:*

  (i)   Workmanship, including procedures and limitations
  (ii) Materials

---

example, the associated planting, wildflower and turf removal and relaying, hard landscape detailing, and the assessment of materials and specifications to meet the environmental requirements of the EAP.

At the construction stage, an environmental clerk of works (ECW) assists the resident engineer in supervising the contract on site. The ECW is responsible for the supervision of all works which may be environmentally sensitive and for ensuring that the contractor complies with all the environmental requirements of the contract. The ECW is encouraged to take a proactive role in such duties, ensuring that all parties are aware of what should happen, and the decisions that need to be taken, to guarantee a sensitive implementation of the works, rather than checking on conditions after mistakes have been made. An environmental protection schedule (EPS), listing all key environmental measures to be undertaken by the contractor, is checked by the ECW on a weekly basis. In the event of a problem occurring on site (for example, one of the environmental parameters being exceeded), an environmental incident reporting system is designed to ensure appropriate assessment and remedial measures are undertaken. This also provides a useful environmental audit trail for use in the post-project appraisal stage.

10.7 Summary

The EA process has been described as a project management tool, and as such can help in managing the implementation of a project from the initial EA scoping stage through to the decision-making point, and on to the successful completion of the project. The problems of integration of environmental and socio-economic issues are regularly faced in the implementation of flood defence projects. The sometimes very different aspirations and needs of the local community, and the wider environment, have to be addressed as part of the assessment and decision-making process, and are key considerations from the scoping stage onwards. The new EA process is still in its infancy and securing its successful development will be an important challenge over the next few years. The Midlands Region of the Environment Agency has used the techniques since January 1995 for all new projects and has seen a marked improvement in the effectiveness and efficiency of the EA process, ensuring that the commitments in the ES are turned into actions on the ground. The use of such management techniques, scoping reports, communication plans and EAPs is recommended for improving the effectiveness of EAs in all future project development work.

References

Boulton, K. (1996), *Internal Guidance Note for the Preparation of a Communication Plan for Construction Projects*, Solihull: The Environment Agency – Midlands Region.

Burdge, R. and F. Vanclay (1995), 'Social Impact Assessment', in F. Vanclay and D. Bronstein (eds), *Environmental and Social Impact Assessment*, Chichester, UK: Wiley.

Canter, L. (1996), *Environmental Impact Assessment*, New York: McGraw-Hill.

Department of the Environment (1989), *Environmental Assessment: A Guide to the Procedures*, London: HMSO.

Department of the Environment (1991), *Policy Appraisal and the Environment*, London: HMSO.

Hickie, D. (1996a), 'A Review and Development of the EA Process for Projects in the Water Environment' in *Conference Proceedings from the International Association for Impact Assessment Annual Conference, 17–23 June 1996 in Estoril, Portugal*, Fargo: IAIA.

Hickie, D. (1996b), *Regional Environmental Assessment Procedures and Guidelines*, Solihull: The Environment Agency – Midlands Region.

Ministry of Agriculture, Fisheries and Food (1993), *Project Appraisal Guidance Notes*, London: Ministry of Agriculture, Fisheries and Food.

Ministry for the Environment (1992), *Scoping of Environmental Effects: A Guide to Scoping and Public Review Methods in Environmental Assessment*, Wellington, New Zealand: Ministry for the Environment.

Morris, P. and R. Therivel (1995), *Methods of Environmental Impact Assessment*, London: University College Press.

Munn, R. (1979), *SCOPE 5: Environmental Impact Assessment*, Chichester, UK: Wiley.

Praxis, (1988), *Public Involvement: Planning Implementing Public Involvement Programs, Calgary*, Canada: Praxis.

UK Government (1988a), S*tatutory Instrument No. 1217 – The Land Drainage Improvement Works (Assessment of Environmental Effects) Regulations 1988*, London: HMSO.

UK Government (1988b), *Statutory Instrument No. 1199 – The Town and Country Planning (Assessment of Environmental Effects) Regulations 1988*, London: HMSO.

11 Integrated environmental assessment applied to river sand harvesting in Kenya

John Kitetu and John Rowan

013
022 p25

11.1 Introduction

In common with many other developing countries, Kenya has based its drive for economic development on the utilization of natural resources. However, it is evident that land and water resources, though in principle renewable, are declining to levels threatening the already fragile economy (Fox, 1988). The heavy reliance of the poorest countries on their natural resources makes them most vulnerable to environmental degradation. Moreover, shortages of capital and personnel severely limit their ability to switch to other economic activities when these resources can no longer sustain them (see, for example, Higgitt and Rowan, 1996).

Sand and gravel extraction is high on the international agenda for environmental action (UNEP, 1990). Rivers have long been exploited as sources of building aggregate; however, the impacts of mining on their stability and ecology have only recently been recognized (Collins and Dunne, 1990). The commercial mining of river sand in Kenya was first described in the early 1950s (Baker, 1954). It has since grown to be an integral element of the national economy with approximately 90 per cent of annual consumption coming from this source.

The environmental effects of sand harvesting are not always obvious and hence have long been underestimated. However, as early as 1982 the Kenyan Government acknowledged that uncontrolled river mining was causing widespread damage to aquatic ecosystems (Diang'a, 1992). The extent and intensity of these problems partly relate to ownership laws giving riparian landowners the right to sell channel aggregates without consultation, and partly to the lack of effective regulation by government and the relevant environmental agencies. For example, county councils (districts) do have licensing schemes, required by all sand-lorries, but their rationale is revenue generation rather than management. The sand harvesters are therefore free to decide where to collect sand, how much to extract, and how to get it to market.

Indiscriminate sand gathering continues to be a major issue and the media frequently refer to conflicts between miners and rural communities, especially where rural water supplies are threatened (for example, Musyoka, 1983; Odongo, 1987). In this chapter we explore the cumulative long-term environmental effects of the Kenyan river sand industry and its relationship to the wider development process. A key objective at the outset of the work was to increase the awareness of environmental planners and policy makers about the extensive threat that mining represents to the stability of the natural resource base.

11.2 Methods

The substantive elements of the assessment approach adopted are shown in Table 11.1. These involved characterizing the mining activities, identifying the key environmental impacts, quantifying the relevant physical processes such as sediment transport rates, and using these data to formulate a sustainable management plan, sensitive to the needs and expectations of the rural population. Collecting data on the harvesting activity involved assembling a range of archive, interview and field survey data. Natural

Table 11.1 Key stages in research

Research stage	Analytical goals and methods
Characterize mining activities	Distribution and scale of sand harvesting operations (*questionnaires, county council records, traffic counts*)
Scoping analysis	Identify key environmental issues (*EIA methods, i.e. matrices supported by local resident questionnaires*)
Baseline surveys	Targeted collection of environmental data (*i.e. archive and field investigation into sediment transport rates*)
Magnitude/ significance	Issue focusing and quantifying the magnitude of environmental impacts (*statistical analysis*)
Mitigation measures	Reach and catchment scale models to predict sustainable extraction rates, natural rehabilitation and restoration programmes (*channel sediment budgets*)
Strategic management initiatives	Management and institutional needs to achieve sustainable development and protect natural resource base (*cost–benefit, environmental quality plan*)

replenishment rates of sand were obtained by reference to the literature and the use of empirical sediment transport equations. Physical impacts on channel systems, water availability and riparian habitats were monitored during field campaigns in 1993 and 1994. Observation timescales were extended using aerial photographs and monumented channel cross-sections found at bridge sites and pipe crossings.

11.3 Baseline environmental data

The distribution of commercial sand harvesting is determined by both geology and proximity to market; transport distances of 30 km can more than double production costs (Bull and Scott, 1974). In Kenya these factors combine to concentrate river mining within the districts situated to the south-east of Nairobi. Historically this area had the best developed transport infrastructure, and the geology is dominated by metamorphic and granitic basement rocks which weather into sandy soils and produce sand-bed rivers. Most of the remaining area around Nairobi, especially to the north and west, is underlain by volcanic deposits which yield unsuitable river substrates.

The importance of the area to the south-east of Nairobi is reflected in the fact that just two districts (Machakos and Makueni) currently supply approximately 90 per cent of the national demand for construction sand (MRD, 1992). Virtually all the area is classed as arid to semi-arid with highly erratic and seasonal rainfall totals ranging between 500 and 1000 mm per annum (Mortimore, 1991). Perennial streams are rare; hence rural communities rely heavily on subsurface water from the sandy river beds which act as natural aquifers. An indication of the importance of such sources is reflected by the fact that 33 per cent of Botswana's ground water is now derived from sand river beds (Shaw, 1989).

11.4 Distribution, nature and economics of river sand harvesting

Sand harvesting is widespread throughout the upper reaches of the Athi basin, but fieldwork concentrated on the most important sand rivers of Thwake, Kiati and Muooni tributaries (Figure 11.1). Intense competition by harvesters means those rivers closest to the urban centres become rapidly depleted. Extensive lengths of channel devoid of sand for several months are testimony to the fact that harvesting rates are exceeding natural replenishment rates. Extraction methods are distinguished by the degree of mechanization. At the simplest level, teams of labourers manually gather sand from the channel and load it directly into lorries driven into the channels (typically 7–12-tonne vehicles). Where the sand deposits are sufficiently thick, mechanized shovels are increasingly employed, obviating the need for large crews and permitting further economies of scale such as 50-tonne lorries.

Official data on harvesting rates were fragmentary and often contradictory, the most reliable evidence suggested 6.3 million tonnes was obtained in 1991. This study found that the total had risen to 9.5 million tonnes by 1994 and confirmed the steady growth in demand for building aggregate, in spite of economic recession in the early 1990s. The market value of the 1994 sand harvest was estimated at Ksh 850 million (UK£8.5 million) which is equivalent to 1.5 per cent of Kenya's GNP (World Bank, 1990). It is estimated that around 30 000 workers are directly involved in the industry, with the majority concentrated in Machakos District.

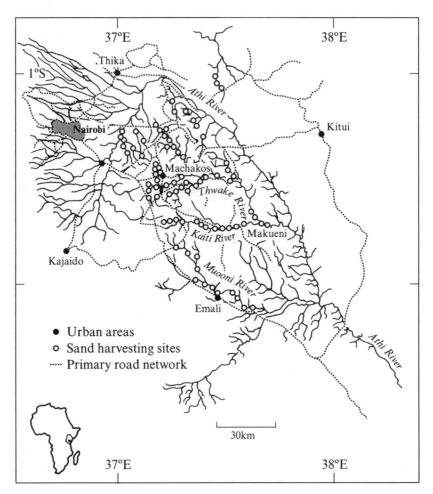

Figure 11.1 Distribution of sand harvesting sites south-east of Nairobi, Kenya

11.5 Scoping survey of local experiences in the main mining area

An essential aspect of the present work was to evaluate the experience of local people living and working within the main sand production area. These results were used to direct subsequent quantitative investigations into the magnitude and impact of physical and socio-economic impacts and as the basis for formulating a management strategy. An extensive interview and questionnaire programme was administered and principally directed towards chiefs, assistant chiefs and village leaders. As spokespersons for their respective communities, these individuals were expected to articulate the wider views of the peoples in the region.

One element of the questionnaire involved asking respondents to score their experience of various impacts on a 1–5 scale, ranging from insignificant to very significant. Two schemes were used to compare responses. In the first, scores of 4 and 5, expressed as a percentage, were considered to represent 'significant impacts'. In the second, an average score was derived to produce an 'impact index', where 1 is the lowest possible score and 5 is the highest. The index was used to rank the impacts, as shown in Table 11.2. The results clearly highlight water supply and quality to be the primary concern of the people. Dust, damage to farmland and crops from sand-lorries and employment from sand-mining industry were the next most important topics. By contrast

Table 11.2 Results of scoping analysis and impact ranking by local resident groups

Environmental parameter	% response in each category					% significant	Impact index
	1	2	3	4	5		
Water supply	1	3	8	20	68	88	4.5
Water quality	3	3	11	32	52	84	4.3
Dust	1	3	29	47	20	67	3.8
Land degradation	5	8	31	36	20	56	3.6
Vegetation damage	5	23	27	20	25	45	3.4
Conflict with miners	12	13	24	40	11	51	3.2
Channel instability	9	16	28	43	4	47	3.2
Stock problems	8	43	24	19	7	25	2.7
Traffic	15	31	40	11	4	15	2.6
Smell	33	24	19	19	5	24	2.4
Flood risk	29	37	21	9	3	12	2.2
Noise	47	29	5	5	13	19	2.1

increased traffic problems, smell, flood risk and increased noise were considered to be relatively unimportant.

11.6 Magnitude and significance of environmental impacts

Impact intensity is heavily dependent on the rate of removal of bed material relative to its replenishment from upstream sediment sources. Where the harvested volume is small in relation to influx, the effects are likely to be minor and short-lived. However, when extraction rates are high, or exceed the replenishment rates, significant and potentially irreversible changes to hydraulic performance and channel stability may result. Field evidence indicates that unsustainable levels of extraction are commonplace, with many areas evidencing harvesting rates three times greater than the annual rate of replenishment (Rowan and Kitetu, 1996).

Uncontrolled sand harvesting is leading to extensive environmental degradation. A useful distinction between off-site and on-site impacts is shown in Figure 11.2. The former are predominantly transport-related, and are associated with the fleets of lorries accessing and collecting sand from the channel network before returning to the urban markets. Soil erosion results from wheel trafficking, and collateral damage to road surfaces and bridges is also widespread. On-site impacts relate to over-deepening of channels, river bank erosion and undermining of bridge piers and pipe crossings.

Long-term degradation was revealed by scour depths approaching 4 m and channel widths doubling over the past 30 years. However, the most significant environmental impacts occur when rural water supplies are damaged by depletion of the sandy channel aquifers. At present more than 95 per cent of the local population receive their water for domestic and livestock use from rivers where sand is harvested. This is illustrated by the fact that as many as 10 000 people depend on wells within a 5 km stretch of the Thwake river for their essential water supplies (MRD, 1992).

The effect of the harvesting activities is to reduce the depth of fill, often resulting in the exposure of water to the atmosphere, leading to enhanced evaporation and reduced recharge. In heavily mined areas ground water levels were observed to drop by between 0.8 and 1.5 m more than in unmined areas. Even a minor reduction in water storage can be critical in the marginal semi-arid environment of the study area. Loss of local water supplies introduces major costs to the rural communities associated with extra travel distances for people and livestock to reach alternative sources, lost income stemming from lower agricultural output and costs associated with the need to establish new sources of water.

SAND AND GRAVEL HARVESTING FROM EPHEMERAL RIVER BEDS IN KENYA

Off-site impacts	On-site impacts

Transport	**Access**	**Excavation**	**Water supply**
Increased number of sand haulage lorries	Impact on land use and soils	Channel bed deepened by sand depletion	Subsurface water exposed
Collateral damage to road network and bridges	Increased use of unplanned access roads	Propagation of excavated pits up/ downstream	Increased evaporation of exposed ground water
Increased risk of traffic accidents	Soil compaction and vegetation damage	River bank height increased	Reduced ground water recharge to local aquifers
Hydrocarbon pollution and exhaust fumes	Reduced infiltration and increased runoff because of reduced plant cover	Bank collapses and increased bank erosion; also trafficking damage	Storage of water for people and livestock especially during drought
	Increased soil erosion by gully and sheet processes, loss of productivity	Changes in channel cross-sections and lateral instability	Water contaminated by oil, gasoline and increased organic pollution
	Ecosystem disruption and loss of genetic resources	Widespread damage to roads and bridges	Conflicts between miners and local communities

ENVIRONMENTAL DEGRADATION

Integrated management solutions

Agency	**Policy and practice**
Government ministries	Resource evaluation
District development committees	Effective monitoring of harvesting activities
Tana and Athi River Development Authority	Appropriate fiscal policy to fund reforms
Sand cooperatives	Ensure provision of rural water supply

Figure 11.2 Environmental management issues in the Kenyan river sand industry, and relevant agencies

11.7 Mitigating measures

The central issue to be resolved by environmental managers is to optimize the utilization of natural resources at sustainable levels whilst satisfying the mutual needs of the various user groups. Applying the terminology of Stocking (1995), these channel systems may be considered both highly *sensitive*, in that they are easily degraded, but also highly *resilient*, because with the appropriate treatment their productive capacities can probably be restored. In response to selected cases of intense local opposition, nominal harvesting bans and site-specific river restoration schemes have been introduced. One method is to construct checkdams across channel sections to provide subsurface water storage dams. These structures serve the dual purpose of stabilizing the channel course, controlling degradation and providing a more predictable supply of sand-filtered water for rural communities and their livestock.

Unfortunately, the success of such schemes has been limited because of ineffective enforcement and general failures to accept responsibility (MRD, 1992). By contrast, the relative success of the Yiika Sand Co-operative (Mwala Division, Machakos District), formed in 1992 with the support of the District Development Committee, may offer a role model for the future development of the river sand industry. The rationale of this cooperative was, *inter alia*, to promote grass-roots participation of the local community in the management of their communal sand resource. The scheme was funded with an initial grant from government, but became self-sufficient following the profitable marketing of its sand. The long-term success and sustainability of the scheme remains to be proved; however, it is a potentially powerful management tool because of its transparency and local accountability.

11.8 Strategic environmental assessment

The Kenyan Government is committed to a policy of sustainable development of its natural resources. However, itinerant sand harvesting normally falls outside these provisions, hence the industry is unregulated and out of control. Exploitation is encouraged by the lucrative market for sand in Nairobi, but management is weak because no single agency has assumed the necessary responsibility to tackle the resulting problems (see, for example, Rowntree, 1990). Sand harvesting must be drawn into a more comprehensive national, regional (provincial), sub-regional (district) and local planning strategy recognizing its mutual dependency with other sectors such as construction, transport and water resources. For this reason incorporating a strategic environmental assessment (SEA) approach to sand harvesting in Kenya has obvious potential (Figure 11.3).

Level of government	Natural resources (SEA)	Policies (SEA)	Plans (SEA)	Programmes (SEA)	Projects (EIA)
National ministries	National resource planning ↓	National mining → policy National economic policy ↘	Long-term national → aggregate plan	Five-year sand-mining → programme	Sand harvesting → from individual river reaches
Provincial development committees	Provincial land use plans ↓		Provincial strategic plan ↘		
District development committees	Environmental action plan ↓			District rural development programme ↘	
Location/site development committees	Sand mining cooperatives				Application of standard EIA protocols

Source: adapted from Lee and Walsh (1992)

Figure 11.3 SEA framework applied to river sand mining in Kenya

SEA recognizes the need to include environmental issues as part of an overall economic policy rather than project by project (Wood, 1995). In principle such concepts are already embraced by the Kenyan Government: the District Focus for Rural Development Strategy (1983) sought to co-ordinate all development policies, plans and programmes at the district level with the goal of sustainable resource management (GOK, 1984). However, this policy has faltered because of the sectoral treatment of both economy and environment, lack of communication between government ministries, lack of enabling mechanisms, lack of resources (data, expertise, financial) and minimal public involvement (see, for example, Partidario, 1995).

Parliament is at the time of writing in the process of debating new EIA legislation outlined in a draft Bill in 1995. Though absent, we suggest SEA should be formally embraced in this legislation because it is applied at an earlier stage, has wider spatial jurisdiction and can consider a much wider selection of project alternatives. This is particularly important because sand harvesting operations are widespread and typically small-scale, but poorly supervised, and generate cumulative impacts on rural communities and the natural environment. Related to this is the need to reinvigorate the role of the National Environment Secretariat (NES) as a supra-ministerial body with capability to coordinate strategic environmental issues across the full spectrum of economic and environmental agencies. However, obvious problems remain in implementing

SEA because the highly politicized government departments may consider these wider structures as an intrusion into their area of competence.

11.9 Conclusions

The harvesting of sand from ephemeral river systems in Kenya, whilst providing an essential raw material for the construction industry, causes widespread damage to catchment ecosystems with concomitantly high social and environmental costs. Strategic environmental assessment offers the most obvious way to coordinate the sustainable development of the rural resource base by providing a framework inter-agency cooperation and resolution of conflicts between stakeholder groups. SEA can promote sustainable development based on detailed appraisal of resources, environmental appraisal of policy decisions and the establishment of management guidelines (that is, tolerable sand extraction rates) based on sound scientific analysis.

New legislation offers the opportunity to establish SEA at the appropriate level and to coordinate sand-mining activities within an environmentally sensitive national mining policy. Weaknesses in institutional structures have hitherto failed to implement these ideals effectively. As an interim measure it is suggested that rural sand harvesting cooperatives, based on the successful example of the Yiika Society, constitute an appropriate management model that could be extended to other areas. Another major problem threatening the sustainability of the Kenyan resource base is accelerated soil erosion from agricultural land (see, for example, Blaikie, 1989). Paradoxically, if effective soil conservation strategies were introduced then the already inadequate sediment replenishment rates to mined river reaches would fall still further. This situation highlights the need for integrated environmental management solutions.

References

Baker, R.G. (1954), 'Geology of the southern Machakos District', Geological Survey of Kenya, Report 27, Nairobi.

Blaikie, P.M. (1989), 'Explanation and policy in land degradation and rehabilitation for developing countries', *Land Degradation and Rehabilitation*, **1**, 23–37.

Bull, W.B. and K.M. Scott (1974), 'Impact of mining from urban stream beds in Southwestern States', *Geology*, **2**, 171–4.

Collins, B.D. and T. Dunne (1990), *Fluvial Geomorphology and River Gravel Mining: A Guide For Planners*, Seattle, WA.

Diang'a, A. (1992), 'Dangers of wanton sand harvesting', *Daily Nation*, 24 April, p. 11.

Fox, R.C. (1988), 'Environmental problems and the political economy of Kenya', *Applied Geography*, **8**, 315–35.

GOK (Government of Kenya) (1984), *Development Plan 1984–1988*, Nairobi: Government Printers.

Higgitt, D.L. and J.S. Rowan (1996), 'Erosion assessment and administration in subtropical China: a case study from Fuijan Province', *Land Degradation and Development*, 7, 1–10.

Kobus, D. and F. Walsh (1994), 'The impact of the environmental assessment processes on mineral planning decisions', *Occasional Paper 39*, EIA Centre, University of Manchester.

Lee, N. and F. Walsh (1992), 'Strategic environmental assessment: an overview', *Project Appraisal*, 7 (3), 126–36.

Mortimore, M. (1991), *Environmental Change and Dryland Management in Machakos District, Kenya: Environmental Profile*, Ministry of Reclamation and Development of Arid, Semi-Arid Areas and Wastelands, Nairobi.

MRD (1992), *Environmental Action Plan (Draft) for Machakos District*, Ministry of Reclamation and Development of Arid and Semi-Arid Areas and Wastelands, Nairobi.

Musyoka, C. (1983), 'MP calls for end to sand row', *Daily Nation*, 12 August, p.5.

Odongo, T. (1987), 'New clashes over sand harvesting', *Daily Nation*, 1 August, p. 4.

Partidario, M.R. (1995), 'Strategic environmental assessment: key issues emerging from recent practice', *Environmental Impact Assessment Review*, 16, 31–55.

Rowan, J.S. and J.J. Kitetu (1997), 'Assessing the environmental impacts of sand harvesting from ephemeral Kenyan rivers', in P.T. Bobrowsky (ed.), *Aggregates: A Global Perspective*, Rotterdam: Kluwer *(in press)*.

Rowntree, K. (1990), 'Political and administrative constraints on integrated river development: an evaluation of the Tana and Athi Rivers Development Authority, Kenya', *Applied Geography*, 10, 21–41.

Shaw, P. (1989), 'Fluvial systems of the Kalahari: a review', *Catena Supplement*, 14, 119–26.

Stocking M.A. (1995), 'Soil erosion and land degradation', in T. O'Riordan, (ed.), *Environmental Science for Environmental Management*, Harlow, UK: Longman, pp. 223–42.

UNEP (1990), 'Environmental guidelines for sand and gravel extraction projects', *Environmental Guidelines* No. 20, UNEP, Nairobi.

Wood, C. (1995), *Environmental Impact Assessment: A Comparative Review*, Harlow, UK: Longman.

World Bank (1990), *World Development Report*, Oxford: Oxford University Press.

12 Potential uses of contingent valuation in the evaluation of dryland resource development projects: a small-scale irrigation case study from south-east Zimbabwe

Chris Lovell, Dominic Moran and Dominic Waughray

12.1 Introduction

The lack of reliable and good quality water sources is one of the principal constraints on development in many dryland areas in Africa (Harrison, 1992; Cleaver and Schreiber, 1994; Scoones *et al.*, 1996). In Masvingo province, south-east Zimbabwe, 32 per cent of people still rely on relatively unsafe water from unprotected wells, rivers, streams and dams (CSO, 1993). Census data for the region have shown that 73 per cent of people walk at least 500 m to their nearest source of water, 32 per cent walking further than 1000 m (CSO, 1993). The basement aquifers which occur in these regions are of particular importance because of their widespread extent and accessibility, and because there is often no other readily available source of water supply for rural communities. In southern Zimbabwe, exploitation of water from the basement aquifer generally occurs through the digging of wells within the residual overburden (the regolith), or by drilling boreholes to intercept fractures in the bedrock (Lovell *et al.*, 1996). Research has shown that collector wells can be used to increase the ground water abstraction from the regolith aquifer. A collector well is a shallow hand-dug well of large diameter with horizontal boreholes drilled radially from the bottom of the well to a distance of 30 m. Lateral drilling can improve the well yield significantly, and can also increase the rate of recovery following abstraction. Thus, even given the low transmissivity of the basement complex, the collector wells can provide a safe daily yield (SDY) of 15 000 litres per day through the use of two bush pumps. This is enough to irrigate a 0.5 ha garden for fresh vegetable production and meet a proportion of the domestic water requirements for the surrounding community.

However, in addition to a lack of reliable and good quality water sources, vegetable production in southern Zimbabwe is also hampered by rigid natural resources legislation, highly inequitable land redistribution initiatives, the threat of uncontrolled grazing or theft, inadequate tenure security and weak rural institutions (Scoones, 1996). This means that for many women the cultivation of fresh vegetables is often regarded as just not worth the effort, being a high-risk activity that cannot be planned for in the long term. As a result, often only the wealthier households with access to a private water source undertake vegetable gardening on a long-term basis. Hence, towards the middle and end of the dry season fresh vegetables are often at a premium in dryland communal areas, and many households, particularly the resource-poor, rely on buying expensive supplies from nearby townships, foraging in the wild or just going without.

Six collector wells, each with a community garden, were established at sites in the communal farming areas of Masvingo province, south-east Zimbabwe. The schemes were implemented jointly by Agritex, Lowveld Research Stations and the Department of Water Development in Zimbabwe, and the Institute of Hydrology (UK) and the British Geological Survey supported by the UK Overseas Development Administration. The pilot project started in October 1991 and finished in January 1996. Detailed technical information on the pilot project can be found in five progress reports (Lovell, 1993; Lovell *et al.*, 1993, 1994a, 1994b, 1995) and in a final report (Lovell *et al.*, 1996) available from the Institute of Hydrology.

12.2 Key economic benefits of the schemes

Extensive monitoring of the collector well and garden schemes over the past four years[1] has shown that a wide portfolio of financial, economic, social and environmental benefits can accrue to the households and communities participating in these schemes over a relatively short timespan (Waughray *et al.*, 1996a). Some of the key benefits are:

- Internal rates of return for the gardens ranging from 11–15 per cent across the schemes. With an overall average gross margin for 1994/5 of Z$67 433 per ha, Z$310 per member and Z$10.76 per labour day, the schemes indicate the impressive returns possible from small, intensively cultivated pieces of land when a reliable source of water can be made available. The returns are generally higher than those given by comparable land use options. For instance traditional *dambo* vegetable cultivation gives an average gross margin per ha of Z$2637 for winter vegetables, or Z$46.26 per member (Meinzen-Diel *et al.*, 1994).
- At sites where the greatest need was for water for vegetable cultivation, communities now say the pilot project has satisfied this need. An estimated 4461 people now obtain fresh vegetables by being a member of one of the six pilot schemes, or in a member's family.

- The community gardens have *reduced* the period of scarcity of fresh vegetables that people in the area face by four to five months, *lowered* the number of people who feel there is a period of scarcity at all by about 25 per cent, and *decreased* the time during scarce periods that people miss out on eating fresh vegetables by about four days in every week.
- At the sites where communities said that one of their greatest needs was for a cleaner and more reliable domestic water supply, the collector wells have helped satisfy this need. An estimated 3882 people, both participants and non-participants in the schemes, now obtain their domestic water from the six collector wells. Furthermore, these wells experience increases in use of up to 55 per cent during periods of water scarcity as and when other water sources fail.
- The community gardens possess considerable potential for income generation and income diversification for garden members. Average income per member obtained from selling vegetable produce during 1994/5 was Z$225 in an area where an estimated 50 per cent of households have annual incomes below Z$400 (Corbett, 1994). It is also important to note not only the *value* of the income generated by the gardens, but also the *number of people* who are participating in this activity. On average, 76 per cent of garden members obtain an income from selling community garden vegetables, on top of their subsistence requirements which the garden meets.
- Of those who joined each scheme, 80 per cent were women and 49 per cent were, on average, among the very poorest in the community (as estimated by the enumerators).
- Women are controlling the saving and investment of cash generated from the schemes. At least 50 per cent of all members in the schemes were found to be involved in savings clubs and revolving funds. Only one fund was said to have existed before the collector well gardens were introduced, and this has expanded. Savings from these funds are being invested in the household or in other income-generating activities.

Clearly, the economic benefits that can be generated from such schemes are significant and the implications this research holds for the improvement in food and income security for households and communities in dryland areas underlain by crystalline basement aquifers are wide ranging (Waughray *et al.*, 1996b).

12.3 Economic concerns surrounding the project
Due to the cross-sectoral nature of its objectives, the collector well and community garden project falls somewhere between a rural water supply

scheme and an irrigation scheme. In standard economic evaluations the wide focus of the project thus tends to count against it at first, when compared to more conventional schemes.

As a water supply scheme, the capital costs properly to implement a collector well and community garden scheme are higher than those incurred by simply siting and sinking a borehole. Capital costs for implementing a collector well and garden average Z$95 984 per scheme, compared to Z$31 000 for a handpump borehole and Z$56 000 for a motorized pump borehole (Lovell *et al.,* 1993, 1994a, 1995, 1996).[2] There is, however, a number of qualifying technical remarks that should be made to contextualize this comparison. First, a different siting technique was used in the implementation of the collector wells. This ensured a 100 per cent success rate as opposed to the 35–50 per cent, on average, success rate of boreholes sited in the region using standard geophysical techniques (Thompson and Lovell, 1996). A full economic comparative-cost analysis of these siting techniques has not yet been completed, but initial findings suggest a financial cost per success of Z$60 784 for handpump boreholes and Z$108 000 for a motorized pump borehole, as compared to Z$95 984 for the collector well and garden scheme (Lovell *et al.,* 1996). However, it is hoped that this new siting technique, when established, will not be exclusive to collector wells, but will also improve the economic viability of *all* types of well and borehole design attempting to exploit shallow crystalline basement aquifers in dryland areas. In this respect, then, the collector well does not seem to be exclusively a cheaper financial option for water supply.

Second, the collector well has two handpumps, compared to boreholes which usually have just one. This means the collector well can pump twice as much water as a borehole. Average capital costs per m³ of water thus emerge as Z$3.70 for the collector well (abstracting 15 121 litres per day SDY), Z$4.06 for the handpump borehole (abstracting 7560 litres per day SDY) and Z$3.61 for the motor pump borehole (abstracting 15 120 litres per day SDY). Again, these figures put the collector well in a more favourable position, but still do not suggest an overwhelming case for implementing a collector well and garden scheme over and above other water supply options. Thus, on a financial basis, the cost–benefit margins for the collector well as an efficient choice of water supply scheme are clearly still quite tight when compared to other options.

Similarly, as an irrigation scheme, concerns have been raised over the relatively high capital cost of irrigating a half hectare of land using the collector well. The typical capital costs per hectare (Z$/ha) of the scheme have been calculated at Z$96 000 (Lovell *et al.,* 1994b), as compared to Z$35 000 for two comparable smallholder irrigation schemes, or Z$5000 for traditional *dambo* gardens (Meizen-Diel *et al.*, 1994). Again, a quali-fying remark to make about these figures is that the gross margins per ha and per unit of water are much more favourable for the collector well garden than for other irrigation schemes (Lovell *et al.*, 1994b).

However, the critical difference between the collector well and garden scheme and other water supply sources (for irrigation or domestic use) is the far greater *reliability* of the well as a source of water and the improved sense of food and income *security* the schemes supply, resulting from a much lower-risk environment in which to grow vegetables. Although these non-market benefits are implicitly recognized as part of the schemes' success, they have never been explicitly quantified or used in an economic evaluation of the project. Yet they are some of the most important economic results of the research and were consistently men-tioned by participating communities as the key benefits of the scheme. It is hypothesized therefore that these non-market benefits would have a high economic value attached to them. Quantification of these values would certainly improve an economic evaluation of the scheme, as com-pared to other water supply choices, and would quantify the key aspects of the project as expressed by the people who actually use it. A contin-gent valuation study was subsequently undertaken to elicit economic values for these non-tangible welfare improvements.

12.4 Key non-market-based benefits of the project
The benefit of cleaner and more reliable water

> *'During the 1991–92 drought we relied on the collector well water to survive.'*
> Headman at a collector well site

Overall, 50 per cent of members and 39 per cent of non-members say they now obtain all their domestic water from the collector well. On top of this, a range of between 3 and 54 per cent of respondents from each site say they also use the collector well for domestic water when their nearest other water source is 'broken'. It is not clear whether 'broken' in this context means a mechanical failure in a pump, or a seasonally dry period for the water source. However, the fact that in times of water scarcity the collector wells experience 'surges' of use by people who would otherwise not use them indicates the *reliability* of the wells as a source of water. The importance people attach to the reliability of the wells was also borne out by an examination of how far the women walked to use them. On average people in and around the schemes walked between 1000 and 1500 m to obtain water from one of the six collector wells, as opposed to the 400–600 m to other water sources. Clearly, time saving does not seem to be a factor in the decision to use the collector wells. This hypothesis was supported by survey results which revealed that the benefit of reliability of water supply was consistently ranked above closeness in importance (Waughray *et al.*, 1996a).

The benefit of an improved water supply is often taken as more than enough economic justification for the implementation of a rural water supply project (Brookshire and Whittington, 1993). However, it would be helpful to know what the perceived value is of a cleaner and more reliable water supply such as that which the collector well supplies, as compared to that of a conventional borehole or well. Although a CV survey was undertaken to elicit a value just for the collector well water, future work plans to research this issue in more depth. Is collector well water valued by project beneficiaries more than water from other sources? Are there seasonal fluctuations in these values? What are the implications of this for comparative economic evaluations of different water supply projects in the area, for potential cost-recovery mechanisms for the collector well schemes and for the price and income elasticities of demand for water supply on which to base a water pricing or water rights strategy?

The benefit of improved food and income security

> *'If I gave up my collector well garden plot, I'd be giving up my future.'*
> Collector well garden member, Gokota.

From evidence obtained during the pilot project, it seems that, before the project gardens were implemented, maintaining a vegetable garden was for the majority of people a risky and uncertain undertaking. Specifically, these risks may have included the illegality of cultivating near to stream banks and the subsequent threat of being thrown off the plot, the uncertainty of unpredictable river flows or privately dug shallow wells and a sense of insecurity regarding loss or theft of produce. Following the implementation of the pilot project, household perceptions of the risks associated with vegetable farming have been changed, through the introduction of some of the following factors:

- a reliable and close-by water supply;
- the official membership of a gardening scheme and recognized ownership of a vegetable plot;
- good security – a chainlink fence surrounding the garden with a padlocked gate;
- the support of the local agricultural extension worker;
- assured markets for selling some of the produce.

If these changes have improved the household's sense of income and food security, it is important to quantify their significance and also understand the wider influence the scheme may have as the catalyst for these changes on coping strategies and perceptions of risk in general. Not only is this an important benefit in itself; it could also be particularly significant in identifying the potential for the gardens to influence production systems decisions on a wider scale within the catchment.

Valuing food security

The possibility of using a market-based approach to find a value for the improvement in food (and income) security that the garden schemes induce was explored. For example, adjusting the trade-off for the household between maximizing the expected profit and minimizing the variance in the whole portfolio of crops may be a key impact of a ground water based community garden scheme. Classically, the household is willing to pay to reduce uncertainty surrounding the whole portfolio of crops (or other sources of income) – to reduce the standard deviation in mean expected income (Varian, 1990). In this context the community garden reduces uncertainty in one aspect of the household's crop portfolio (vegetable production and the income obtained from it). However, to achieve this the scheme requires an initial reduction in overall expected household income for that year equivalent to the cost of membership of the community garden. Thus, the willingness to pay (WTP) the cost of membership of a garden scheme could be used as a proxy for the perceived improvement in security of future household food and income flows that a garden plot may represent.

To join a garden a new member is usually obliged to pay a one-off down-payment to the organizing committee for a plot in the garden. This 'price per plot' has increased at every site since the project's inception, sometimes quite dramatically, but as of February 1995 it ranged from Z$45 to Z$260 across the schemes. Corbett (1994), cited in Scoones (1996), estimated that 50 per cent of households in the pilot project area in 1990 had annual incomes below Z$400, and under 10 per cent of households had incomes above Z$1200. The MLARR national survey 1989–90 stated that crop incomes account for 58 per cent of total gross average income per rural household (MLARR, 1990). Based on these figures, rain-fed crop incomes on average bring an annual income of Z$232 to 50 per cent of rural households in the area, and Z$696+ for less than 10 per cent of households. It may be possible, therefore, to express the perceived value of a garden plot to a household as a willingness to forfeit gross crop income to pay the price for a plot. Taken from February 1995 plot prices, this figure, even for the richest 10 per cent of households, ranges from a willingness to forfeit 6 per cent to 37 per cent of one year's income from crops to purchase a plot of land in the garden. These figures can be used as a coarse financial indication of a risk premium that households are willing to pay to ensure a stream of benefits accruing to them over time as a result of the garden scheme (Waughray and Dube, 1995).

However, using these figures as a revealed or indirect WTP to reduce risk is not satisfactory. Constrained by poorly developed markets for plots in the community gardens and high marginal utilities of money in rural households the figure may well be an *under-representation* of the true value households attach to the gardens. Thus, a direct valuation approach using CV techniques to ascertain the WTP to join a scheme, with a proxy for money (as households rarely have access to reasonable amounts of cash) seems preferable.

Moreover, in using CV techniques to elicit a WTP for joining the schemes, field experience suggests that the value being obtained is actually a combination of both this risk premium *and* the direct use values attached to the garden. In formal surveys and informal discussion groups both members and non-members of the gardens stated that the plots were valuable for the produce and income they yielded *and* for the security of tenure and other inputs necessary for long-term vegetable growing which the schemes provide. All these aspects, however, appear embedded within the overall value they would place on a collector well garden plot. Thus if a WTP bid to join the garden were elicited, it would include both aspects of the direct use value attached to the garden (vegetable yields and income flows) *and* a non-use risk premium or option value (the non-market benefits of a secure fence, membership of a committee and so on). Any WTP bid for membership of the garden needs therefore to be treated as a 'total value', in essence perhaps a WTP for the food and income security the scheme offers.

Interestingly, the field observation of respondents expressing a mixture of use and non-use values for the garden plot is echoed in other recent CV studies and research. In particular, Cummings and Harrison (1995) note the impossibility of de-constructing CV responses into constituent value categories. Evidence from this survey would tend to agree with their finding, and suggests that rather than being a weakness in CV, the elicitation of total values could be of benefit in project needs assessment and appraisal, particularly in food or income-insecure areas.

Obtaining a total value for the food and income security perceived to be offered by a project could significantly improve the economic evaluation process for identifying and implementing the 'right type' or most cost-effective design of an intervention. This approach may be particularly applicable to those types of projects implemented in resource-poor areas that are designed to carry a range of non-market benefits, such as the collector wells and community gardens. They are often justified on the basis of the welfare benefits they could bring alone, although these are often seen as difficult to quantify or evaluate. Often the recipient community has no input to the exact design of the project it might prefer and value most and the donor agency has limited ability to compare objectively the economic benefits of the project in relation to others it might support in the region. Furthermore, the elicitation of total values for the food and income security perceived to be offered by a project could significantly improve the construction of accurate and simple pricing strategies for related resource management, operation and maintainence or cost-recovery purposes.

12.5 The use of CV methods

Methodology

To quantify the value of the welfare improvements of the garden, the stated preferences of scheme users were elicited through a contingent valuation survey which invited willingness-to-pay responses (WTP) from respondents. Details on the construction of the CV questionnaire used can be found in Waughray *et al.* (1996a). The survey was conducted in October 1995 across each of the pilot project sites. In total 60 households were surveyed, including both members and non-members of the schemes. Detailed socio-economic information on all the households surveyed had already been collected as part of the monitoring and evaluation process of the project. Respondents were asked in a discrete choice (yes/no) format about their WTP for maintaining the water supply from the collector well and their WTP to join a scheme. In order to eliminate biases, an iterative bidding game, using different opening bids as starting points, was used. The survey was conducted in Shona by a female enumerator, and most respondents took the exercise very seriously, with lengthy discussions ensuing between husband and wife, or whichever female member took an interest in the vegetable garden.

For the question about joining the schemes, where larger sums of money were involved, bags of maize were used as a proxy for cash. In October 1995, one bag of maize was equivalent to Z\$75. Households on average grow about four bags of maize a year. Eight outliers were removed from the sample on the basis of their bids being two or more standard deviations from the mean and three stages of analysis were undertaken: frequency analysis, cross-tabulation between responses and socio-economic characteristics and multivariate statistical analysis using a logit model.

Analysis of results

Frequency and cross-tabulation. The mean WTP for maintenance of the collector wells was Z$4.67 per month, or Z$56.04 per year. Seventy per cent of respondents expressed WTP between Z$3.5 and Z$7.5 per month.

Cross-tabulation of the WTP maintenance bids:

By wealth

Wealthy $(n = 5)$	mean WTP = 6.1pm (s.d. 0,8)	= Z$73.2 pa
Average $(n = 34)$	mean WTP = 4.53pm (s.d. 1.31)	= Z$54.36 pa
Poorest $(n = 1\ 3)$	mean WTP = 4.50pm (s.d. 1.24)	= Z$ 54.00pa

By distance

0 to ≤ 500m from water source $(n = 32)$ WTP = 5.41 pm (s.d. 2.68)= Z$64.92
> 500m from water source $(n = 20)$ WTP = 8.90 pm (s.d. 8.94)= Z$106.8

The mean WTP to join a scheme was Z$165.00 (s.d. 88.7) as a one-off payment. Sixty per cent of the sample expressed WTP between Z$150 and Z$300.

Cross-tabulation of the WTP to join bids:

By wealth:

Wealthy $(n = 5)$	mean WTP = Z$225.00 (s.d. 118.5)
Average $(n = 34)$	mean WTP = Z$170.85 (s.d. 88.9)
Poorest $(n = 13)$	mean WTP = Z$131.25 (s.d. 62.2)

By distance:

0 to ≤ 500m from garden $(n = 32)$	WTP = Z$166,40 (s.d. 93.25)
> 500m from garden $(n = 20)$	WTP = Z$162.50 (s.d. 80.03)

Membership:

Members (n = 29)	WTP = Z$175.00 (s.d. 91.3)
Non-members (n = 23)	WTP = Z$153.26 (s.d. 84.2)

Multivariate analysis For the collector well maintenance question the most incentive-compatible method of analysing the data was considered to be the treatment of the initial discrete response to WTP $2, $5 or $10. Three design points are considered sufficient to cover the approximate location of the true mean. For the scheme membership question using the maize numeraire a double-bounded format was analysed (see Hanemann *et al.,* 1991). The double-bounded dichotomous choice (DC) format censors respondent WTP (1 bag, 2 bags, Z$ equivalent) in tighter intervals bounded by a response pattern which is one of yes yes, no no, yes no, no yes. The more precise location of the respondent's true WTP in a smaller interval of the integral leads to more efficient parameter estimation by maximum likelihood. Because of estimation problems caused by the possibility of a no no response (censoring the individual between zero and the lowest bag amount $75) this region was arbitrarily restricted as a range 0.1–75.

Table 12.1 presents only the multivariate regression results for the single-bounded model as the parameter values of the regressors were not improved in the double-bounded model. The table also presents estimated means and associated confidence intervals for both models. Recall that the payment vehicle in the double-bounded model is discrete bags of maize (value equivalent). Figure 12.1 shows how the function predicted by the logit model over the bid value range can be used to bound the expected WTP value. Apart from the bid amount, the selected explanatory variables were poor predictors of the probability of WTP the proffered amount. In both regressions neither wealth nor distance from a

Table 12.1 Multivariate logit single bid (well maintenance), double-bounded mean (scheme membership)

Variable	Additional covariates in logit regression Coefficient	*t*-statistic
Constant	5.35	2.54
Bid	−1.006	−3.16
Wealth	−0.337	−0.702
Distance	0.0003	0.45
Member	−0.811	−0.866
Use collector well	0.885	0.895

Notes:
$n = 51$
Log-likelihood (LL) = −17.38
LL (slopes = 0) = −35.10
Chi-squared test for significance = 35.44
% correct predictions= 80.3%
Single-bound question mean WTP for maintenance per month (alpha/grand beta) = $4.53 (95% =3.81 – 5.8)
Double-bounded question mean WTP for scheme membership (one-off payment) = $224.55 (95% = 197.21 – 260.52)

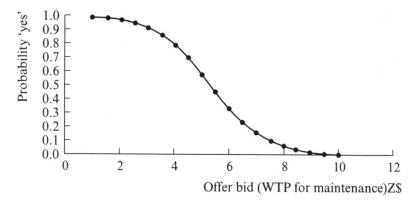

Figure 12.1 Predicted logit function

water source conformed with *a priori* expectations. Only in the double-bounded regression did membership appear to play any role and, as expected, members were more likely to express WTP. Interestingly, the response proportions vary between the elicitation formats. In the case of single question, yes and no responses to the offered amount are approximately equal. In comparison the double-bounded elicitation format provided a WTP value for all but one household (that is, a no no response pattern). This may be due to the different good on offer, but one may speculate about the combined effect of the maize numeraire and the bidding process leading to more careful decisions.

Discussion

The WTP to join a scheme On the basis of the double-bounded logit model the survey suggests a 95 per cent confidence interval for the WTP a one-off joining fee for the schemes of between Z\$197 and Z\$260. In reality the garden plot prices that people are paying to join when a space arises range from Z\$47 to Z\$260. The hypothesis that the mean of these actual plot prices, Z\$105, might well under-represent the total value people attach to the gardens seems to be correct. Perhaps due to garden committees distorting the markets for the plots by setting fixed low prices, or because of the high marginal utility of money as a payment vehicle, the cash price of the garden plots can be seen as an inadequate reflection of the value people place on them. It is also interesting to note that the proxy for cash, in this case bags of maize, produced a stable result which is consistent with the higher prices some people do actually pay for the garden plots.

On the basis of these results it can be shown that in terms of (hypothetical or actual) cost recovery potential, there is a 95 per cent degree of certainty that between Z$16 960 and Z$22 405 could be elicited from a recipient community in one-off joining fees, representing a matching of between 18 per cent and 23 per cent of the initial capital costs of the scheme. A payment vehicle of bags of maize, for example, could be set equivalent in value to the prearranged amount to join per member. The garden committee could sell the collected maize payments at the farm gate price, thus raising the matching funds. Or a series of payments totalling the identified WTP value per household could be constructed to offset the problem of access to lump sums of cash. These systems could be further stratified for different income groups.

The WTP for maintenance of the collector well On the basis of the logit single-bid model, the survey suggests that the mean WTP for maintaining the collector well water supply would be Z$4.33 per month or Z$51.96 per year. With an average 82 households using each scheme constantly (rising to 100 towards the end of the dry season), the model suggests that over Z$5000 could be obtained each year to assist with the operation and maintenance costs of each well. This figure compares favourably with the actual recorded operation and maintenance costs of the schemes, which ranged between Z$25 and Z$100 for the 1995 growing season. Excess funds could thus be invested in fertilizer, pesticides, marketing strategies, transport or other community-based amenities such as toilet facilities.

In terms of the *economic* value of the water the collector wells supply, if the mean WTP is taken as an economic value for clean and reliable water attached by the female head of household to each person within her household, then 647 people on average gain benefits from the collector well constantly, rising to 789 towards the end of the dry season. Discounted over the schemes' 20-year time horizon at 13 per cent this value aggregates out at Z$287 986 or £22 152, a significant economic benefit. A comparison of the economic value of water gained from the collector well to that of other water sources – borehole, hand-dug well – would be fruitful. It can be hypothesized that the collector well water would have a higher value attached to it, and the difference in this value from that of other water sources would represent a value for the reliability and/or cleanliness of the water supplied. The size of this 'reliability' value may itself be quite large and would therefore justify the implementation of the reliable collector well over other maybe cheaper water supply options. This finding would support the hypothesis of the World Bank water demand research team that 'reliability is crucial: households are typically willing to pay much more if the water from an improved source is reliable' (World Bank Water Demand Research Team, 1993).

A WTP for food security? Given that this survey covered user and non-user households, one can speculate that numerous motives are behind the observed WTP for joining a scheme. In particular the recent history of drought in the region, and the legal uncertainty surrounding garden cultivation might have instilled a strong option motive in the respondents' bids. When the field-based experience of respondents' concerns and motives in this case study is added to the academic concerns over the ability to disaggregate CV bids into use and non-use values, particularly for water resources (Cummings and Harrison, 1995; Brookshire *et al.,* 1986), the idea of a total value having been elicited for the economic benefits of the scheme seems applicable. It is suggested that this total value could be taken as a WTP for the food and income security the scheme offers, or is perceived to offer. This value constitutes both the direct value of subsistence crop and cash income generated from the scheme and the value of the flow of benefits the scheme offers the household in the future, in terms of an improvement in food and income security.

Further work is needed on this issue, particularly with regards to averaging out seasonal fluctuations in bid values and comparisons of the mean bid with similar 'control' studies undertaken in relatively food-secure regions. Nevertheless the essential hypothesis of a total value representing food security seems strong. As a result, the implications for the use of CV in this context are wide ranging. One of the clearest uses seems to be in the arena of needs assessment. The accurate targeting of the 'right type' of water and irrigation projects in food- and income-insecure dryland areas is critical. Current needs assessment methodologies, however, often rely on the qualitative characteristics of participatory methods such as rapid rural appraisal or participatory rural appraisal (PRA) (Chambers, 1994). However, the ability of these techniques to supply quantitative economic information to donor and implementing agencies in relation to the economic comparison of the benefits of alternative projects, price and income elasticities of demands of these benefits for the recipient community, the potential for cost recovery and information for the construction of sustainable or equitable resource management systems, is limited. In contrast, the potential for CV studies to learn from the participatory techniques and games of PRA in order to elicit more stable 'total values' for food or income security, given the nature of the proposed project and the socio-economic status or background of the respondent, in order to deliver this economic information to the donor, is great. The blending of aspects of PRA and CV in the search for more accurate total values may be a research area which could prove fruitful to both stakeholder and donor in improving project identification, design, cost-effectiveness and the implementation of equitable and sustainable water resource initiatives and management systems.

12.6 Conclusions

The conclusions to be drawn from the application of CV to the collector wells and community-based small-scale vegetable gardens project are many and wide ranging.

First, it is clear that CV can help address the immediate concerns about the benefit–cost ratio of the project, by quantifying some of the non-market-based benefits the schemes supply, such as reliable and clean water. These economic values can be added to a social cost–benefit analysis and should substantially improve the project's net present value. Importantly, the use of CV in this case captured values of the project that participants rated quite highly, such as a reliable and clean water supply and a secure plot on which to grow vegetables, but which would not have been included in a standard financial appraisal of the project.

Second, on the basis of the values that the CV survey elicited, systems for cost recovery and water resource management can be designed. In particular price and income elasticities of demand can be derived from the data and will be of great help in improving the sustainability and equity of the project by managing the increasing demands on the exploited water and tackling the problems of rent seeking.

Third, however, is the conclusion that the WTP value elicited should be thought of as a *total* value. In this respect it encompasses both direct use and non-use risk or option values. This total value should be regarded as a WTP for the improved food or income security the project is perceived to offer, given the respondents' own needs and desires. It is hoped that further work on this issue can reinforce the validity of CV responses as a total value and, by using CV in conjunction with more sensitive participatory techniques developed within other disciplines (Chambers, 1983; Chambers *et al.*, 1989; Okali *et al.*, 1994), illustrate to donor agencies that stable and comparative economic data can be elicited from rural communities on which accurately targeted water development projects and sustainable demand management systems for natural resources can be effectively and efficiently designed and implemented.

Acknowledgements

Funding for the work reported here was provided by the British Overseas Development Administration and the Government of Zimbabwe. The authors wish also to acknowledge the advice and assistance of many colleagues and friends in Zimbabwe and the UK. Particular thanks should go to Mr I. Mharapara, Mr G. Mtetwa, Mrs M. Mtetwa, Mr T. Dube, Mr C.J. Lovell, Mr C.H. Batchelor, Mr A.J. Semple, Mr J.A. Butterworth and Mr P. Moriarty.

Notes

1. Particular effort was given to assessing the economic and social impact of the schemes on participating communities. In 1993/94, 180 households were interviewed as part of a socio-economic baseline survey undertaken before each of the schemes was implemented, and in September 1995, 169 households were interviewed in a return socio-economic survey. Participative monitoring of each garden's agro-economic performance has also taken place continuously during the pilot project. The surveys obtained replies from both 'members' and 'non-members' of the community garden schemes. Consequently, aspects of the results presented in this chapter differentiate in places between members and non-members. A member is taken to be a person who has joined and remains part of one of the community garden schemes. Each scheme member is taken to represent a different household within the area, the number of households directly receiving benefits from the garden being equal to the number of members of the garden. A non-member is taken to be a representative of a household from one of the kraals in the area who has not joined one of the collector well community garden schemes. Each non-member is taken to represent a different household within the area which does not participate directly in the community garden.
2. £1 is taken as Z$13 (as of February 1995).

References

Brookshire, D.S. and D. Whittington, (1993), 'Water resources issues in developing countries', *Water Resources Research*, **29** (7) 1883–8.

Brookshire, D.S., L.S Eubank, and C.F Sorg (1986), 'Existence values and normative economics: implications for valuing water resources', *Water Resources Research*, **22** (11), 1509–18.

Chambers, R. (1983), *Rural Development: Putting the Last First*, Harlow, UK: Longman.

Chambers, R. (1994), 'The origins and practice of participatory rural appraisal', *World Development*, **22** (7) 953–69.

Chambers, R., A. Pacey and L. Thrupp (1989), *Farmer First: Farmer Innovation and Agricultural Research*, London: Intermediate Technology Publications.

Cleaver, K. and G. Schreiber (1994), 'Reversing the spiral: the population, agriculture and environment nexus in sub Saharan Africa', Washington, DC: World Bank.

Corbett, J. (1994), 'Livelihoods, food security and nutrition in a drought prone part of Zimbabwe', Final Report to UK ODA ESCOR, Centre for the Study of African Economics, Oxford and CSERGE, London.

CSO (1993), 'Census 1992: provincial profile, Masvingo', Central Statistical Office, Harare.

Cummings, R.G and G.W. Harrison (1995), 'The Measurement and Decomposition of Nonuse Values: A Critical Review', *Environmental and Resource Economics*, **5**, 225–47.

Hanemann, M., J. Loomis and B. Kannine (1991), 'Statistical efficiency of double bounded dichotomous choice contingent valuation', *American Journal of Agricultural Economics* **73**, 1255–63.

Harrison, P. (1992), *The Third Revolution: Environment, Population and a Sustainable World*, London and New York: IB Taurus.

Lovell, C.J. (1993), 'Small scale irrigation using collector wells: Pilot Project – Zimbabwe', First Progress Report, October 1992 – March 1993, Institute of Hydrology, Wallingford, UK.

Lovell, C.J., C.H. Batchelor, M.W. Brown, P.J. Chilton, M. Murata, A.J. Semple and D.M. Thompson (1993), 'Small scale irrigation using collector wells: pilot project – Zimbabwe', Second Progress Report, April 1993 – October 1993, ODA Report 94/4, Institute of Hydrology, Wallingford, UK.

Lovell, C.J., C.H. Batchelor, M.W. Brown, P.J. Chilton, M. Murata, A.J. Semple and D.M. Thompson (1994), 'Small scale irrigation using collector wells: pilot project – Zimbabwe' Third Progress Report, October 1993 – March 1994, ODA Report 94/4, Institute of Hydrology, Wallingford, UK.

Lovell, C.J., M. Murata, M.W. Brown, C.H. Batchelor, D.M. Thompson, T. Dube, A.J. Semple and P.J. Chilton (1994b), 'Small scale irrigation using collector wells: pilot project – Zimbabwe', Fourth Progress Report, April 1994 – September 1994, ODA Report 94/9, Institute of Hydrology, Wallingford, UK.

Lovell, C.J., E. Mazhangara, G. Mtetwa,T. Dube, D.M. Thompson, D.M.J. MacDonald and C.H. Batchelor (1995), 'Small scale irrigation using collector wells: pilot project – Zimbabwe', Fifth Progress Report, October 1994 – March 1995, ODA Report 95/6, Institute of Hydrology, Wallingford, UK.

Lovell, C.J., C.H. Batchelor, D.K. Waughray, A.J. Semple, E. Mazhangara, G. Mtetwa, M. Murata, M.W. Brown, T. Dube, D.M. Thompson, P.J. Chilton, D.M.J. MacDonald, D. Conyers and O. Mugweni (1996), 'Small scale irrigation using collector wells: pilot project – Zimbabwe', Final Report October 1992 – January 1996, ODA Report 95/14, Institute of Hydrology, Wallingford, UK.

Mazahangara, E., G. Mtetwa and T. Dube (1995), 'Collector well garden performance – winter 1995', Lowveld Research Stations, PO Box 97, Chiredzi, Zimbabwe.

Meinzen-Diel R. *et al.* (1994), Agro-economic performance of a smallholder irrigation scheme in Zimbabwe', in M. Rukini *et al.* (eds), *Irrigation Performance in Zimbabwe*, Harare: UZ/AGRITEX/IFPRI, University of Zimbabwe.

MLARR (1990), 'Second annual report of farm management data for communal area farm units 1989–90 season', Farm management research section, economics and marketing branch, Ministry of Lands, Agriculture and Rural Resettlement, Harare.

Okali, C., J. Sumberg and J. Farington (1994), *Farmer Participatory Research: Rhetoric and Reality*, London: Intermediate Technology Publications.

Scoones, I. *et al.* (1996), *Hazards and Opportunities: Farming Livelihoods in Dryland Aftica; Lessons from Zimbabwe*, London: Zed Books.

Thompson, D.M. and C.J. Lovell (1996), 'Hydrogeological evaluation of potential areas by exploratory drilling and pumping test analysis', ODA Report 95/16. Institute of Hydrology, Wallingford, UK.

Varian, H. (1990), *Intermediate Microeconomics: A Modern Approach*, third edition, New York: W.W. Norton.

Waughray, D.K. and T. Dube (1995), 'Small scale irrigation using collector wells: pilot project – Zimbabwe. An environmental economic reconnaissance', ODA Report 95/4, Institute of Hydrology, Wallingford, UK.

Waughray, D.K. *et al.* (1996a), 'Small scale irrigation using collector wells: pilot project – Zimbabwe. Return to households survey report', ODA Report 95/13, Institute of Hydrology, Wallingford, UK.

Waughray, D.K. and E.M. Mazhangara and C.J. Lovell (1996b), 'Generating economic benefits in dryland areas: exploiting basement aquifers for small-scale irrigation schemes', mimeo.

World Bank Water Demand Research Team (1993), 'The demand for water in rural areas: determinants and policy implications', *The World Bank Research Observer*, **8**, 47–70.

13 Public valuation of solid waste impacts: a case study in Bangkok

Q26 Q22 Q13

Ian Blore and Fiona Nunan

Q24 (Thailand)

13.1 Solid waste management in Bangkok

Solid waste collection in Bangkok rose by 17.6 per cent between 1987 and 1991, from 5100 tons to approximately 6000 tons of garbage per day (Setchell, 1995). In 1994, the figure had risen to 6500 tons per day (*Bangkok Post*, 18 April 1995). All this waste has to be managed in a safe and cost-effective manner. The Public Cleansing Department of the Bangkok Metropolitan Administration (BMA) and the associated District Offices are responsible for collecting and disposing of solid waste in Bangkok. Being such a compact, densely populated city, land space and availability are at a premium.

Bangkok has several operating dumpsites and landfill sites, and is undergoing considerable developments in solid waste management. Dumpsites are being closed, and replaced with more managed sanitary landfill sites and composting plants. Two dumpsites that have recently been closed are in the Nong Khaem and On-Nooch districts. A significant amount of the decomposing garbage at the Nong Khaem site is being transferred to a sanitary landfill site at Khampaengsan, over 70 kilometres away. The same procedure is being carried out at On-Nooch, with some of the decomposing garbage being taken to the selected research site in the Lat Krabang district, on the far eastern side of Bangkok.

The Lat Krabang landfill site was opened in August 1994, with the intention of it having a very short life. The local residents, politicians and industrial companies have been vociferous in their complaints about the site. The site, on the edge of Bangkok, next to an industrial estate and situated on clay soil, would suggest an ideal place for a landfill site. However, as a headline of an article in the *Bangkok Post* suggests, ('*Lat Krabang residents set to move out*', (14 April 1995), the site appeared, in the media, not to be acceptable to the neighbouring community.

The residents of Bangkok pay for the collection of their garbage through the garbage collection fee. The amount charged in 1995 was 4 baht a month for up to a 20-litre bin (US 17 cents). It has been estimated that only about 10 per cent of the costs of solid waste collection and disposal are covered by this fee (Phantumvanit and Liengcharernsit, 1989).

At the time of the research, the BMA was keen to raise the fee to 40 baht a month. This would be a first step to achieve a realistic fee for the cost of collecting and disposing of waste. However, it faced considerable political opposition with elections due in 1996. An additional, unofficial, payment is made by households, of about 20 to 30 baht a month, to the crews of the trucks to ensure that their garbage is collected.

13.2 Landfill externalities and their economic valuation

Externalities exist where the costs of an activity are not compensated for (Serageldin and Steer, 1993). In the case of landfilling solid waste, external costs are borne by the environment and society, and the magnitude and nature of these costs will generally be site-specific. The economic valuation of external costs is a complicated and sometimes subjective procedure, but can provide useful information for public policy makers and to the private sector involved in managing landfill sites. The internalization of external costs may raise the costs of landfilling solid waste, and enable policy makers to make informed decisions concerning solid waste management. The information should allow a municipal authority to review waste management options and the charges made for solid waste collection and disposal.

The potential environmental impacts from dumping solid waste are well documented. They include the formation of leachate, landfill gas, particulate air pollution, smell, traffic, vermin and flies, and the disamenity caused by the existence of the site. For any economic valuation exercise, particulate air pollution, flies and vermin, traffic, smell and visual impacts can be grouped together into a disamenity category. It is these effects that this research was concerned with. Disamenity effects can be reduced by engineering efforts and management policy, but not entirely removed. They are also often indivisible and so do not vary with quantities of solid waste. These effects may be the most important, in terms of complaints by the local residents and their political representatives. These factors may make disamenity costs very important but difficult to estimate and value.

Leachate, landfill gas and particulate air pollution pose risks to health. Such health risks may be valued using dose–response methods or by using clean-up costs or the costs of better collection, treatment and monitoring equipment at the site. The latter will provide a less accurate measure than the dose–response costs, but will give a guide to the value (CSERGE *et al.*, 1993). Dose–response relationships are however, notoriously difficult to establish and site-specific information and data are almost impossible to collate. Figure 13.1 shows the different economic valuation techniques that can be used to value the effects of these externalities.

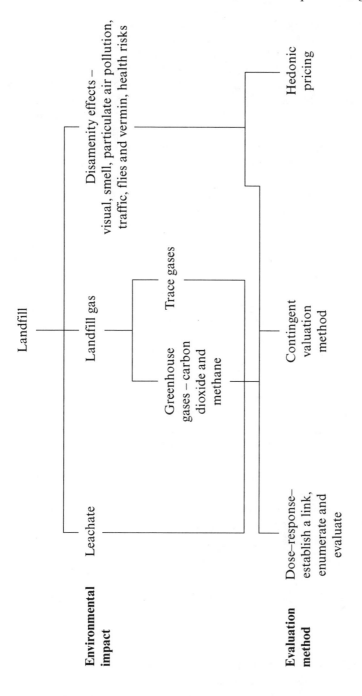

Source: adapted from Bateman and Turner (1992).

Figure 13.1 The potential externalities of landfill sites and possible economic evaluation techniques

13.3 Estimation of disamenity effects

There are two economic valuation methods that can be, and have been, used to estimate the disamenity effects of landfill sites – the hedonic pricing method and the contingent valuation method (CVM) (OECD, 1995). The hedonic pricing method involves an examination of property prices (Whittington, forthcoming). Similar house types are chosen in different environments to ascertain how much of a depreciation in the market value of a house is due to the presence of a landfill site. This type of calculation requires much information and many assumptions. Housing markets may be distorted and price information may be difficult to collect. This is certainly true of Bangkok, as it is of many other Asian cities. In Bangkok, the landfill site chosen was unsuitable for such a method, with so much uncertainty as to how long it would remain open. The presence of the industrial estate may also have affected house prices. This leaves CVM as the most appropriate approach to valuing disamenity effects. However, only two examples of such studies are recorded by Carson *et al.* (1995).

One difficulty that may arise when eliciting willingness-to-pay responses for the disamenity effects of a landfill site is that the value given may include respondent's estimation of other risks (Diamond and Hausman, 1993). This is illustrated in Figure 13.1, where the positioning of CVM indicates that within some of the responses, the risk of pollution or adverse health implications arising from leachate and landfill gas may be included in the value given by a respondent. This makes the exercise of assigning the given value to the disamenity effects of a landfill site alone contentious. In the Bangkok surveys people were aware of the potential health effects of leachate, if not the possibility of landfill gas explosions. There may be two approaches to the question as to what people are valuing:

- construct a survey that tries to focus respondents only on disamenity values;
- provide as much information as possible about health risks and interpret the values as containing respondents' subjective expected values of those risks.

The Bangkok survey followed the latter approach. Respondents, however, tended to object to the disamenity effects of the landfill rather more than to the health risks. Smell was the main concern of the residents in the survey results.

13.4 Questionnaire and survey design

The research was designed to present a scenario to a sample of respondents, to ask how much they would be willing to pay for the landfill site to be closed and the waste taken elsewhere, and to collect possible explanatory information. Two surveys were carried out around the Lat Krabang landfill site. An open-ended (OE) survey of 140 households was conducted in February 1995, the results of which were fed into a dichotomous-choice and iterative-bidding (DC/IB) survey, to set the starting points of the bidding process. The DC/IB survey was carried out in March–April 1995. A number of socio-economic, awareness and attitudinal questions were included in the questionnaire to seek explanations for willingness, or not, to pay, and to determine whether there are any explanatory variables for the amount the respondents are willing to pay.

The valuation scenario briefly described how the BMA was considering closing the landfill site at Lat Krabang, and taking the waste to a site out of Bangkok. It was explained to the respondents that this would result in increased haulage costs which would have to be met by the residents of Bangkok. The garbage collection fee would therefore be raised throughout Bangkok. It was suggested that the new landfill site would have a lifetime of 30 to 40 years, which implies a requirement for the residents to be aware that it is not a one-off payment. The residents would benefit by no longer having to tolerate the landfill site. A question was then posed to the respondents, asking them if they would be willing to pay more garbage collection fees for the waste to be taken to a landfill site away from Bangkok. The purpose of this question was to validate a zero willingness-to-pay response. This was followed, in the case of the OE survey, by a question seeking their maximum willingness to pay per year. The scenario presented was realistic in that, at the time, the company managing the site had found another location, which was ready for operation, but was meeting with opposition. Residents were aware of this.

In the DC survey, respondents were asked if they would be willing to pay a specified amount. A 'triple-bounded' process was used, where respondents were offered higher or lower bids based on their response to the starting and subsequent bids. The bidding process is illustrated in Figure 13.2, where an initial bid of 10 baht is presented, followed by 20 or 7, and then 40 or 5, depending on the response. A final maximum

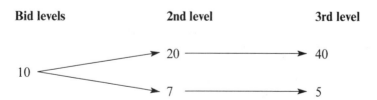

Figure 13.2 Iterative bidding for DC questionnaire

willingness-to-pay question completed the valuation. The starting bids were chosen using the results of the OE survey. The number of starting points was determined by the expected sample size and by the desire to produce a spread across the range provided by the lowest and highest starting bids. The starting points were in baht per month and the maximum willingness to pay values were per year. The respondent was then asked what was the main reason they did, or did not, support an increase in the garbage collection fee. A number of sensitive socio-economic questions concerning household income and occupations completed the questionnaire.

13.5 Results of the open-ended survey

In answer to the question whether or not they would be willing to pay a higher garbage collection fee for the landfill site to be closed, 40 respondents (28 per cent of the sample) said 'no'. Table 13.1 shows the most common reasons for not being willing to pay for both the OE and DC surveys. Reasons for refusing to value included disposing of their refuse by themselves (by burning it); a belief that the landlord should pay for any increase in garbage collection fee; that the private operator who manages the site should pay; and that, as people were not informed of the decision to allow a landfill site to be sited there, it is not their responsibility to pay for it to be 'moved'.

The respondents who stated that they were willing to pay more in their garbage collection fee were asked the main reason for their response. The results of this question are shown in Table 13.2, and are compared to the results from the DC/IB survey. The table shows that environmental and health concerns were important reasons, as well as people believing that the amount they stated was a reasonable amount to pay. These reasons have important implications for the BMA, in terms of the level of garbage collection fee charged, the management of the site and communication with the general public.

Table 13.1 Main reason for not being 'willing to pay' in OE and DC surveys

	OE		DC	
	% of sample	% of non-payers	% of sample	% of non-payers
BMA should pay	11	40	11	45
Pay too much fee already	6	20	2	9
Do not mind the landfill site	1	5	6	24
Refused to value	6	20	3	11

Table 13.2 Main reason for WTP responses

Reason	Open-ended survey		Dichotomous choice	
	%	Valid %	%	Valid %
Reasonable amount to pay	19.7	28.6	13.3	19.8
Lives close to landfill site	4.9	7.1	4.7	7.0
Health concerns	14.1	20.4	16.4	24.4
Environmental concerns	20.4	29.6	17.5	26.0
Income level	8.5	12.2	13.9	20.7
Other	1.4	2.0	1.4	2.1

Note: 'Valid %' is the percentage of the total sample, not only of those willing to pay a higher collection fee.

The mean WTP value was 44.4 baht per month (95 per cent confidence intervals, 34.89, 53.92), with a 5 per cent trimmed mean of 36.65 baht. This indicated a 17 per cent reduction and is closer to the median of 30 baht per month.

13.6 Results of the dichotomous-choice survey
The DC/IB questionnaire was refused by 28 respondents, giving a total sample size of 332. The valuation section began with the question to validate zero WTP. A total of 89 of the 332 respondents answered 'no' to this question (26.8 per cent), which is comparable to the level found in the OE survey. The main reasons for not being willing to pay are shown in Table 13.1.

The respondents who were willing to pay a higher garbage collection fee numbered 243, 67.5 per cent of the total sample, and 73 per cent of those to whom the question was posed. These respondents were asked for their main reason for being willing to pay, the results of which are shown in Table 13.2. A number of factors was found to influence the answer to this question, including the location of the respondent in relation to the landfill site, whether or not they pay the garbage collection fee, and the level of household income.

The bid function of the response to the DC starting bid levels was analysed using a logit link function between the dependent variable and the potential explanatory variables. This approach is described in Zylicz *et al.* (1995), and is used to analyse the probability of saying 'no' to a bid level. The mean value of WTP can be calculated from the bid function. Possible explanatory variables for the bid level may be explored. The mean value is shown in Table 13.3, with the OE and IB means for comparison.

Table 13.3 Mean values of WTP (baht per month)

	DC	OE	DC/OE	IB
Mean	71.67	44.4	51.12	54–56

Notes:
DC   = expected WTP value of the starting bid responses
OE   = mean WTP value of the OE survey responses
DC/OE = mean of the open-ended WTP question at the end of the bidding process
IB   = range of mean values obtained from different models for the triple-bounded
       bidding process

The analysis of the triple-bounded process (IB) revealed a lower mean than the single-level DC analysis, at 56 baht a month (for details of the approach used see Langford *et al.*, 1995).

13.7 Discussion of the results
The explanatory variables of the bid function, although weak, do offer some interesting information. The ownership of a house and the level of household income have the strongest associational relationship with willingness to pay. This supports the intuitive hypothesis that once people have settled in an area, and plan to continue living there, they will be more concerned about the siting of a landfill in the locality, whilst those with higher incomes will be prepared to pay more. The number of years lived in the house and concern over health effects also point to concern about the existence of the landfill site, with its potential environmental and health consequences, and possible effects on property prices.

It would be unwise, however, to use the functional relationships as predictive models. The overall power of explanation provided by the best fitting models is poor. This is fully consistent with other applications of CVM. There may be two explanations for this in the case of Lat Krabang, both reflecting the attitudes of respondents to the survey. The first concerns the adverse publicity given to the Lat Krabang landfill site. The English-language newspaper, the *Bangkok Post*, has carried a number of controversial articles concerning pollution from the site. The Thai-language newspapers have carried similar pieces, and may have influenced the responses given in the survey. Information about the number of landfill site articles read by the respondents was not sought; neither was there a question asking whether they had complained to the BMA about the site. The level of sensitivity about the site became apparent during the surveys, and some way of ascertaining the respondents' knowledge of the debate concerning the future of the landfill site would have been informative. However, it can be assumed that the debate would have been known by some, and will have influenced some of the responses, but by what amount cannot be ascertained.

Another factor that may have influenced the WTP amount could be the idea of a 'social norm'. This may be guided by the level of the unofficial 'fee' given to the garbage collection crews to ensure the garbage is collected. Again, if this has influenced the WTP amounts, this cannot be measured from the questionnaire data obtained. Although this is a question to be debated elsewhere, the discussion about 'social norming' appears to reflect a misconstruction of WTP values as somehow 'pure' and unbiased by other factors conditioning behaviour. We would argue that in the Lat Krabang case it is entirely reasonable that people would relate a possible fee to be rid of the landfill with an unofficial payment to ensure their garbage is collected. Social norming is a basis of behaviour. It should affect contingent behaviour. What is important is having some information about what is possibly affecting any social norms in a specific case.

13.8 What are valid CV results?

The Thai respondents to the contingent valuation survey appeared to have no difficulty in answering the valuation questions. On the basis of the experience gained in Bangkok and on general guidelines on conducting CV surveys (see Mitchell and Carson, 1989), it can be stressed that a realistic and understandable scenario is extremely important to the success of the survey. Culture is also an important consideration in designing a CV survey and questionnaire. The Thais' familiarity with bargaining for goods and services may have contributed towards residents' ability to respond to valuation questions.

How the results of CV surveys are used in relation to policy decisions depends on how they are achieved and interpreted. Mitchell and Carson (1989) suggest that CV surveys should be assessed for their validity. One of these validity tests, *criterion validity*, involves comparing the mean values of WTP to congruent market prices. This test is essentially asking whether the mean values are 'sensible', as there is no market price for the goods being valued in such a survey. There can be no 'true' value for such goods, but comparisons can be made to assess the mean values obtained. The question of what the mean values actually include, or how they may be interpreted, is interesting and is discussed in Blore (1996). Tests of validity generally involve trying to find comparable values that exist and to ascertain whether the mean values are in the right 'ball park'. The researchers involved in this project would generally suggest that the values obtained in such surveys should be used as one source of information in a decision-making process rather than as the answer to a policy question. The information provided by CV surveys should be used in context, with reference to information obtained from a variety of sources. Attempts to mark the mean values as a 'price', for the good in question should be treated with caution.

One test of criterion validity was a comparison of the mean values of WTP, from both the OE and DC/IB surveys, with the actual present and proposed garbage collection fee. Respondents' willingness was roughly similar to the proposed, but not publicized, new collection fee. Validity tests of this kind are useful, particularly for policy makers, where a comparable market price does not exist. The high level of estimated mean values of WTP obtained in the analysis of the starting bid responses in the DC survey was reduced when the bidding process was brought in. Policy makers can take these values into consideration in decision-making processes. It is interesting that even those who do not currently pay the fee, and many of those who do not have their solid waste collected by the BMA, were also willing to pay for the landfill site to be closed.

A second test of criterion validity is perhaps the existence of 'private' payments to garbage crews by households. Although these are to ensure collection rather than to improve disposal, they do indicate that Bangkok households are willing to pay more for solid waste management generally, up to 24–34 baht a month.

13.9 Dose–response and CV methods
The main conclusions of the research concern the application of CVM and the problems that may be encountered in the valuation of external costs of landfilling and recycling solid waste using dose–response techniques. The most important conclusion concerning CVM is that undertaking such surveys in a southern city is possible, cost-effective and can provide meaningful and useful information. The cost-effectiveness of conducting CV surveys is reflected in the fact that the surveys took seven days to complete in total, and trained students can adequately undertake such work (see Glass and Corkindale, 1994 for a discussion of value for money in environmental valuation). The design of the questionnaire, gathering background information and conducting the analysis, does require resources, but may require comparatively less than other methods that could be employed, such as hedonic pricing or dose–response approaches.

In Bangkok it was almost impossible to gather sufficient information to establish and evaluate dose–response relationships, for either landfilling or recycling solid waste. Many assumptions have to be made and extrapolation of data, from other sites or plants, may be inappropriate. Nor can dose–response estimates capture disamenity values. This makes the use of CVM even more important in assessing and evaluating external costs to the environment and society. The final point concerning the results obtained from the CV surveys is that it may be suggested that the mean values give a more realistic guide to the concern that the residents may feel than does the rather hysterical media coverage of the Lat Krabang landfill site.

13.10 CV methods and public policy

Most public policy analysis requires hypotheses about predicted behaviour. Actual behaviour may sometimes deviate from that predicted but this is not a good argument that analysis should not therefore be used (Sen, 1973). The question is how the information of the analysis can and should be used. Most CV surveys are used to generate information that can be fed into a decision-making process. Such information will normally be used alongside other information and certainly requires judgement about its validity. Assessing a value of willingness to pay is not usually followed by the imposition of a tax, price or even voluntary donation and therefore criterion validity usually needs to be judged qualitatively, although its application to water supply is easier (Briscoe, 1990). It is not usual to have such a policy test as that provided in the Bangkok survey.

If hypothetical information is commonly used by policy makers, why is the use of such information provided by CV methods often criticized? One reason may be that the language of CV methods is laden with terms that are emotive to many. A further set of objections to using hypothetical scenarios lies in the psychology of the response. These are often categorized as 'embedding problems', warm glow effects or social norm values. The criticism is that these effects distort an answer to many questions about an environmental change. The counter-argument has been simply put (Willis, 1994). It suggests that all values, even those emerging in a real price, are the outcome of an interplay between individual psychology and social factors.

Research into respondents' psychology can be reduced to the problem of whether the questions used to elicit responses make sense and what sort of sense to different people. There are methods that attempt to improve this 'content scenario' and the way it is presented to respondents. Many of the guides to good practice are well publicized (the seminal being Mitchell and Carson, 1989). Ultimately the judges of whether a hypothetical scenario is good or not are the users of the survey data. These may be either respondents or decision makers (they are probably different people).

Two benefits may arise from the recommended elaborate scenario-testing and dialogue methods in conducting a CV survey. The first is that they force very careful consideration of realistic options. Thinking aloud about contingencies is often healthy in public policy making. Discussing them and their realism with stakeholders to a decision is perhaps even healthier. Maybe we could even advocate that the process should stop after the construction of the survey and its questions. If guidelines such as those of the NOAA Blue Ribbon Panel (Arrow *et al.*, 1993) were to be taken seriously, they would ensure both rigour and creative imagination. These are not a bad basis for good public policy.

13.11 CV methods and risk

The advocates of CV claim that it is something more than just a salutary process (Hanley and Spash, 1993). There is a fundamental belief that a question can be so framed and posed that it elicits an answer that is meaningful and gives some information that can be understood by the questioner. This belief in a meaningful dialogue between the public and policy makers is a bedrock of CV methods. So is its inherent treatment of risk as subjective probabilities. A hypothetical scenario is truly contingent. It may be best to imagine the scenario as a risk assessment in the sense that it asks people to imagine the likelihood of a change in their environment if they were to pay something. We would expect the answer to depend on the subjective probability of the hypothetical scenario. Were the respondent to have little knowledge of the likelihood of the scenario, such as saving a species or reducing global warming, the response is more likely to be guess-work than if the scenario, such as increasing the garbage collection fee in Bangkok, were to be better known in terms of its likely outcome.

Treating CV surveys like opinion polls about risk and insurance may both help their operational practice and assist in bringing the theories of environmental precaution and contingency assessment together. In practice, treating the results of such surveys as values for insurance eliminates the sterile arguments about the impossibility of valuing the invaluable. People can effectively insure against the risks to them of public decisions such as the siting of a new landfill site. They can buy houses in areas that are unlikely to be affected. They can lobby or campaign. They can bribe policy makers.

The treatment of environmental values as insurance premia against risky events allows us to compare survey estimates more realistically with other similar contingent values. 'Pain and suffering does not have a valid economic equivalent' (Griliches, 1993) outside insurance valuation. There is, however, an insurance market for it just as there is for certain classes of 'inconvenience'. Insurance routinely covers such non-use costs as option use and bequest losses. Disamenity losses are less well covered by actual insurance markets although contingent liability insurance is often an addition to loss-of-use insurance. In the absence, as yet, of well-developed contingent markets for disamenity the use of CV methods may play a significant role in estimating the likely behaviour of people in such markets.

References

Arrow, K., R. Solow, P.R. Portney, E.E. Leamer, R. Radner and H. Schuman (1993), *Report of the NOAA Panel on Contingent Valuation*, Washington DC: Resources for the Future.

Bangkok Post (1995), '*Lat Krabang Residents Set to Move Out*', 14 April.

Bangkok Post (1995), '*Sanitary Landfill "to End Garbage Woes"*', 18 April.

Bateman, I.J. and R.K. Turner (1992), *Evaluation of the Environment, the Contingent Valuation Method*, CSERGE Working Paper GEC 92-18, UEA, Norwich.

Blore, I. (1996), 'How Useful is Contingent Valuation to Decision-Makers?', *Public Administration and Development*, **16**, 215–32.

Blore, I. and F. Nunan (1996), 'Living with Waste: Public Valuation of Solid Waste Impacts in Bangkok', *Papers in the Administration of Development*, **57**, Development Administration Group, University of Birmingham.

Briscoe, J., P.F. de Castro, C. Griffin, J. North and O. Olsen (1990), 'Toward Equitable and Sustainable Rural Water Supplies: A Contingent Valuation Study in Brazil', *World Bank Economic Review*, **4** (2), 115–34.

Carson, R.T., J. Wright, N. Carson, A. Alberini and N. Flores (1995), *A Bibliography of Contingent Valuation Studies and Papers*, Natural Resource Damage Assessment, San Diego, CA.

CSERGE, Warren Spring Laboratory and ENTEC (1993), *Externalities from Landfill and Incineration*, a study for the Department of the Environment, London: HSMO.

Diamond, P.A. and J. Hausman (1993), 'On Contingent Valuation Measurement of Non-use Values', in J.A. Hausman (ed.), *Contingent Valuation: a critical assessment*, New York: North-Holland.

Glass, N. and J.T. Corkindale (1994), 'Value for Money in Environmental Valuation', in K.G. Willis and J.T Corkindale (eds), *Environmental Valuation: New Perspectives*, Wallingford, UK: CAB International.

Griliches, Z. (1993), 'Discussion of Papers Presented at the Symposium', in J.A. Hausman (ed.), *Contingent Valuation: A Critical Assessment*, New York: North-Holland.

Hanley, N. and C. Spash (1993), *Cost–Benefit Analysis and the Environment*, Aldershot, UK: Edward Elgar.

Langford, I.H., I.J. Bateman and H.D. Langford (1995), 'A Multilevel Modelling Approach to Triple-Bounded Dichotomous Choice Contingent Valuation', *Environmental and Resource Economics*, **5**, 1–15.

Mitchell, R.C. and R.T. Carson (1989), *Using Surveys to Value Public Goods: The Contingent Valuation Method*, Washington, DC: Resources for the Future.

Organization for Economic Cooperation and Development (1995), *The Economic Appraisal of Environmental Projects and Policies*, Paris: OECD.

Phantumvanit, D. and W. Liengcharernsit (1989), 'Coming to Terms with Bangkok's Environmental Problems', *Environment and Urbanization*, **1** (1), 31–9.

Sen, A.K. (1973), 'Internal Consistency of Choice', *Econometrica*, **61** (3), 495–521.

Serageldin, I. and A. Steer (eds) (1993), *Valuing the Environment*, Proceedings of the First Annual Conference on Environmentally Sustainable Development, Washington, DC: World Bank.

Setchell, C.A. (1995), 'The Growing Environmental Crisis in the World's Mega-cities: The Case of Bangkok', *Third World Planning Review*, **17** (1), 1–18.

Willis, K.G. (1994), 'Contingent Valuation in a Policy Context: The NOAA Report and its Implications for the Use of Contingent Valuation Methods in Policy Analysis in Britain', in K.G. Willis and J.T. Corkindale (eds), *Environmental Valuation: New Perspectives*, Wallingford, UK: CAB International.

Whittington, D. (forthcoming), 'CVM and HPM Approaches to Valuing Water and Sewerage Schemes in a Developing Country', in I.J. Bateman and K.G. Willis (eds), *Valuing Environmental Preferences: Theory and Practice of the Contingent Valuation Method in the US, EC and Developing Countries*, Oxford: Oxford University Press.

Zylicz, T., I. Bateman, S. Georgiou, A. Markowska, D. Dziegielewska, R.K. Turner, A. Graham and I. Langford (1995), 'Contingent Valuation of Eutrophication Damage in the Baltic Region', *Global Environmental Change Working Paper* 95-03, Centre for Social and Economic Research on the Global Environment, University of East Anglia, Norwich and University College London.

14 The environmental impact of irrigation: the social dimension. A case study of Sultanpur, India

Behrooz Morvaridi

14.1 Introduction

This chapter suggests that environmental impact assessment could be redefined as environmental and social impact assessment, since by definition environmental issues are social issues. Designing analytical tools and methodologies to take account of not only the economic but also the environmental and social effects of development projects is problematic. However, we should endeavour to establish a framework that assesses the qualitative as well as quantitative impacts of environmental change under the umbrella of sustainable development (Morvaridi, 1994).

It is important to base any decision making on a clear understanding of what is meant by 'impact', 'environment', 'social' and 'environmental degradation'. The environment is the geographical and physical location in which we live, work and produce, and is therefore locale-specific. The need for familiarity with local resource management strategies and the socio-economic constraints within which they operate is paramount for project design as well as policy planning. Any change in the environment, whether positive or negative, is usually defined by the impact that it has on resource availability and/or quality. Environmental degradation, whether of soil, water or air, for example, is understood as decline in the quality and/or quantity of that resource in the structure of a locale's ecosystem. In the reality of everyday life, this definition is only valuable if the impacts of changes in resource quality on people's well-being, in particular the poor's livelihoods and standards of living, that is, the social impacts, are appreciated. Indeed, current environmental concern stems from evidence that natural processes are being disrupted by productive activities to such an extent that the quality of life in the North and livelihoods in the South are being threatened.

According to World Bank guidelines, the objective of environmental assessment procedures is to ensure that development projects are sustainable (World Bank, 1995). This implies that appraisal of individual projects recognizes the cumulative interaction of economic, social and environmental concerns so that best productive use can be made of resources in order to eliminate poverty and improve human welfare. However, even though environmental impact assessment of development projects has moved away from a purely technical bias, it tends to focus on identifying and quantifying the impact of projects on the production and consumption of environmental resources from an economics perspective. For an EIA to cover social and economic impacts, several disciplines need to be involved. This begs the question of whether traditional appraisal techniques are adequate to address the measurement and valuation of sustainability or whether it is essential to devise new techniques. Attempts at expanding cost–benefit or multi-criteria analysis to include sustainability have tended to draw on a narrow definition of ecological or environmental sustainability (van Pelt, 1990). Such definitions limit themselves to resource use and avoid the issue of measuring social as well as environmental change. Although the measurement of costs and benefits is useful in project appraisal, socio-economic sustainability is too complex to be disaggregated into 'rules' for the purposes of cost–benefit analysis.

Part of the problem in carrying out EA on rural projects is lack of success in assigning weights to causal factors or establishing links between environmental change and socio-economic variables. This is particularly true with regard to explaining the relationship between environmental degradation and productivity, as this chapter shows. The case study, which relates to an irrigation project in Sultanpur, Uttar Pradesh (UP), provides an example of the complexity of the relationship between the perceived essential technology for development and the consequences for the environment and local people.

14.2 The case study: Sultanpur District
Environmental degradation is a process – environmental impact does not simply happen. Its assessment, therefore, should not be fixed in time such as happens in project planning or design but should be continuous. EA procedures are in favour of monitoring and good management and of establishing the necessary institutions or institutional strengthening. Project operation is important, not just design. This case study is not an example of environmental impact assessment, but rather an evaluation of the socio-economic impact of environmental change that the irrigation project induced. In the case study, many of the negative impacts of the irrigation project only became apparent after project completion and utilization. Poor management and weak infrastructural maintenance have contributed to salinization and waterlogging in the irrigation area. The impacts of this process are compounded by differential access to inputs,

resources and mitigating strategies. Severe patterns of land degradation are evident in UP, and many large areas of land suffering from salinization are found, particularly in eastern UP. Of the estimated 1.2 million ha of wasteland in UP as a whole, 800 000 ha are found in eastern UP. Many are degraded lands which have been abandoned once the costs of cultivating land suffering from soil degradation prove higher than the productive returns (Sharma, 1990).

Sultanpur District is located on the central eastern plain of Uttar Pradesh. Total population is 2.5 million with high population density. Ninety-six per cent of the population of the district live in rural areas where farming generates the main source of employment and income. Twenty-five per cent of the labour force are landless labourers and 59 per cent are engaged in cultivating crops and raising livestock (State Planning Institute, 1992).

Small farming dominates agrarian structure in Sultanpur. Eighty-two per cent of farmers own less than 1 ha and the average farm size was 0.63 ha in 1981. A reasonable amount of good quality land for an average household with eight members to farm for subsistence is 2.5 ha. If a household owns less, or has degraded (waterlogged or salinized) land, then they will have survival problems. Only 1 per cent of holdings own more than 5 ha in Sultanpur even though they account for 11 per cent of the cultivated area. Changes in the land size distribution over time show a systematic increase in the smaller categories.

In Sultanpur District several development initiatives were implemented in the late 1970s and 1980s, when Rajiv Ghandi was the elected MP for one area of Sultanpur. Some factories and roads were built and irrigation, land development, reclamation and forestry projects implemented. As a result, the district is relatively better off than the state average in terms of road and rural electrification, health and education facilities. The impact of these development initiatives on agriculture production has been limited, partly due to the political motivation behind them. For example, according to a local NGO officer, 'sugar factories came without sugar cane. We cultivated sugar cane a few years after the factory was established. And many couldn't cultivate sugar cane because their land was salinized or waterlogged.' Since Rajiv Ghandi's death, the area no longer receives the same level of investment.

The introduction of new technology to the region during the late 1970s and 1980s induced some changes in cropping patterns and allowed expansion of the cultivated area. Agriculture is mainly subsistence, consisting of 42 per cent paddy crop and 38 per cent wheat. Eighty-one per cent of the cropped area is under foodgrains – paddy and wheat – and about

11 per cent is under pulses. Only 2.1 per cent is under sugarcane cultivation (State Planning Institute, 1992). The area under wheat has doubled since 1950. By contrast, the area under paddy cultivation has changed little and increases in paddy yields are due to productivity growth per unit.

14.3 The Sarda Sahayak Irrigation Project

Irrigation has played a major role in developing agriculture to feed a growing population in Sultanpur, which has a semi-arid climate with around 95 per cent of annual rainfall received in 40 days (985 mm between June and October). Successful production of crops such as paddy and wheat is reliant on adequate irrigation of the cropping areas outside the monsoon season. Forty-two per cent of the cropped area is irrigated under the Sarda Sahayak Canal Irrigation Project. This project irrigates the lower reaches of the Sarda Canal Command area, diverting flows from two rivers – the Ghaghara and the Sarda. The area reached by canal irrigation via the two branch canals, Sultanpur and Jaunpur, lies between the Ghaghara and Ganga rivers, extending up to their confluence.

Since the inception of the Sarda Sahayak feeder channel in 1976, the ground water table in the canal area has risen. In 1974 the water table rose from 8.5 m in the pre-monsoon season to 6.7 m in the post-monsoon season. In 1984 the table rose from 5.3 m pre-monsoon to 3.9 m post-monsoon. In 1993 the ground water table varied from 0.5 m to 2 m below ground level. This has contributed to surface waterlogging and an increase in salinized areas. Waterlogged land is land where water is at or near the surface and stagnates for most of the year. There is very little ground slope in this region so water does not drain away easily. The drainage system in Sultanpur is poor and from June to September large areas are under water. The natural basin has been further blocked by the canal system and its inadequate infrastructure.

The causes of irrigation-induced salinization are primarily technical. Environmental problems such as waterlogging have been attributed to excessive seepage from the canals and poor drainage: 'the intensity of seepage is high because of faulty repairing of the sides of the canals and silting up the bottom of the canal'. Generally canals are not well maintained and when repairs are made the work is inadequate and low-quality materials are used. Soil and other particles are not removed from the water and they silt up the canal, reducing its capacity to hold water. This capacity in turn decreases and, with increases in water pressure, seepage occurs. Canal courses overflow and contribute to the rising water table in fields adjoining the irrigated area. As a result the areas suffer from waterlogging.

14.4 Assessment of the environmental impact of poorly managed irrigation: increases in wasteland

Initial data collection shows increasingly large areas of degraded land in Sultanpur District. Degraded land is land that has suffered 'a loss of intrinsic qualities or a decline in its capabilities' through loss of soil, or a change to a simpler floral/faunal composition through any number of processes (Barrow, 1991). With respect to this case study, land degradation means loss of qualitative and quantitative land productivity. At its worst, degraded land is abandoned and becomes wasteland. The patterns of degradation which render cultivated land to wasteland may differ widely – different types of water abuse or wind erosion, the manner in which land is used, land impoverishment through overgrazing or shifting cultivation.

Two kinds of wasteland are found in Sultanpur. The first is barren lands, such as rocky areas, which are under-utilized due to their physical properties. These are lands which could be brought under vegetation cover with investment. The second is lands degraded because of inappropriate soil and water management.

Some studies have estimated the extent of salt-affected and waterlogged lands within the Sarda Sahayak Irrigation Project (Joshi and Jha 1991; Shah 1989; Afroz and Singh, 1986). Joshi and Jha's primary data collection shows that 30 per cent of the farms were 'problem-affected'. On these farms 29 per cent of the area was uncultivated, whereas on 'normal' farms only 11 per cent was uncultivated. Most of these soils were alkaline. The cropping intensity was 110 per cent in the problem-affected and 166 per cent in the normal category farm. The Remote Sensing Agency reveals that in an area of about 1.43 million ha, about 74 000 ha were waterlogged on the surface. According to the director of Remote Sensing, 'land up to 2 km to 3 km away from canals can be affected. The water level in EUP has never been as deep as in WUP and this area does not suit canal irrigation for this reason, in fact over 130 years ago the British surveyed the area and decided against irrigation in the East for this reason, choosing the West instead. A low water table makes an area more vulnerable to degradation of the kind witnessed in Sultanpur.'

The Remote Sensing Director believes that the use of tubewells or a traditional system of lifting up water, which is more labour intensive, could make water resources more efficient if used alongside canal irrigation. The number of pump sets for tubewells has grown significantly in the district to substitute for poor access to canals and poor service from the irrigation scheme. The area under canal irrigation has increased from 16 per cent in 1964 to 35 per cent in 1991 and the area under tubewell irrigation has increased from 8 per cent to 54 per cent during the same years. Small farmers often prefer to purchase water from those who own tubewells, and many tubewell owners are making water supply a profitable business. Water from the irrigation canals is charged by crop and costs are higher. Furthermore, as one farmer pointed out, supplies from the canals are more unreliable than from tubewells: 'We never know when they are going to release water and when they do we do not know how long it will last and how much we will get.' However, one of the problems with tubewells is that many remain out of order due to inadequate maintenance, since responsibility for repair costs lies with owners, or because of lack of regular power supplies.

A high ground water table itself does not substantially reduce crop production, but it can restrict the kind of crops that can be cultivated on waterlogged land. Paddy is the obvious crop to cultivate on waterlogged land, although net incomes from paddy grown on waterlogged lands can be up to 55 per cent lower than from paddy grown on normal land (Joshi and Jha, 1991).

Even though yields per hectare in eastern UP have increased for most crops since the 1970s, they remain lower than yields in western UP. Low yields are attributed to low productivity from areas affected by the problems of soil salinity and alkalinity. The impact of salinization, that is, the excessive presence of salts in the soil or subsoil water as a result of waterlogging, can have devastating consequences for productivity. A high water table, poorly applied irrigation and drainage, and canal seepage can result in the upward movement of salts. When water evaporates, the salts are left in the soil and often accumulate in the root zone, inhibiting plant growth and reducing agricultural productivity. High temperatures in April, May and June induce capillary action to bring harmful salts to the surface, known as secondary salinization. Saline lands are known locally by a variety of names and by far the most common term used is 'usar' derived from the Sanskrit word 'ushtra,' meaning barren or sterile.

Some crops are more affected than others by salinization. Yields of wheat grown on salt-affected lands are only 60 per cent of yields from normal lands, and yields from waterlogged lands only 50 per cent. Production efficiency losses are the net result of increased costs of production on degraded lands. Paddy per unit costs rise by 60 per cent on saline land and by 20 per cent on waterlogged land. Costs for wheat increase by 85 per cent on salinized land (Joshi and Dayanatha, 1991).

The effect on cropping and productivity for small households can be devastating. A typical household has nine members who own 2.1 acres of land (an elderly mother, one married son with three children, another son and two daughters). Even though the family's land is situated about 5 km away from the canal and its distributors, the land still suffers from excess water. The household cultivates paddy and sometimes, when the land is suitable, wheat. In the Rabi (winter) season the land remains fallow and wheat cannot be cultivated or is cultivated late because it is not possible to plough the land, due to waterlogging. If the right time for sowing in the agricultural cycle is missed, yield per hectare is low and the labour requirement is high. As the farmer explained: 'the water table is high when I prepare the fields for sowing the seeds in Rabi season. We have to sow our land late because we still have water on our land and it cannot be prepared. I have given up as it is not worth farming for such a low yield which anyway is insufficient for our own needs.' This shows how farmers are restricted in their choice of crop and how they are forced to select crops that are more tolerant of saline soil waterlogging, such as paddy. Household incomes decline when they cannot cultivate cash crops or high-value crops, and the food cultivated for their own consumption is restricted. As one household head said with embarrassment, 'we would like to invite you to come and be our guest for a few days but we can only offer you bread and salt during the monsoon period'.

At very high levels, salinization renders land uncultivable. In Sultanpur, partial to complete loss of productivity has occurred in many areas, to the extent that cultivated land has been converted into uncultivable land or wasteland. In aggregate figures, wastelands are often categorized as 'fallow land' and regional level data imply that 'fallow' land is increasing. This provides an example of how misinterpretation of the processes of degradation and their impact on farm productivity can easily be made from aggregate analysis. Regional and district level data, as well as an extensive literature, attribute salinization and abandoned wasteland to bad management of the irrigation system. Initial data collection at village and household level indicates that the processes of degradation are extremely complex.

14.5 The socio-economics of degradation: access to resources
Symptoms of over-exploitation, such as waterlogging-induced salinization, have been identified in many different socio-economic and ecological situations, but there is generally little success in assigning weight to causal factors or establishing patterns of links between environmental, demographic and socio-economic variables. In this case study the poor maintenance of the irrigation canals over the past 20 years has been a cause of land degradation. However, the problems associated with waterlogging and salinization have been compounded by socio-economic and institutional conditions.

Initial data collection shows that increasingly large areas of wasteland, which are either privately or government-owned or community 'Panchayat' lands, are being abandoned in Sultanpur District. Land is in high demand due to increases in the ratio of people to land, and any surplus land available tends to be wasteland, that is, degraded land that has been abandoned or land of little productive value. These areas tend either to belong to marginal farmers, having been sold to them by the Zamindars after the Zamindari Abolition Act of 1951, or to have been distributed to landless or low-caste farmers by the government (Chauhan, 1990).

In Sultanpur villages, the impact on household survival of land degradation caused by the inefficient management of irrigation and poor management of land will depend on a household's ability to install mechanisms to mitigate negative impacts. The most fertile land belongs to the larger farmers. A low caste sharecropper complained that 'the government gave all the bad lands to us. We cannot grow crops, or if we can the yield is so low that it costs us to grow crops. We cannot afford to reclaim the land even with the help of the government. The rich farmers even have their eye on our lands because they can afford to reclaim land.'

The soil alkalinity is the main problem and is very high. Average soil pH is 9.5 and the maximum is 10.5. Investment in wasteland-improving measures in Sultanpur has the potential to extend the cultivated area to achieve optimal utilization of land in this densely populated zone. However, in the wasteland areas where low castes live, poverty is at its worst. Few of the poorer farmers are in a position to make these lands workable since reclamation and land development are expensive, and even with government support and subsidies they cannot afford it. Attempted reclamation programmes have, therefore, had a slow response since the poor are more concerned with their immediate needs and survival. It takes a minimum of four to five years to reclaim land, sometimes more, and it requires funding, technology, skill and time. The cost of reclamation is high – between Rs 30 000 per hectare for less severely degraded land to Rs 50 000 per hectare in 1993 for very degraded land (£1 = 45): Table 14.1.

Many smallholdings have sold their land to the larger farmers who can afford to invest in developing wasteland, and have become either landless themselves or sharecroppers to meet household food demand. Alternative land tenure arrangements to ownership are often a response to a largely unchanging resource base, especially under conditions of continued growth in family size. When the ratio of land to the number of household members is low, productivity may not meet household subsistence demands. This is often the case where the application of new technology to increase productivity per unit is low. In this case study changes in land quality through degradation have led to marginal farmers relying on sharecropping arrangements. Even though sharecropping is illegal in India, it provides households with access to more land or better-quality land, even if only in the short term.

*Table 14.1 Costs of land reclamation: unit cost for
reclaiming 1 ha of salt-affected area for each
component of work (1993) prices*

Component items	Cost per hectare (Rs)
Cost of boring	3 000
Cost of pumpset	4 500
Drainage development	3 000
On-farm development	5 000
Cost of soil amendment	12 500
Cost of green manuring	1 500
Total	30 000

Source: Field Survey

Degradation in Sultanpur is not always a direct result of the poorly maintained irrigation system. Land management and differential access to
resources is also affecting soil quality and long-term productivity in the
area. Sharecropped land, for example, is vulnerable to degradation in the
villages of Sultanpur due to lack of continuity of land management.
Farmers do not know how much fertilizer or what kind of fertilizer a previous sharecropper has applied, because sharecropping arrangements are
only for short periods (one year). Sharecropped land often suffers from
continuous cropping and imbalanced applications of fertilizer, which
exacerbates soil acidity in the affected areas. Sharecroppers as well as
poorer farmers tend to use nitrogenous fertilizers alone rather than combined with phosphatic and potassic fertilizers because it aids crop growth
and is all they can afford. Acidic soil is the result of not applying the correct balance of inputs.

Many small farmers, who do not cultivate commercial crops but operate on a consumption basis, simply cannot afford to leave land fallow and
so cultivate their land every year. This means that land does not have time
to recover soil nutrient content, and because these farmers have limited
access to inputs, they do not add fertilizer to compensate. They rely on
working as seasonal labourers for others to sustain the household. In
good seasons they may be able to make some surplus, but they rarely
accept the membership of cooperatives that provide credit because they
fear they would never be able to guarantee repayment and would therefore suffer harassment.

Larger holdings that are integrated into the commercial market
produce a higher yield per hectare than smaller farmers, reflecting differ-

Table 14.2 Average yield per acre by size and crops

Size in hectares	Crop, kg/ha	Yield
1–5	Paddy	700
	Wheat	500
5–10	Paddy	1000
	Wheat	700
>10	Paddy	1500
	Wheat	1000

Source: Field Survey

ential access to resources. Only commercial farmers are rich enough to take up offers of formal credit. Table 14.2 shows that the yield per acre of those who own above 1 acre is high compared to smaller farms.

14.6 Environmental degradation, gender and social relations
Within the household the social impacts of degradation differ according to age, gender and role. When the land is insufficient for survival, many marginal farmers take manual jobs throughout the year, work in other villages or release one labourer during the off-peak season to work in towns or cities as wage labourers. A fairly recent trend has been seasonal migration for agricultural work since there is insufficient alternative employment in the area. Men tend to go after harvesting and sowing their land in December and return to the village in April in time to harvest the wheat. Due to the lack of off-farm opportunities, many farmers migrate some distance away from their villages for work.

High rates of male out-migration from the area because of degradation increase the labour demands on women. Two brothers who inherited the family holding from their father decided not to divide that land but remain as a joint household along with their mother and two sisters. This is a strategy adopted by a number of households to cope with productivity declines linked to degraded land, since the larger the size of the holding, the greater the chances of maintaining productivity and household survival. Despite the fact that their land is 5 km away from the canal, seepage has reached their land, damaging not only the land but also their house. Since the holding has continued to suffer from decline in productivity and income, one brother who is married with three children has migrated to Delhi, where he works as a watchman, returning to the village every three months to visit his wife and children: 'That is how we can survive,' said the wife. 'We all also work for other people as share-croppers and to get wheat for ourselves. But even this is not enough because half of my share goes to the landowner. My share will last for only four to five months. We have to work as labourers for the rest of the year and purchase grain from the wealthy people or those who have larger land in the village, that is if we can find jobs. Often it is very diffi-cult to find jobs, which is why some families have to eat salt and bread. If we did not have enough people who could work, we would have to go without too'.

When a household decides to sharecrop or work as wage labour, the age and sex distribution of household members will influence the choices made. 'We have enough labour at home, that is why we are in a better position to rent land', said the son. 'Some landowners rent us their saline land that they cannot be bothered to work themselves'. A strict division of labour by gender operates in the area. Therefore when making land management decisions a household must be sure that labour for all peri-ods of the agricultural cycle can be guaranteed. If women harvest and weed and a household has several women of working age, then they can be employed as wage labour for these key tasks when they have finished their own land or provide sufficient labour for sharecropping. In this family the two unmarried sisters and the wife of the son working in Delhi provide labour. The grandmother looks after the young children but even she works in the field in peak periods.

Village women complained that they have to work much harder on land that is degraded and it takes a longer time to weed and harvest. Labour inputs are much higher on waterlogged land than on normal soil. Saline land requires more labour for low productivity. At the time when there is drought many farmers have to purchase grain from the larger holding households who act as merchants in the village: 'But often in drought period we do not have enough money and then we have to buy it and pay later with interest for every rupee that we borrow. When these people buy grain from us we sell it at one-third of the price. When we buy grain from them they sell it three times higher than our price'.

14.7 What can be learnt from the case study?
The synergism of environmental and socio-economic interactions, as seen in this case study, means that environmental and social impact are interrelated. This is the crux of sustainable development and all it sets

out to achieve. For the purposes of assessment, therefore, social impact and environmental impact should be integrated into one framework that is interdiscplinary and draws on the epistemology of social and natural sciences.

Assessment during project design and planning, although essential, will always be based on potential impacts so that measures to avoid or mitigate them can be built into the project. It is also necessary, however, for assessment to relate to the dynamics of the development process by assuming a time-frame that incorporates not only predicted responses but also post-operative monitoring.

The following measures, if emphasized in environmental assessment procedures, could help to recognize and integrate social impact into the project cycle. They focus on issues of operational relevance.

Monitoring

The case study demonstrates the complexity of environmental change and how different forms of degradation do not operate exclusively, but often reinforce each other. The degradation originally induced through poor irrigation is compounded by unsustainable land management practices. The degradation has been gradual and cumulative – in this case study the process of degradation, measured by changes in the water table, rates of waterlogging and declines in productivity linked to damaged lands, has been continuing for 20 years. As the degradation has increased, its social impact has intensified.

EA involves assessment of the locale's socio-economic as well as geographic and physical conditions. It is important that study of the field or village level includes analysis of socio-economic conditions and that this is integrated into monitoring and mitigation plans so that they can be effective. In this case study, since land is scarce, in particular good-quality land, a household's ability to counteract environmental degradation is important if land is to maintain some productivity. Reclamation measures are available but at a cost. Survival strategies such as migration and sharecropping that offer little long-term security are often the option for families with damaged land who cannot afford reclamation measures. This both reflects and accentuates social differentiation.

Monitoring of project implementation would include assessment of the mitigating measures in place. In particular, monitoring can help to establish mechanisms to take account of the specific needs of different groups.

Management

Irrigation projects have been implemented as a driving force behind the intensification of agriculture in densely populated agricultural areas. In the case of Sultanpur the inefficient management of a major irrigation project has been cited as the main cause of severe land degradation in the study area. Much of this damage could have been avoided if management of the project had been more rigorous so that maintenance was carried out. Furthermore, water pricing and availability to poorer farmers needs to be incorporated into management so that the poor are not dependent on richer farmers who own their own wells.

The case study shows that the environmental impacts of the poorly maintained irrigation system had severe social consequences. Environmental assessment involves mitigation plans to assure sustainability of a project's infrastructure. For the purposes of irrigation projects institutional and technical capability must go hand in hand with improved water management to mitigate against the potential problems of waterlogging and salinization.

Community participation

The success of linking environmental effects to social impacts will depend on the extent of community or local involvement with a project. Development projects are planned for a particular locale. Suitable mitigating or monitoring measures can be built into the project if 'local people's' involvement with the project cycle is improved. This will involve assessment of the varied impacts on different groups in society, including gender differentiation, so that their specific needs can be taken into account.

The means by which local involvement is accommodated in current environmental assessment procedures (of the World Bank and other donor agencies) is through 'consultation'. But what do we mean by 'consultation'? Scheduled public meetings, or similar, are simply not sufficient. Communities are not comprised of homogenous groups of people, and if environmental assessment is expected to include 'effects on human beings', it is necessary to be clear that all interested parties are included. The problem with using the concept of 'consultation' is that often only the local representatives are consulted, and they tend to be the educated or richer members of a community, for instance large landowning farmers or the heads of the village. They do not necessarily represent the interests of all community members. Many are easily neglected – the women who are the main actors in rural areas, sharecroppers, landless farmers and the poor.

Rural households are dependent on land as a source of income and livelihood. Local people understand their environment; they know the social and economic history of their forefathers' relationship with the land. 'Consultation' needs to be effective and this means involving local people with the project – decisions on its operation or its management. Many of the elites who are involved in the establishment, infrastructure and management of projects find communication with local people difficult. Qualified staff who are trained in consultation techniques are necessary to encourage local people to participate in the project cycle and to establish trust and mutual support.

References

Afroz, A. and P. Singh (1986), 'Assessment of environmental impacts of Sarda Sahayak Canal irrigation project of Uttar Pradesh', *International Journal of Environmental Studies,* **28**, 123–30.

Barrow, C.J. (1991), *Land Degradation*, Cambridge: Cambridge University Press.

Chauhan, K.N. (1990) 'The fallacy of wastelands in Uttar Pradesh' in S.C. Sharma, R.B. Chaturvedi and O.P. Mishra (eds), *Utilisation of Wastelands for Sustainable Development in India*, New Delhi: Concept Publishing Company.

Indian Agricultural Research Institute (1989), '*Resource Analysis for Integrated Development*', Water Technology Centre Sultanpur District, New Delhi: IARI.

Joshi, Pramod K. and Dayanatha Jha (1991), 'Farm level effects of soil degradation in Sharda Sahayak irrigation project', International Food Policy Research Institute, *Working Papers on Future Growth in Indian Agriculture,* 1.

Morvaridi, B. (1994), 'Sustainable development and project appraisal', in J. Weiss (ed.), *The Economics of Project Appraisal and the Environment,* Aldershot, UK: Edward Elgar.

Pelt, M.J.F. van (1990), 'Project appraisal and sustainability: methodological challenges', *Project Appraisal ,* **5** (3) 139–58.

Shah, P.N. (1989), 'Assessment of surface waterlogging in the Sarda Sahayak Canal Command Area of UP through digital analysis of IRS-A data', mimeo.

Sharma, C.S. (1990) 'User land reclamation measures in India with special reference to Sangrampur Block, District Sultanpur (UP)', in S.C. Sharma, R.B. Chaturvedi and O.P. Mishra (eds), *Utilisation of Wastelands for Sustainable Development in India*, New Delhi: Concept Publishing Company.

State Planning Institute of Uttar Pradesh (1992), *Statistical Report of Sultanpur*, Finance and Statistical Department, UP.

World Bank (1995), *Mainstreaming the Environment: The World Bank Group and the Environment Since the Rio Earth Summit*, Washington DC: World Bank.

Index

Abaza, Hussein 14, 135
Abdalla, C. W. 163
Abelson, Peter 21, 113
actual carbon sequestration index
    (ACSI) 79
Adams, W. M. 64, 66
Africa 31, 93, 110, 191
Afroz, A. 235
agricultural policies 34
    changes in 88, 89–90, 93, 97–9,
        109–10
    decision making on 15, 93–4
    in developing countries 15, 88–111
    EIA 15, 88–111
    non-price policies 104–5
    on prices 93, 94–104, 110
    sustainability issues 88–92
agricultural sector
    in developing countries 15, 17, 35,
        36, 39, 88–111, 233–4
    natural resources and 90–92
    population pressure on 92, 93–4,
        233
agricultural subsidies 36, 93
Agritex 201
aid agencies 8, 9, 29, 73, 112, 128, 129,
    134
Alexandratos, N. 100
altruistic value 169, 171
America see United States
analytical methods 6, 16, 46–52
    cost–revenue analysis 140, 141
    discounting 15, 119–20
    dynamic analysis 93–4
    impact chain technique 146, 147
    investment appraisal 8–9, 127
    modelling 68, 74–83, 169
    multi-criteria analysis 126, 130,
        131, 135
    multi-variate analysis 209–11
    net present value 6

for policy decisions 15, 93–4
rational-choice model 10
static analysis 93
valuation methods 6, 130
    see also contingent valuation;
        cost–benefit analysis
Anderson, Dennis 113
Anderson, G. D. 164
Andrasko, K. K. 74
appraisal see economic appraisal;
        environmental impact assessment;
        project-level appraisal; social
        impact assessment
Arts, J. 135
Asian Development Bank 8, 20, 21,
    135
Atkinson, G. 70
avoided costs 160–61
    see also economic valuation

Baker, R. G. 189
Bangladesh 100
Bangkok
    landfill refuse sites 17–18, 217–30
    see also Thailand
Barrow, C. J. 235
Basel Convention, 1989 47
Batchelor, C. H. 214
Bauer, P. 66
behaviour prediction 227
benefit transfers (BT)
    in economic valuation 120–21, 122,
        160–61
    in SAPs 32, 43
bequest value 171
Bergstrom, J. C. 157, 159, 160, 163
biodiversity 74, 75, 77, 79
    see also global climate change
Bird, Catherine 113
Bishop, R. C. 163
Bisset, Ron 27–8

Blore, Ian 17–18, 134, 225
Bogen, K. T. 163
Bond, M. 110
Boothroyd, P. 135
Boserup, E. 92, 100
Boyle, K. J. 157, 159, 160
Bradford University 4, 20
Bregha, François 26
Brew, D. 134
Briscoe, J. 227
British Airways 143, 144
British Geological Survey 201
Bromley, Daniel W. 122
Bronstein, D. A. 4, 139
Brookshire, D. S. 213
Brown, Katrina 113
Brown, L. 110
Bruen, M. P. 135
Brundtland Commission 63–4
Bull, W. B. 191
Bumb, B. 93
Burdge, R. J. 7, 20, 184
Burgher, B. M. 169
Burt, O. 163
Butterworth, J. A. 214

Canada 7, 54, 55
Canter, Larry W. 6, 16, 63, 133, 145,
    155, 181
Carpenter, R. A. 135
Carson, R. T. 220, 225, 227
cash crop farming 36
    see also farming practices
Central Statistical Office (Zimbabwe)
    200
Centre for Social and Economic
    Research of the Global
    Environment (CSERGE) 64, 218
Chambers, R. 213, 214
Chauhan, K. N. 238
chemical hazards 47–8
    see also environmental degradation
choice
    dichotomous 210, 221–4
Chowdhury, A. 20
circular models
    of land use 74–83
    of sustainable development 66
Cleaver, K. 93, 99, 100, 200

Cline, W. 10
coastal defence projects *see* flood
    defence projects
collector wells 201–6, 215
    see also water supplies
Collins, B. D. 189
commercial criteria
    decision making based on 125–6,
    134
Commission for Sustainable
    Development *see* UN
    Commission
    for Sustainable Development
communications plans 16, 176, 179,
    180–2, 183
community impact evaluation (CIE)
    131, 135
    in the development process 141–52
    evolution of 139, 141–3
    integration issues in 143–4
    in Kenya 7, 189–99
    methodology 144–6
    options process 146, 148–9, 150,
    151
    project descriptions 144–5
    reconciliation process 150, 151
    stakeholders in 146–7, 150
    in UK 16, 143–4
    see also cost–benefit analysis
compensation schemes 74–5
    willingness-to-accept (WTA) 122
competitiveness 34, 37
Comprehensive Environmental
    Response, Compensation, and
    Liability Act (CERCLA), 1980
    (USA) 155
consistency issues 15–16, 125–33
consultation process *see* public
    participation
contingent valuation (CV) studies 15,
    17–18, 73, 113, 115–17, 121,
    160–61, 180
    criterion validity 225–6
    field studies and 204–7
    of landfill sites 219, 220, 224–9
    methodology 208–13, 226–9
    risk assessment in 228–9
    of water supply studies 17, 200–16
    see also economic valuation

Corbett, J. 206
Corkindale, J. T. 226
cost internalization 42, 62, 64, 125, 218
cost manuals 168–9
  see also data collection
Costa Rica 72, 113
cost–benefit analysis (CBA) 8–10, 18 20, 21
  consistency issues 15–16, 125–33
  discounting in 9–10, 130, 135
  distributional consequences 131, 135, 142
  EIA and 9–10, 15–16, 19–20, 62, 63, 114, 117, 139–41, 157, 164, 178, 180
  environmental 157, 164, 168, 171–2
  evaluation methods 130–32
  evolution of 139, 140, 142
  failures in 142–3
  of flood defence projects 178, 180
  of ground water remediation 164–71
  of policies, plans and programmes 10, 21, 114
  relevance issues 15–16, 125–33
  risk assessment in 9, 131
  scope of 129–30
  SIA and 9, 10, 18, 130, 135
  uncertainties in 9, 131, 135
cost–revenue analysis (CRA) 140, 141
costs
  of environmental degradation 41–2, 119–20
Counce, R. M. 169
Council of Environmental Quality (USA) 7, 8
Country Wildlife Trust (UK) 181
Countryside Commission (UK) 181
credit/interest rates 93
criterion validity 225–6
  see also contingent valuation
Cropper, Maureen 112, 118, 121
Crutchfield, S. R. 163
Cruz, W. 20, 37–8, 68, 89
Culpepper, M. 169
Cummings, R. G. 207, 213
currency devaluation 34, 36
Curry, S. 20, 135

data collection
  benefit transfers 120–21, 122, 160–61
  cost manuals 168–9
  for EIA 41, 79, 113–14, 176, 190–91
  geographical information systems 77, 79
  information management and 176
  policy sites 120
  by satellite 79, 235
  study sites 120
Daubert, J. T. 162
de Boer, J. 20
de Jough, P. 135
decision making
  on agricultural policies 15, 93–4
  on commercial criteria 125–6, 134
  cost–benefit analysis and 125–38
  economic appraisal and 10–11, 125, 164–71
  EIA and 3–4, 6, 14–15, 37–8, 125–38, 164–71, 175–6
  on flood defence projects 175–6
  integration issues in 11–13, 16, 18–19
  SEA and 27–8
deforestation
  acceleration of 34, 35, 36
  in Brazil 69
  control of 62, 75–81
  effects of 39, 75
  in Thailand 75, 77–81
  in USA 69, 81
  see also forestry sector
Department of Defence (USA) 169
Department of Energy (USA) 169
Department of the Environment (DOE) (UK) 9, 69, 114, 135, 176, 180
Department of the Interior (USA) 169
Department of Water Development (Zimbabwe) 201
Deren, B. 20
desertification 36, 62
Devarajan, S. 20, 135
developed countries 4, 5, 7, 18, 62, 64, 110
  see also United Kingdom; United States

developing countries 4, 5, 8, 48–9,
    61–2
  agricultural policies 15, 88–111
  agricultural sector 15, 17, 35, 36,
    39, 233–4
  balance of payments 29–33
  cost internalization 42, 62, 64, 125,
    218
  cost–benefit analysis in 8, 10, 20
  deforestation 34, 35, 36, 39, 62, 69,
    75–81
  economic problems 29–31, 37, 74–5
  EIA in 14–15, 61–87, 128
  environmental degradation 17–18,
    30, 35, 36, 43, 47–8, 61–2, 189
  external intervention in 73–83,
  forestry sector 35, 36, 37, 39, 49,
    50, 62, 69,72, 73, 74, 75–81, 120
  policy making 88–111
  project-level appraisal in 20
  SAP in 29–45
  SEA in 26
  sustainable development in 61–87
  trade liberalization policies 31, 32,
    33–4, 36, 40
  see also farming practices;
    individual countries
development *see* sustainable
  development
development balance sheets (DBS)
  142
development banks 9, 128, 129, 134
developmentalist approach 66
Devine, P. J. 8
Diamond, Peter A. 73, 116, 220
Diang'a, A. 189
dichotomous choice (DC) 210, 221–4
disamenity costs *see* environmental
  damage
discounting
  in cost–benefit analysis 9–10, 130,
    135
  differential 119
  in economic valuations 119–20
  procedures for 15, 119–20
disease *see* health and life
distributional consequences 9, 10, 15,
    29, 66
  in CBA 131, 135, 142
  in EIA 131, 135

Dixon, J. A. 73, 112, 134
Djeddour, Mohammed 26
Dorfman, J. H. 163
dose-response relationships 218, 219,
    226–7
double-counting problem 129–30, 131,
    135
Dreze, J. 20
Dube, T. 207, 214
Dunne, T. 189
Durdag, M. 21
dynamic analysis 93–4

Eckstein, O. 142
eco-imperialism 62, 63
ecological value 157
economic appraisal 3–4, 8–11
  contingent valuation 15, 17–18, 73,
    113, 115–17, 121, 160–61, 180,
    200–216, 219, 220, 224–9
  decision making and 10–11, 125,
    164–71
  EIA and 6, 9, 14–15, 16, 21,
    112–24, 125, 126, 134
  investment appraisal 8–9, 127
  see also cost–benefit analysis
economic and fiscal policies
  in EU 51–2
  in Kenya 197
  reform of 89
  SAPs for 30–31, 32–3, 34
economic growth 29–30, 31, 32, 42
  sustainable development and 62,
    64, 65, 189
economic problems
  in developing countries 29–31, 37
economic reform 29, 30
economic valuation 72–3
  applications of 112–15
  avoided costs 160–61
  benefit transfers 120–21, 122,
    160–61
  contingent valuation 15, 17–18, 73,
    113, 115–17, 121, 160–61, 180,
    200–216, 219, 220, 224–9
  controversy about 115–21, 126, 134
  discounting in 119–20
  of environmental impacts (EVE) 6,
    9, 14–15, 16, 21, 112–24, 125,
    126, 134

existence value 116–17, 157, 171
of flood defence projects 178, 180
future of 121–2
of ground water remediation 157–64
of health and life 15, 117–18
hedonic pricing 160–61, 180, 219, 220
integration issues in 164–71
of landfill sites 218–29
market valuation of physical effects 121
methodology 164–71, 208–13
options exercises and 121–2, 157, 220–26, 228
risk assessment and 117–18, 201, 205, 228–9
total economic value 157–61
US bias in 115, 118–19, 121
of water supplies 17, 200–216
willingness-to-accept compensation 122
willingness-to-accept risk 176
willingness-to-pay 115–16, 117–19, 121–2, 180, 206–7, 208–13, 219, 220, 221–6, 227
education 39, 65
Eduljee, G. 135
Edwards, S. F. 162
efficiency costs 142
see also cost–benefit analysis
EIA Centre 135
electricity generation 114
endangered species 47, 48
energy policies 34, 36
energy supplies 47, 74, 114
English Nature 181
Environment Agency (UK) 16, 114, 175–6, 180, 181–2
environment industry 47
environmental action plans (EAPs) 17, 178, 185–7
environmental cost–benefit analysis (ECBA) 157, 164, 168, 171–2
see also policies, plans and programmes
environmental degradation 10, 17, 27, 29
chemical hazards 47–8
costs of 41–2, 119–20

desertification 36, 62
in developing countries 17–18, 30, 35, 36, 43, 47–8, 61–2, 189
endangered species 47, 48
farming practices and 96–9
by ground water remediation 160–61, 164
hazardous wastes 47
by irrigation projects 18, 231–44
land degradation 17, 189–99, 234, 235, 236, 237–44
by landfill sites 17–18, 218–19, 224
population level and 92
salinization 234, 235, 236
of sand harvesting 17, 189–99
SAPs and 30, 35, 36, 43
social effects of 240–41
water pollution 36
see also deforestation
environmental impact assessment (EIA)
of agricultural policies 15, 88–111
consistency issues 15–16, 125–33
cost–benefit analysis and 9–10, 15–16, 19–20, 62, 63, 114, 117, 139–41, 157, 164, 178, 180
data collection for 41, 68, 79, 113–14, 176, 190–91
decision making and 3–4, 6, 14–15, 37–8, 125–38, 164–71, 175–6
definition of 3–11, 62–3, 139, 176, 231–2
in developing countries 3–4, 5, 14–15, 61–87, 128
economic appraisal and 6, 9, 14–15, 16, 21, 112–24, 125, 126, 134
of flood defence projects 16–17, 175–88
of ground water remediation projects 155–74
in India 231–44
integrated management of 175–88
integration issues in 4, 11–13, 16–17, 18, 67–73, 231–44
of irrigation projects 231–44
in Kenya 17, 189–99
of land degradation 240–44
of landfill refuse sites 17–18, 217–20

methodology 6, 52–5, 93–4, 128, 130–32, 134, 164–71, 176–80, 190–91, 193
OECD studies of 14, 46–57, 89, 120, 121, 127, 134, 220
of policies, plans and programmes 5–6, 7, 8, 14, 141–4
project-level appraisal and 5–6, 7, 8, 15–16, 63, 125–38
relevance issues 15–16, 125–33
of sand harvesting 17, 189–99
SAPs and 4, 5, 14, 25, 29, 30, 33–45
scope of 129–30, 135
SIA and 130, 133–4, 175–6, 184
sustainable development and 61–87, 195, 197
trade liberalization policies and 4, 5, 14, 46–57
in United Kingdom 143, 144
in United States 133, 155–74
see also economic valuation; strategic environmental assessment
environmental indicators *see* natural resource accounting
environmental management 43, 62, 64, 190
see also sustainable resource management
environmental pollution 47, 48, 54, 62, 74, 110, 113, 121
from landfill sites 218–19, 224
see also global climate change
Environmental Protection Agency (USA) 157, 168–9, 171
environmental protection schedules (EPS) 187
environmental quality 65, 77, 127
environmental statements (ES) 6, 176, 177–8, 179, 182, 183, 185
environmentalist approach 66
error predictions 145
Eskeland, G. S. 134
European Union 5, 51–2, 134
exchange rate policies 32, 34, 93
existence value 116–17, 157, 171
see also economic valuation
exploitation *see* environmental degradation

exports 34, 36, 37, 43, 93
Exxon Valdez oil spillage, 1989 115

farming practices 35, 36, 89–92, 93, 94
cash crops 36
changes in 97, 100
environmental degradation and 96–9
fertilizer use 50, 51, 105–6
herbicide use 105, 106
intensive 92, 93, 96, 100
land degradation and 93, 96, 110
monoculture 92
pesticide use 50, 51, 105–6
sharecropping 236–7, 238, 239
shifting cultivation 92
subsistence 35, 36, 233–4
technology and 88, 92–4, 99, 100–104, 109, 110, 233
types of 95–6, 105–6
see also agricultural sector
feasibility studies *see* project-level appraisal
Feather, P. M. 163
Federal Remediation Technologies Roundtable 169
fertility levels *see* population levels
fertilizers 50, 51, 105–6
see also farming practices
financial analysis (FA) 140, 141
see also economic valuation
financial sector reform 34
fiscal policies *see* economic and fiscal policies
fisheries sector 48–9
Flood Control Act, 1936 (USA) 139
flood defence projects
cost–benefit analysis of 178, 180
decision making on 175–6
EAP for 17, 178, 185–7
economic gains from 178, 180
economic valuation of 178, 180
effects of 184
importance of 175–6
integrated management of 175–88
in UK 16–17, 175–88
Food and Agriculture Organization (FAO) 105
food supplies 88, 110
garden schemes 201–8, 215

global climate change and 113
global food debate 88, 110
security of 205–8
water supplies and 200–208, 215,
236–7
willingness-to-pay issues 213
forestry sector 49, 50, 62, 83
conservation issues 73, 74, 75, 81
global climate change and 113
logging 81
reforestation 37, 74, 75, 76, 79
tropical forests 62, 72, 73, 74, 120
see also deforestation
Foster, S. S. D. 162
Foster, V. 162
Fox, G. 89, 93, 99
Fox, R. C. 189
Franck, B. 9
Frank, A. G. 65
Freeman, A. Myrick 94, 112
Freshwater Foundation (USA) 162
fuel supplies *see* energy supplies
future benefits 119–20
bequest value 171
future developments 19–20

garden schemes 201–8, 215
see also food supplies
General Agreement on Tariffs and
Trade 55
geographical information systems
(GIS) 77, 79
Ghandi, Rajiv 233
Gianessi, L. P. 163
Gisser, M. 162
Glass, N. 226
Glasson, J. 139
global climate change 61, 62, 73, 74,
75
costs of 113
food supplies and 113
see also environmental pollution
Global Environment Facility 113
global food debate 88, 110
see also food supplies
goals achievement matrix 131, 135
Goldsmith, E. 62
Goodland, Robert 26, 28, 30, 35, 37,
43, 48
Graham-Tomasi, T. 163

Grainger, Alan 14, 70–71, 72, 74, 75,
77, 81, 82, 135
Grainger's S index 70–71
Great Britain *see* United Kingdom
Green GDP concept 70
Griffin, C. C. 163
Griliches, Z. 228
Grima, A. P. 135
Grindle, M. S. 10
ground water remediation projects
cost manuals for 168–9
cost–benefit analysis 164–71
costs of 164
ecological value 157
economic valuation 157–64, 168–71
EIA 155–74
environmental degradation from
160–61, 164
impacts of 160–61, 164
in situ value 157
methodology 164–72
modelling of 169
remedial studies 164, 168
total economic value 157–61
traditional impact studies of 155–7
in USA 16, 155–74
valuation case studies 162–3
valuation methodology 157–61

Hanemann, W. Michael 116, 209
Hanley, N. 21, 228
Hansen, S. 30
hard approach
to sustainable development 64–5
Harrison, G. W. 207, 213
Harrison, P. 200
Hauser, A. 163
Hausman, Jerry A. 73, 116, 220
hazardous wastes 47
see also environmental degradation
HDI *see* UN human development
index
health and life
disease 48
economic valuation of 15, 117–19
risks to 17–18, 113, 218
safety 54, 118
health services 39, 65
see also social welfare
Heaney, D. 135

Hearne, R. 126, 134
Heathrow Airport 143
hedonic pricing 160–61, 180, 219, 220
  see also economic valuation
Hellerstein, D. R. 163
herbicides 105, 106
  see also farming practices
Hickie, David 16–17, 176, 177, 184
Higgitt, D. L. 189
Hill, M. 135
Hoel, M. 74
Holland, M. M. 163
Holtz, Susan 26
housing 175, 176
  house prices 160–61, 180, 219, 220
Howe, Charles W. 114
Hughes, J. 20
human capital 64, 65, 66, 72, 82
  see also natural capital

impact chain technique 146, 147
implementation caps 33–4
in situ value 157
income flows *see* benefit transfer
    measures
Index of Sustainable Economic
    Welfare (ISEW) 70
India
  EIA in 231–44
  environmental degradation 18,
    231–44
  farming practices 233–4, 236–7,
    238
  gender relationships 240–41
  irrigation projects 232–40
  social problems 18, 240–41
  water supplies 18, 231–44
indices
  ACSI 79
  data integration for 72–3
  on environmental impacts 68
  hard 70–71
  improvements in 71–2
  indicators used in 69
  national 14–15
  PCSI 79
  soft 68–9
  on sustainable development 71–3
  see also monitoring
Indonesia 50, 70, 113

Industrial Economics Inc. 169
industrial policies 34
information management 176
  communications plans 16, 176, 179,
    180–82, 183
Institute of Hydrology (UK) 201
institutional framework 11, 31, 32, 34,
    127–9, 132–3
  failures in 35
  for SAPs 40–41
  for SEA 28
  for sustainable development 81–2,
    197–8
insurance 228–9
  see also risk assessment
integrated management
  communications plans 16, 176, 179,
    180–82, 183
  of the environment 43, 62, 64, 190
  of flood defence projects 175–88
  of land degradation control 242–3
  of natural resources 67, 69, 72–83
  procedures and guidelines 177–8
  by project teams 177–9, 180–81,
    186–7
  of project-level appraisal 175–88
  of sand harvesting 193, 195, 196,
    197
  scoping studies for 16–17, 179, 182,
    183, 184
  stages in 176–80
  of sustainable resources 67, 69,
    73–83
integration issues 4, 16, 18
  consistency issues and 15–16,
    125–33
  in decision making 11–13, 16,
    18–19
  in the development process 139–52
  in economic valuation 164–71
  in EIA 4, 11–13, 16–17, 18, 67–83,
    231–44
  in project-level appraisal 132–3
  relevance issues and 15–16, 125–33
  in SEA 25–45
  in SIA 18, 27
  strong 11–13, 18
  in sustainable development 25–45,
    231–44
  weak 11–13, 18

intellectual property rights
  trade-related (TRIPS) 53
intensity studies 194
intensive farming 92, 93, 96, 100
  see also farming practices
Intergovernmental Panel for Climate
  Change (IPCC) 74, 77
international agreements 26, 63–4,
  82–3
international cooperation 42, 47, 62
  in agricultural policy making
    88–111
  standards harmonization 51–2
  trade agreements 53, 82–3, 84
international issues 41–3
International Monetary Fund (IMF)
  15, 29, 30, 31, 34, 68, 73, 84
International Tropical Timber
  Agreement, first, 1983 81
International Tropical Timber
  Agreement, second, 1994 81
International Tropical Timber
  Organization 83
International Union for the
  Conservation of Nature (IUCN)
  62, 63, 113
international value transfers *see* benefit
  transfers
Inter-organizational Committee...
  Social Impact Assessment 8, 20
investment appraisal 8–9, 127
investment measures 37
  trade-related (TRIMS) 53
irrigation projects *see* water supplies
iterative bidding 221, 223–4, 226
Iverson, L. R. 79

Jacobs, P. 38
Jansson, A. 73
Jha, Dayanatha 235, 236
Jimenez, E. 134
Jones, R. M. 8
Joshi, Pramod K. 235, 236

Kanbur, R. 10
Kenya
  CIA in 17
  District Focus for Rural
    Development... 197
  EIA in 17, 189–99
  institutional framework 197–8
  legal framework 197
  sand harvesting in 17, 189–99
  water supplies 190, 191, 193, 194
Kirkpatrick, Colin 15–16, 20, 134
Kitetu, John J. 17, 194
Knetsch, J. 135
Kopp, R. J. 163
Krupnick, Alan J. 114, 164

labour supply 103, 110, 241
  migratory workers 240–41
Lal, D. 62
land degradation 17, 35, 36, 39
  farming practices and 93, 96, 110
  integrated management of 242–3
  irrigation projects and 234
  living standards and 240–41
  monitoring of 242
  sand harvesting and 189–99
  SIA of 240–44
  see also environmental degradation
Land Drainage Improvement
  Works...1988 (SI 1217) (UK)
  177, 179, 182
land reclamation 238–9
land reform 34, 36, 93, 104
land use 100
  modelling of 74–83
  national scale for 74
  transition periods in 75
  trends in 75–7
  types of 79, 81
  see also farming practices
land use planning 16, 175–88
landfill refuse sites
  in Bangkok 17–18, 217–30
  community reactions to 217–18,
    220
  cost of 217–18
  CV studies 219, 220, 224–9
  economic valuation of 218–29
  EIA of 17–18, 217–20
  environmental pollution from
    218–19, 224
  hedonic pricing of 219, 220
  options exercises on 220–23
  willingness-to-pay issues 220,
    221–6, 227

Langford, I. H. 224
Lazo, J. K. 163
Lee, Norman 5, 8, 15–16, 20, 134
legal framework 5, 11, 41
  Basel Convention, 1989 47
  European Union 5, 134
  in Kenya 197
  litigation 115
  regulatory systems 127–9, 132–3
  United Kingdom 143–4, 177, 178, 179, 180, 182
  United States 3, 5, 7, 114, 115, 133, 139, 155, 169, 171
Lerman, Peggy 26
Lichfield, Dalia 6, 16, 135, 144
Lichfield, Nathaniel 6, 16, 135, 139, 140, 141, 142, 143, 144, 146
Lichtenberg, E. 163
Liengcharernsit, W. 217
life *see* health and life
linear models 66
Little, I. M. D. 9, 10, 20, 21, 135
living standards 17, 18, 31, 236–7
  food supplies 88, 110, 113, 200–208, 215, 236–7
  land degradation and 240–41
  poverty levels 18, 30, 32, 34, 35, 36, 37, 39–40, 65, 201, 206
  unemployment 35, 37
  water supplies 17, 18, 190, 191, 193, 194, 200–216, 231–44
Livingstone, I. 135
logging 81
  see also forestry sector
Londero, E. 10
Lovell, Chris J. 17, 134, 200, 201, 203, 214
Lutz, Ernst 89, 114

Mackenzie, Craig 114
Maddox, B. 72
management *see* information management; integrated management
Manchester Airport 146
Manchester University 4, 40
man-made capital *see* human capital
Mapp, H. P. 162
Marinov, U. 139
Markandya, Anil 10, 120, 135

market failures 8, 35, 48–9
market valuation of physical effects (MVPE) 121
  see also economic valuation
market values 120, 130, 131, 180
marketing 32, 104–5
McCalla, A. 110
McClelland, G. H. 169, 171
McDonald, G. T. 43
Meinzen-Diel, R. 201, 203
Mercado, A. 162
Mexico 55, 113
Mharapara, I. 214
Michaels, R. G. 163
Mickle, Craig 114
migratory workers 240–41
Mills, A. J. 117
Ministry of Agriculture, Fisheries and Food (UK) 178
Ministry of Agriculture and Food (NZ) 90
Ministry for the Environment (NZ) 184
Ministry for the Environment (UK) 181
Ministry of Lands, Agriculture and Rural Resettlement (MLARR) (Zimbabwe) 206
Ministry of Reclamation and Development (MRD) (Kenya) 191, 194
Mirrlees, J. 9, 10, 20, 135
Mitchell, R. C. 225, 227
modelling
  computer models 169
  of environmental performance 68
  of ground water remediation 169
  of land use 74–83
  see also analytical methodologies
Moffat, I. 70
Moldan, B. 134
monitoring 72, 201, 215
  of compliance with international agreements 64, 68
  of environmental performance 15, 41, 53, 64, 67–83
  of human development 65
  of land degradation 242
  reliability of 72
  see also indices

monoculture farming 92
  see also farming practices
Moraes, A. S. 134
Moran, Dominic 17, 134
Morel-Seytoux, H. J. 162
Moriarty, P. 214
Morris, P. 145, 175, 184
Morrison, Jamie 15, 135
Mortimore, M. 191
Morvaridi, Behrooz 18, 231
Mtetwa, G. 214
Mtetwa, M. 214
multi-criteria analysis (MCA) 126,
  130, 131, 135
multi-national corporations *see*
  transnational corporations
multivariate analysis 209–11
Munasinghe, Mohan 20, 37–8, 89, 134
Munn, R. 176
Musyoka, C. 190

national accounting systems (SNA) 42
national budgets 26
National Environment Secretariat
  (NES) (Kenya) 197–8
national environmental indices 14–15
National Environmental Policy Act,
  1969 (USA) 3, 5, 7, 139
National Index of Sustainable
  Development (proposed) 15
national indices *see* indices
National Oceanic and Atmospheric
  Administration (NOAA) (USA)
  115
national surveys *see* monitoring
natural capital 65, 66, 72, 73, 82
  see also human capital
natural disasters 35, 155
  see also environmental degradation
natural resource accounting 71–2,
  113–14
natural resources 35–7, 41–2, 43, 66
  agricultural sector and 90–92
  depletion of 42, 43, 48, 54, 61, 66,
    189
  integrated management of 67, 69,
    73–83
  value of 72–3
  see also deforestation;
    environmental degradation

nature conservation
  economic valuation of 113
net present value criterion (NPV) 6
New Zealand 7, 51, 90, 184
Newbery, David 114
newly industrialized economies (NIEs)
  5
Niekerk, F. 135
Nijkamp, P. 6, 135
non-governmental organizations
  (NGOs) 81, 113, 181
non-market value 120, 204–8
non-use value 171
North, J. H. 163
North American Commission on
  Environmental Cooperation
  (CEC) 55
North Atlantic Free Trade Association
  (NAFTA) 47, 52, 54–5
the 'numeraire' debate 9
  see also cost–benefit analysis
Nunan, Fiona 17–18, 134

Oates, Wallace 112
Odongo, T. 190
Oh, S. I. 163
oil prices 29
oil spills 115
Okali, C. 214
O'Loughlin, C. 72
open-ended surveys 221–3, 224, 226
  see also public participation
options exercises 121–2, 157, 220–26,
  228
  see also willingness-to-pay
Organization for Economic and
  Cultural Development (OECD)
  5, 20, 21, 112, 113
  EIA studies 14, 46–57, 89, 120, 121,
    127, 134, 220
  trade liberalization studies 14,
    46–57
Overseas Development Administration
  (UK) 8, 20, 201, 214
ozone depletion 113
  see also global climate change

Pagiola, S. 100
Palmer, Karen 114
Panayotou, Theodore 31, 34, 42, 134

Parliamentary Office of Science and Technology (POST) (UK) 114
participatory rural appraisal (PRA) 213
Partidario, Maria Rosario 26, 27, 29, 197
Partido, M. 5, 20
Paulson, G. 164
Pearce, David W. 10, 21, 64–5, 66, 70, 73, 92, 93, 112, 113, 120, 134, 135, 140
Pearce, Richard 15
Pearce and Atkinson's Z index 70
pesticides 50, 51, 105–6
    see also farming practices
Peters, G. H. 139
Peterson, W. L. 110
Petts, J. 135
Phaneuf, Y. 6
Phantumvanit, D. 217
Philippines 49, 72, 82, 83, 113
Picciotto, R. 10
Pinheiro, A. C. 118
planning balance sheet method (PBSA) *see* community impact evaluation (CIE)
Poe, G. L. 163
Poffenberger, M. 82, 83
policies, plans and programmes (PPPs) 11, 15
    CIE of 16
    cost–benefit analysis of 10, 21, 114
    decision making on 19
    EA of 17, 178, 185–7
    EAP and 17, 178
    EIA of 5–6, 7, 8, 14, 141–4
    planning processes 17, 141–4
    scoping studies 16–17, 179, 182, 183, 184, 190
    SEA of 26, 27–8, 131, 135
policy appraisal 15, 114, 227–8
policy changes 10
    in agricultural sector 88, 89–90, 93, 97–9
policy failures 35, 48–9
policy making 26, 28, 31
    in agricultural sector 88–111
    in developing countries 88–111
    international harmonization of 51–2

procedural guidelines for 52–5
pollution *see* environmental pollution
Poore, M. E. D. 62, 83
population levels 39, 88
    agricultural sector and 92, 93–4, 233
    environmental degradation and 92
    growth rate (PGR) 92
population planning 41
Porter, G. 62
Portney, Paul R. 114, 115, 117, 164
potential carbon sequestration index (PCSI) 79
Potier, Michel 14, 135
poverty levels 18, 30, 65, 206
    food supplies and 201
    increases in 18, 35, 36, 37
    reduction of 32, 34, 35, 39–40, 232
    see also living standards
Praxis 181
preservation values 120
    see also economic valuation
pressure groups 81, 217, 228
Prest, A. R. 20, 139
price reforms 34, 35–6
pricing policies
    agricultural sector 93, 94–104, 110
private sector projects 127–9
private sector role
    in SAPs 41
privatization programmes 26, 31, 34, 127
process approach
    to project-level appraisal 10
product effects
    of trade liberalization 47–8, 54
project management *see* integrated management
project-level appraisal 8
    CIE and 144–5
    consistency issues 15–16, 125–33
    cost–benefit analysis and 10, 15–16, 125–38
    economic valuation and 112–13
    EIA and 5–6, 7, 8, 15–16, 63, 125–38
    of flood defence projects 175–88
    integrated management of 175–88
    integration issues 132–3
    relevance issues 15–16, 125–33

SEA and 26
  stages in 177–8
  types of 139–41
  see also policies, plans and
    programmes
property rights 41, 43, 48, 189, 238
Provencher, B. 163
psychology of response 227
public accountability 180–82
public participation 10–11, 17–18,
    193–4, 197
  communications plans 16, 176, 179,
    180–82, 183
  in EIA 243–4
  options exercises 121–2, 157,
    220–26, 228
  in SAPs 41
  willingness-to-accept compensation
    122
  willingness-to-accept risk 176
  willingness-to-pay 115–16, 117–19,
    121–2, 180, 206–7, 208–13, 214,
    220, 221–6, 227
public sector projects 127–9
public sector reform 32, 34
public utilities 114
Puffer, C. A. 163

qualitative predictions 131, 178, 213
quantitative predictions 131, 157, 178,
    193, 204, 213

rainforests *see* tropical forests
rational-choice model 10
Rau, J. G. 139
recreational values 120
Redclift, M. 64, 66
Reed, D. 20
Rees, J. 72
referenda *see* public participation
reforestation 74, 75, 76, 79
  see also forestry sector
regional planning 141–2
regulatory effects
  of trade liberalization 51–2, 54
regulatory impact analyses (RIAs) 157
regulatory systems 127–9, 132–3
  see also legal framework
relevance issues 15–16, 125–33

remediation projects *see* ground water
    remediation projects
Remote Sensing Agency 235
Repetto, Robert 68, 70, 72
resource allocation 32, 34
resource capital 65, 77
Resource Conservation and Recovery
    Act (USA) 169, 171
resource sustainability capital (RSC)
    82–3
resources *see* natural resources
Richardson, N. 38
Ridell, J. B. 30
Riebveld, P. 6
Rio Summit *see* UN Conference on
    Environment and
    Development...
risk assessment
  in contingent valuation 228–9
  in cost–benefit analysis 9, 131
  in economic valuation 117–18, 201,
    205, 228–9
  in EIA 131, 135
  willingness-to-accept risk 176
Rogers, M. G. 135
Rostow, W. W. 66, 74
Rowan, John S. 17, 189, 194
Rowntree, K. 195
rural development 18, 31, 34, 35, 39,
    232, 233, 243–4

S index *see* Grainger's S index
Sadler, Barry 5, 20, 28, 38, 43, 135
safety issues 54, 118
  see also health and life
salinization 234, 235, 236
  see also environmental degradation
sanctions *see* trade sanctions
sand harvesting
  conflict over 189–90
  damage mitigation 195
  distribution of 191–3
  economic importance of 191–2
  EIA of 17, 189–99
  environmental degradation by 17,
    189–99
  integrated management of 193,
    195, 196, 197
  process of 195–8
  SEA of 196

Sarda Sahayak Irrigation Project
    (India) 234–40
satellite data 79, 235
scale effects
    of trade liberalization 48–9, 54
Schofield, J. A. 139
Schreiber, G. 93, 99, 100, 200
scoping studies 16–17, 179, 182, 183,
    184, 190
    see also policies, plans and
    programmes
Scoones, I. 200, 201, 206
Scott, K. M. 191
Sedjo, R. A. 62
Semple, A. J. 214
Sen, A. K. 227
sensitivity analysis 9
Serageldin, I. 218
set-aside arrangements 73, 74, 75
Shah, P. N. 235
sharecropping 236–7, 238, 239
Sherman, P. B. 73
shifting cultivation 92
    see also farming practices
significance studies 194
Simpson, E. S. 65
Singh, P. 235
Sites of Special Scientific Interest
    (SSSIs) (UK) 185
Smith, V. K. 163
social impact assessment (SIA) 4, 7–8
    cost–benefit analysis and 9, 10, 18,
        130, 135
    definition 6, 7
    development process and 3–4,
        14–15
    EIA and 130, 133–4, 175–6, 184
    integration issues 18, 27
    of land degradation 240–44
    SAPs and 32, 38–43
    in US 7
social relationships 18, 240–41
social welfare 35, 232
    health services 39, 65
soft approach
    to sustainable development 63–4
soil erosion *see* land degradation
solid waste *see* landfill refuse sites
Soloman, R. A. 62

Solórzano, R. 72
Spash, C. 21, 228
Spofford, W. O. 164
Squire, L. 10, 20, 21
stabilization policies 30–31
the state
    role of 40–41
State Planning Institute of Uttar
    Pradesh 233, 234
state subsidies 31, 36
static analysis 93
Steer, Andrew 114, 218
Stern, N. 20
Stockholm Environment Institute
    (SEI) 113
Stocking, M. A. 195
strategic environment assessment
    (SEA) 5, 14, 20
    in decision making 27–8
    definition 5–6, 28–9, 63
    in developing countries 26, 195–8
    influence of 18–19, 26
    institutional framework 28, 197–8
    integration issues in 25–45
    in Kenya 17, 195–8
    of policies, plans and programmes
        26, 27–8, 131, 135
    at project-level 26
    purpose and objectives 26, 43–4
    of sand harvesting 17, 195–8
    SAPs and 43–4
    sustainable development and
        25–45, 195–8
Streeten, P. 110
strong integration 11–13, 18
structural adjustment programmes
    (SAPs)
    benefit transfer measures in 32, 43
    in developing countries 29–45
    for economic policies 30–31, 32–3,
        34
    effects of 34, 35–7, 43
    EIAs and 4, 5, 14, 25, 29, 30, 33–45
    environmental considerations 25,
        29, 30, 33–43
    environmental degradation and 35,
        36, 43
    implementation caps 33–4
    integration issues 38–43

international issues 41–3
poverty reduction and 32, 34, 35, 39–40
purpose and objectives 25, 30–31, 33, 34
for resource allocation 32
SEA and 43–4
SIA and 32, 38–43
sustainability assessment of 39–40
structural effects
of trade liberalization 49–51, 54
subsistence farming 35, 36, 233–4
see also farming practices
Suffolk County, NY (USA) 162
Sugden, R. 150
Sun, H. 163
Superfund Amendments and Reauthorization Act (SARA), 1986 (USA) 155
Superfund CASHOUT model 169
Superfund sites (USA) 16, 155, 164, 170, 171
supply elasticity
in agricultural sector 94, 110
surveys *see* monitoring;
options exercises
Susangkarn, Chalongphob 31, 34
sustainability constraint 120
sustainable development
in agricultural sector 88–92
as CBA constraint 10
conditions for 67
cost of 42, 62, 64
definition 69
in developing countries 61–87
economic growth and 62, 64, 65, 189
EIA and 61–87, 195, 197
institutional framework 81–2, 197–8
integration issues in 25–45, 231–44
international issues in 41–3
measurement of 67–73
SAPs and 39–40
SEA and 25–45, 195–8
in UK 69
sustainable development theories 63–73, 77, 82–3
circular models 66

hard approach 64–5
linear models 66
soft approach 63–4
surrogate indicators 83
sustainable development index (SDI) (proposed) 71, 72–3
sustainable resource management 67, 69, 73–83
see also environmental management
Suthiwart-Narueput, S. 20

tax systems 34, 93
Taylor, P. J. 62
technical appraisal
of development process 3–4
technological choices
in agricultural sector 88, 92–4, 99, 100–104, 105–6, 109, 110, 233
Thailand 72, 83
Bangkok 17–18, 217–30
land use 75, 77–81
landfill sites 17–18, 217–30
Therivel, R. 5, 20, 26, 63, 145, 175, 184
Thomas, C. O. 169
Thomas, J. W. 10
Thompson, R. E. 169
Tietenberg, T. H. 42, 65
Tillman, Gus 26, 30, 35, 37, 68
timber *see* forestry sector
timing considerations 9
for cost–benefit analysis 130, 135
for EIAs 53, 130
for forest management 83
Tom, B. J. 162
total economic value (TEV) 157–61
Town and Country Planning (Assessment of Environmental Effects) Regulations, 1988 (SI 1199) (UK) 143–4, 178, 180, 182
trade agreements 53, 82–3, 84
trade liberalization policies
in developing countries 31, 32. 33–4, 36, 40
effects of 47–52
EIA and 4, 5, 14, 46–57
guidelines on 52–5
OECD studies of 14, 45–57
product effects 47–8, 54
scale effects 48–9, 54

trade regulation 34, 51–2, 53, 54
trade sanctions 81
trade tariffs 34, 53
trade-related intellectual property
    rights (TRIPS) 53
trade-related investment measures
    (TRIMS) 53
transitional economies 4, 5, 18
transnational corporations 26
transport systems 34, 47, 49, 50
travel cost studies 113, 120, 121, 180
HM Treasury (UK) 135
Tribe, M. 135
tropical forests 62, 72, 73
    conservation of 73, 74
    value of 120
    see also forestry sector
Tsur, Y. 163
tubewells 235–6
    see also water supplies
Turner, R. K. 66, 69, 73, 112, 134
Turvey, R. 20, 139
Tyson, W. J. 8

UN 62
UN Commission for Sustainable
    Development 64, 68, 73
UN Conference on Environment and
    Development (UNCED), Rio de
    Janeiro, 1996 25, 43, 64, 68
UN Environment Programme (UNEP)
    27–8, 43–4
UN human development index (HDI)
    65, 66
UN Industrial Development
    Organisation (UNIDO) 9, 20
UN Social Summit, 1995 35
uncertainties
    in CBA 9, 131, 135
    in economic valuation 172
    in EIA 9, 131, 135
unemployment levels 35, 37
United Kingdom 128
    CIE in 16, 143–4
    EIA in 143, 144
    environmental policies 114
    flood defence projects 16–17,
        175–88
    land use planning 16, 175–88

legal framework 143–4, 177, 178,
    179, 180, 182
sustainable development in 69
underground water levels 114, 121
water supplies 114, 121
United States
    deforestation 69, 81
    EIA in 133, 155–74
    ground water remediation in 66,
        155–74
    health costs 118–19
    legal framework 3, 5, 7, 114, 115,
        133, 139, 155, 169, 171
    NAFTA and 55
    public utilities in 114
    SIA in 7
United States Air Force 169
United States bias
    in economic valuation 115, 118–19,
        121
United States Trade Representative
    54, 55
United States Agency for International
    Development (USAID) 8, 20
urban planning 141–2
urbanization 35, 88
use value 169
utilities *see* public utilities

valuation methods 6, 130
values
    altruistic 169, 171
    bequest 119–20, 171
    existence 171
    future benefits 119–20, 171
    market 120, 130, 131
    market valuation of physical effects
        121
    non-market 120, 204–8
    net present 6
    non-use 171
    preservation 120
    recreational 120
    see also economic valuation
van der Tak, H. 20
Vanclay, F. 4, 7, 20, 139, 184
van Pelt, M.J.F. 135, 232
Varian, H. 206
Vaux, H. J. 162
Verheem, R. 5, 20, 135
Voogd, H. 6

wages and incomes 31, 88, 117, 206, 237
see also poverty levels
Ward, W. A. 20
Warford, J. 92, 93
waste management *see* landfill refuse sites
water pollution 36
see also environmental degradation
Water Resources Research (WRR) 120
water supplies
    collector wells 201–6, 215
    economic valuation of 17, 200–216
    environmental degradation and 17, 18, 160–61, 164, 189–99, 231–44
    food supplies and 200–208, 215, 236
    in India 18, 231–44
    in Kenya 190, 191, 193, 194
    reliability of 204
    sources of 200
    tubewells 235–6
    in UK 114, 121
    in USA 16, 155–74
    willingness-to-pay issues 206–7, 208–13, 214
    in Zimbabwe 17, 200–216
waterlogged land 234
see also land degradation
Wathern, P. 62
Wattage, P. M. 134
Waughray, Dominic 17, 134, 201, 205, 207, 208
weak integration 11–13, 18
Weaving, R. 10
Weiss, J. 20, 21, 135
welfare *see* social welfare
Welsh Brown, J. 62
Whittington, Dale A. 118, 220
wildlife species *see* endangered species
Williams, A. 150
Williams, M. 69, 81
willingness-to-accept compensation (WTA) 122
    see also compensation schemes

willingness-to-accept risk 176
    see also risk assessment
willingness-to-pay (WTP)
    in economic valuation 115–16, 117–19, 121–2, 180
    for food supplies 213
    for landfill refuse sites 220, 221–6, 227
    for water supplies 206–7, 208–13, 214
Willis, Ken G. 73, 115, 118, 227
Wilmhurst, J. 10
Wilson, J. H. 169
Wilson, M. D. 70
Winpenny, James T. 15, 21, 110, 112, 113, 126, 134
women 18, 39, 201, 241, 243
Wongpakdee, Somboon 83
Wood, Christopher 26, 134, 197
Wood, E. F. 164
Woolf, Tim 114
Wooten, D. C. 139
World Bank 8, 15, 20, 29, 30, 31, 32, 34, 68, 69, 73, 84, 134, 192, 231
World Bank Water Demand Research Team 212
World Commission on Environment and Development (WCED) 62, 63–4
World Resources Institute 69, 70
World Wildlife Fund (WWF) 39, 42, 113

Yang, E. C. 168
Yiika Sand Cooperative (Kenya) 195
Young, M. 89
Young, R. A. 162

Z index *see* Pearce and Atkinson...
Zamindari Abolition Act, 1951 (India) 238
Zieger, W. 169
Zilberman, D. 163
Zimbabwe 17, 200–216
Zylicz, T. 223